AHEAD OF OUR TIME

Reflections on Diversity

Jefferson High School, Daly City, CA
1968–1972

Carol Badran

Always celebrate diversity!
Carol B

YBK Publishers   New York

Ahead of Our Time: Reflections on Diversity

Copyright © 2022 by Carol Badran

YBK Publishers, Inc.
39 Crosby Street
New York, NY 10013

ISBN: 978-1-936411-81-8

Library of Congress Cataloging-in-Publication Data
Names: Badran, Carol, author.
Title: Ahead of our time : reflections on diversity : Jefferson High
    School, Daly City, CA, 1968-1972 / Carol Badran.
Description: New York : YBK Publishers, [2022] | Summary: "A high school's
    past history of diversity as viewed by students of that period"--
    Provided by publisher.
Identifiers: LCCN 2022037173 | ISBN 9781936411818 (Paperback)
Subjects: LCSH: Jefferson High School (Daly City, Ca.)--History. |
    Multicultural education--California--San Francisco Bay Area--Case
    studies. | Cultural pluralism--California--San Francisco Bay Area. |
    High school students--California--San Francisco Bay Area--Interviews. |
    High school teachers--California--San Francisco Bay Area--Interviews.
Classification: LCC LC1099.4.C2 B34 2022 | DDC
    370.11709794/6--dc23/eng/20220815
LC record available at https://lccn.loc.gov/2022037173

Cover and map design by Lecia Badran-Doane

Manufactured in the United States of America
for distribution in North and South America
or in the United Kingdom or Australia
when distributed elsewhere.

For more information, visit
www.ybkpublishers.com

In memory of my sisters who paved the way for me.

Jean Badran (Class of '68)

Peggy Badran (Class of '70)

Contents

Introduction

by Carol Badran

What Are You?

At my tiny elementary school in Daly City, California, while not fully understanding what it meant, we children asked each other that question with genuine curiosity. My classmates' answers were varied: "Italian and Filipino," "Jewish," "Chinese," "Mexican," and so forth.

My own answer was longer: French, English, Welsh, Indian, Lebanese. When I stopped at Lebanese, there was inevitably a pause—one I came to dread—followed by the question, "What's *that*?" As a seven- or eight-year-old I enjoyed playing this little question game with my classmates. However, the fact that nobody else was Lebanese, and no one had ever even heard of it, made me feel different.

Once we had finished sharing our backgrounds, we got on with the business of playing and continuing our friendships. We were so mixed that it didn't seem as if anyone cared what we were. In hindsight, it's interesting that no one ever answered that they were American.

Although my father was born in California, his parents were immigrants and his first language was Arabic. His mother spoke broken English. Until her death when I was nine, I remember the smells of lamb kibbeh, warm Syrian flatbread, and other tasty Lebanese dishes when we visited her home every week. Ten years later I lost my father, so I never got to know him when I was an adult.

My mother came from a tiny all-White town in Oklahoma. She and my father met in 1947 while she was working at Standard Oil in California, where some of her colleagues referred to Arabs as "sand n—s" (the n-word, which I refuse to speak or write). As I got older, I often wondered how my mother came to be so open-minded about race, but it wasn't something we talked about at home.

As an adult, when anyone had asked me about my high school, I casually described it as "half White, half you-name-it-we-had-it," without knowing the actual numbers. Recently I pulled out my yearbooks to see if my description was accurate. Without doing an exact count, it looked like we were about fifteen percent Black, fifteen percent Latinx, fifteen percent Asian Pacific Islander, five percent mixed race, and fifty percent White.

While each minority percentage was low, what stood out throughout my four high school years was that many non-White students consistently had a high profile: as class president, team captain, cheerleader, or homecoming queen. We chose our classmates for these roles based on their qualifications and personalities, regardless of race, ethnicity, or religion. That was our normal: a beautiful mix of adolescents growing, learning, and exploring their interests together. We were doing exactly what adolescents do, figuring out how to get to adulthood.

If I had grown up somewhere other than Daly City, with its "What are you?" and "you-name-it-we-had-it" schools, I may have felt that my father's Arab roots were something to avoid mentioning—but I never questioned it. This may be connected to the fact that I "passed for" and reflexively identified as White until college, when I began to think more about my mixed heritage.

It's not surprising that I married someone from another culture. When I was twenty-four, I went to Ecuador as a Peace Corps volunteer, and I fell in love with an Ecuadorian man. As my service was ending, we discussed the possibility of his coming to the U.S. He had saved enough money to live and study abroad for a year, and he was accepted to an English language school in San Francisco. We wanted to see how things went before deciding about marriage, but he was denied a student visa. I always wondered whether this was because of his darker skin color or because he didn't come from a wealthy family. To get around the visa problem, we decided to get married. After arriving home, I asked my mother how she felt about my marrying someone she'd never met. She said, "If you think he is a good person, he must be." I appreciated how accepting she was. What might have been a racial minefield was a non-issue in my family.

Some kind of inverse racism also applied: my Afro-Ecuadorian mother-in-law was proud of her White daughter-in-law and showed me favoritism.

My Growing Awareness

My obviously non-White husband and I sometimes attracted unwanted attention in mostly liberal, progressive San Francisco in the early 1980s: occasional hard stares, angry looks, and shrugs, as if we posed an insoluble problem. Some people treated him as if he was stupid because he was learning English and was not yet fluent. These critics were almost certainly among the majority in the U.S. who, themselves, never take the trouble to learn another language. It didn't seem to occur to them that English was my husband's second language—he already had a language he spoke perfectly well.

My husband had a bachelor's degree in business administration, and in Ecuador he'd had a prestigious job in accounting. His first job in the U.S. was as a cashier at a gas station. After several months he came home early one day, looking despondent, and told me that he had been fired. Wow! I didn't know what to say. I couldn't imagine what he'd done. It turned out that there was money missing, and he was accused of being the thief. It's a terrible feeling to have someone you love be accused of stealing. Eventually the truth came out: the older White man who did the nightly cash pick-ups and deposits had been skimming money. But my husband, with the darkest skin and heaviest accent among the cashiers, was the perfect fall guy.

In 1994, I attended the American Public Health Association's annual conference in New York City. I was managing an AIDS prevention education program targeting youth for the San Francisco Department of Public Health. I was attending the APHA conference to share about our program. While there, I encountered a taxi driver who turned out to be Egyptian. He was very excited to discover my last name, Badran. "*Badran*," he said, pronouncing it correctly. He told me there were many Badrans in Egypt, even a well-known cheese company, Badran Cheese. It felt good that, for the first time, someone recognized my Arab ancestry without my having to tell them. On our taxi ride to the airport he played a tape of Arab music while he sang along with it. When I got out of the cab he presented me with the cassette, a touching gesture from a nice man.

I checked in, went through security, and found my gate. A colleague who had also been at the conference was already there. I told her about the Egyptian driver and the cassette he'd given me. She got very serious about the rule, "accept no packages from strangers." She had a terrible fear of flying and insisted that I go back through security with the cassette tape. It didn't make sense to me since I'd already been through it. I complied and all was fine, but an unexpected, sweet experience was turned sour. I wondered if she would have been so paranoid if the driver wasn't Arab. Reconsidering the issues today, I shudder to think how it might have been had it happened soon after September 11.

On a beautiful spring morning that same year, I was driving up Market Street in the Castro District of San Francisco with my good friend and colleague, Percy, in the passenger seat. We stopped at a traffic light. I glanced toward Percy and noticed a police car facing us as it exited a parking lot. I realized that the two officers inside were staring intently at Percy, so intently that they didn't notice I was looking, equally intently, at them. When the light changed, and I drove away, I saw them pull in behind me. I drove very carefully as they followed us closely for several blocks. Eventually they turned, but I have never felt so uncomfortable about having a police car behind me.

Percy is a dark-skinned Black man. He wore his hair short and neatly trimmed, and a crisply starched white shirt, buttoned up to the collar. He always looked professional, much more so than I. But I knew why the cops were staring at him and why they followed us. If Percy had been White, it would not have happened unless we were actually doing something wrong. I never discussed it with Percy, but I'm sure it wasn't the first time he'd been followed, nor would it be the last. For me, however, it was a first. It was a small window into the everyday lives of Black people in our country. (Percy told me that whenever he hailed a cab it took forever for one to stop for him.)

A few years later I got a call early on a Sunday afternoon from Tito A, a young staff member, telling me, "I need you to either bail me out or I'm calling in sick tomorrow." It took me a few minutes to process this. Was he joking? Why on earth was he arrested? I'd never posted bail for anyone before, and quickly learned how to do it; the risks, etc. When I picked Tito up later that afternoon, he explained what had happened.

Several family members were celebrating his sister's thirtieth birthday at a club the night before. When they left the club, the police showed up and hassled them. Tito was arrested. He was a young, dark, Brown-skinned Guatemalan Mayan man with a smile that could light up a room, but some people still read him as intimidating. As so often happens, the charges against him were dropped. There weren't any legitimate charges in the first place, but he'd spent a night locked up.

Anyone old enough to remember the brutal 1991 beating of Rodney King by the Los Angeles police knew that cops harassed Black (and Brown) people, at least occasionally, but most of us hoped it was an isolated event. I had never been aware of anyone close to me experiencing such intimidation by the police. Both Percy and Tito were/are wonderful people, doing hard and important work. Yet, at any moment, their lives could be disrupted and put at risk by public servants who abuse their power over people with Black and Brown skin.

Dividing Races

Racism came to the "New World" with the first Europeans. North American history is based on taking land from the people who were here before us and persecuting them, along with importing enslaved people and using them and generations of their enslaved offspring to build our country. Racism is still with us, but many of us are privileged not to experience or witness it with any frequency. While I know what it's like to be treated a certain way because of my gender, I can't comprehend what it's like to move in a world where, at any moment, people might treat me harshly and unfairly because of the way I look.

In my perception, it is undeniable that Black and Brown people are often targeted and harassed by some of those who are supposed to "protect and serve" all of us, and by racist systems and policies in our country. It has been proved now that everyone with a cellphone is a potential or actual witness to almost daily episodes of violence.

But, clearly, that is not everyone's view.

Planning this book, I began by reaching out to former classmates from Jefferson High School to ask them to participate in my project. One exchange with a White classmate caught me off guard. His response to my reaching out was:

Him: Why are you doing this and who is your audience?

Me: Good questions. Since our country is rapidly becoming fifty percent or more minority, I'm hoping to show that it actually can (and did) work. At Jeff, while I don't know the exact numbers, I've always casually explained to friends that we were "50% white, 50% you-name-it-we-had it." The picnics we have yearly are so popular. They demonstrate how people did like each other and had friends of all ethnicities and races. Were you aware that while we were at Jeff, the population of our country was 88% white? I had no idea about this because my experiences growing up were so completely different. I know everything at Jeff wasn't perfect, but it seemed like most people mixed harmoniously in some way, even if it was just in class, on a sports team, or in band.

Him: For my two cents, I see that the far left continues to divide races by saying that there is systemic racism going on. I don't see it, but if you keep saying it in the mainstream media, some people start to believe it. We have so many people of color in companies: mayors, city councils, President!

For that former classmate, it seems that this country is done with racism. I don't see it that way at all. While I am not an expert on racism, I have always been an observer of humankind, an avid reader, and a critical thinker. Why is the life expectancy of a young Black man shorter than that of a young White man in our country? Why is the percentage of incarcerated Black and Brown people in any given state much higher than the percentage of incarcerated White people in that state? Why is it that Black college graduates are about as likely to be unemployed as White Americans with only a high school diploma, and Black Americans with a college education hold less wealth than White Americans who have not even completed high school? (Per Ibram X. Kendi, Director, Center for Antiracist Research, Boston University.)

While I am half Arab, I "look" White, and I have been aware of my White privilege my entire adult life. The problem with White privilege is that many people who have it, don't realize, or don't want to acknowledge, that this privilege is bestowed them at the expense of others. White people didn't do anything to earn this privilege. It's not as if any of us can choose our skin color. When White people (like the former classmate referenced earlier) see this privilege being questioned, many of them lash out, so it's essential to begin with the understanding that our privilege came at a huge cost to humanity. In fact, in the U.S., "the system"—the collective policies and practices we live under—was designed over time with the intended outcome of giving White people more advantages than people of color. This began as soon as Black people emerged from slavery after the Civil War (per Heather McGhee, in *The Sum of Us*, p.79) and continued into modern times with segregation, redlining, mass incarceration, inequities in school funding, racialized hiring practices, and so on.

Growing Inequality

When I was in high school in the late sixties and early seventies, most people—at least where I lived and went to school—believed that everybody, regardless of race, ethnicity, creed, or social class, had opportunities to work hard and move up the socioeconomic ladder. That was what we were taught under the rubric of the "American Dream." It was a time when most people who worked in low-wage jobs, as cashiers and so on, were teenagers and young adults, getting work experience while making extra money for themselves, sometimes to lessen the burden on their families .

Many of us Baby Boomers had parents who had proudly served in World War II. Numerous White veterans benefited from the GI Bill (officially the Servicemen's Readjustment Act of 1944) through being given housing loans, scholarships, and other financial assistance. The GI Bill helped my father to buy the house I grew up in. Only much later did I learn that many of these same benefits were either denied, or were very limited, for non-White veterans: a vastly higher percentage of the benefits went to White veterans, per the *1619 Project* (a 2019 endeavor of *The New York Times*).

Not having the same access to GI loans made it harder for people of color to buy a home. This had a compounding effect on a family's intergenerational wealth—assets that may be inherited, such as property, stocks, and other investments. Passing down assets to children and grandchildren allows an ordinary family to accrue wealth over time, rather than each generation having to start from scratch. Black and Brown people, after WWII, were blocked from the opportunity to accrue intergenerational wealth, a contributing factor to the immense inequalities of wealth in our nation today.

Additionally, there was the practice of redlining, in which real estate lenders drew actual red lines on maps to mark predominantly Black or mixed-race neighborhoods. People who lived in those areas were often refused credit, loans, or insurance, or they might have "special" clauses in their contracts that imposed certain conditions—conditions that did not apply to White borrowers. In *The Sum of Us* (pp.80–81), Heather McGhee talks about how the Federal Housing Administration's (FHA) subsidy of house purchases made it easy for working-class White people who had never owned a house to buy a place in the suburbs. It was often cheaper for them to do this than to rent, again contributing to their growing prosperity, a prosperity in which non-Whites were not allowed to share.

While I'm not personally aware of redlining in Daly City while I was growing up, some of the non-White people I interviewed mentioned that their families had been steered to other neighborhoods when they were looking to buy a house, and sometimes were flatly rejected when trying to buy in a newer development. Some were steered from more affluent areas to the working-class area of Daly City, and others were steered to primarily Black neighborhoods in San Francisco.

Redlining and other discriminatory practices have led to great disparities in intergenerational wealth in our country. According to the Federal Reserve's 2019 *Survey of Consumer Finances* (published 9/28/20), a typical White family had $188,200 in assets with Black families having about $24,100 and Hispanic families having $36,100. For families with fewer assets, there is no extra money to help pay for a college education. Their children will need loans to go to college, loans which can take decades to pay back, further setting them back in terms of building intergenerational wealth. These same families have little, if anything, to pass on to their heirs.

Inequality in the U.S. is greater today than ever. Millions of people of all races and ethnicities are struggling to get by. Yet, if we remain divided by prejudice, we all lose. The truth is, we all gain when the poorest among us is lifted up. Many White people who oppose access to better education, jobs, health care, and housing for people of color, do not even themselves have such access, yet they persist to continue to deprive their own selves by espousing that cause. Rampant prejudice benefits the wealthiest, while the rest of us must keep fighting for crumbs, instead of enacting fairer tax laws and policies that would lift us all.

Another impact of racism today is that, during the COVID-19 pandemic, a disproportionate number of Black and Brown people got sick and died because they worked on the front lines doing essential, but low-paid, work. They did not have the luxury of working from home and staying safe. Many of them do not have access to good health care, or do not trust the health care system.

The former classmate, whom I quoted earlier, believes that with "so many people of color" achieving success, there is no problem with racism. But the proportion of people of color who are actually successful does not correspond in comparative percentage to the numbers in which those people are present in our country. The American dream posits that they should all have the same opportunities, but we know this is far from the truth.

In 1977, after I graduated from college, I worked in San Francisco with men who were completing their prison sentences at Vacaville, Folsom, and San Quentin. I helped them to prepare for reentry into society and the job market. The White men coming out of prison got more support from families and agencies. While many of the Black and Brown men also got support from their families, the agency support they received was different. Theirs was more dependent on people like me, a young college graduate trying to do good, but who didn't have many more skills than they had themselves. A picture of the structural inequalities and racism in our society began forming in my head at that time.

Finally, there is another facet of racism that is more psychological: the issue of representation. Many people in the community in which I grew up had immigrant parents or grandparents who either spoke English with an accent, spoke "broken" English, or had not had the opportunity to learn English. The Internet was still a few decades away, and social media even longer away, so our information came from friends, teachers, newspapers, and/or television news. Most people on television had fair skin and appeared to be White. What was it like growing up seeing no one who looked like you on popular television shows?

This Project: What I Hoped to Find, and How I Went About It

Several years ago, my high school began having annual barbeques in addition to periodic class reunions. The numbers of those attending grew year after year, with people flying in from all over the country. Partners of fellow classmates marveled at our "little United Nations." This is a wonderful thing.

However, as our country moves closer to a racial and ethnic make-up more like the one we had at school—50% rather than 88% White—there are people who obviously struggle with this fact, who blame divisiveness on everything except its actual causes. During the pandemic, with time on my hands, and horror-struck by the senseless, wanton killings of George Floyd, Ahmaud Arbery, Breonna Taylor, and others, I decided to investigate our high school experiences, to learn more about my classmates' perceptions, and to compare them to my own.

This book began after I talked with Jennifer, one of my closest friends from high school, who confirmed my sense that our experiences at Jefferson High School in Daly City during the late sixties and early seventies were unique. I set out to interview other classmates to see if they, too, confirmed my sense of Jefferson's specialness.

I developed a set of questions to guide my interviews. I reached out to a variety of people, hoping to have a racially and ethnically representative sample of classmates from our time in high school. Facebook was helpful for locating people. Some people connected me with other people to interview.

I also thought it might be interesting to interview teachers who were at Jefferson during those years. Particularly, I was curious as to whether they received any special training or preparation to work at such an ethnically and racially diverse school. I also interviewed Teresa (see page 234), who started out at Jefferson but suddenly had to move to the much-less-diverse Midwest.

These stories are snapshots of the lives of forty-one people, including me, whose lives intersected at Jefferson High School between 1968 and 1972. At Jefferson, we were pretty much accepted for who we were, and not judged based on the color of our skin, our ethnicity, or our background.

This is a book about a "normal" that was very different in the U.S. from that of the great majority of high school students between 1968 and 1972. In many ways, our normal wasn't much different from that of a similar socioeconomic class, but in terms of our diversity and how we mixed with each other, we were ahead of our time. People chose friends based on personality and common interests. However, the big difference at our school was the mixture of races and ethnicities, which was our normal.

Through the following stories I hope to show how community can be enriched through diversity; that having a mixture of people and cultures allows everyone to broaden their knowledge and appreciation of what may have at one point seemed to be "other."

Notes
(To Help You Better Understand the Stories)

A few things to keep in mind while you read the stories that follow:

The stories are taken from interviews conducted by telephone or on Zoom over a period of a year and a half during the pandemic of 2020/2021. In order to be a part of this project, the person had to have spent some time as either a student or a teacher at Jefferson High School (aka Jeff) between 1968 and 1972, the four years when I attended Jeff. The stories rely on peoples' memories of what they witnessed and experienced several decades ago. No fact-checking has been done to confirm these events.

Jefferson High School, located in Daly City, is about a mile from the border of San Francisco. It is on Mission Street, a very long street, lined with businesses and other buildings (some apartments), that begins at the waterfront of the Embarcadero in San Francisco. Mission Street passes through numerous San Francisco neighborhoods, eventually having a gradual incline up to where Daly City begins, past numerous businesses and Jefferson High School, and ends where Daly City ends and El Camino Real begins. Just past the boundary between San Francisco and Daly City, that incline reaches its highest point. This is frequently referred to as "**The Top of the Hill**," which you will read of in some of the stories.

Being so close to San Francisco, our part of Daly City was a kind of hybrid city; semi-suburban, but with lots of minority families. We were literally located on the other side of the tracks, since there used to be railroad tracks that bordered the back (west) side of the school. A freeway was built, and Bay Area Rapid Transit (BART) tracks were installed. BART officially opened in 1972, the year that many of the people in this book graduated. On the western, the opposite, side of the tracks, there were newer, more expensive homes which minority families were steered away from buying. That area was known as **Westlake**.

Over the hill from Daly City, to the east, is a very small, majority-White town called **Brisbane**. While Brisbane had its own elementary and junior high schools, it did not have a high school, so students were bussed over the hill to Jefferson.

Most students who attended Jefferson, first went to Colma Junior High School, also known as Colma Intermediate. One of the feeder schools to Colma was Jefferson Elementary, known as "**Little Jeff**." For those who attended Little Jeff, they may refer to Jefferson High School as "Big Jeff."

The Jefferson High mascot was the **Indian**. We loved being Indians, which I later realized is offensive to people who are indigenous to our country. The school mascot was recently changed to the Grizzlies. The name Jefferson remains, in spite of our third president's history of owning enslaved people.

When growing up, people referred to themselves, or others, as Italian, Filipino, etc. Most likely, the person was Italian American, born here, but of Italian descent. Someone who is Filipino may or may not have been born in the Philippines.

Some people, in their interviews, say they "did not see color." While, of course, they were aware of the color of a person's skin, what they mean is that they did not judge others or choose their friends based on that.

Some people use the word "gang" to refer to their circle of friends, not in any negative sense. We did not have organized gangs during the four-year period that the people in this book, who were students, were at Jeff.

Several people mention the **War Memorial Community Center**, which was on Mission Street. Teens could play sports there, do arts and crafts, attend dances, etc.

Some people mention "**The Road**" at Jeff, which was located on the northwest part of campus, notorious for people hanging out there to cut class or get high. There was also "**The Field**," which ran parallel to The Road, just south of it, and was where many people hung out during lunch and other times, played frisbee, and other sports. Another hangout spot was "**The Wall**," overlooking The Field.

Our rival high school, **Westmoor High School**, mentioned frequently in the stories, was southwest of Jeff and up the hill, in a predominantly White area.

We had several cultural clubs at Jefferson, including the BSCO (Black Student Cultural Organization which had a Black Drill Team), the Latin Heritage Club, and the Filipino Club.

In the stories, either a person's actual name or, sometimes, a fictitious name is used.

One of our classmates, Teresa (see Chapter 39), did not graduate with our class because her family suddenly moved to the Midwest in the middle of her sophomore year. I was interested in comparing her experiences with those of people who spent their entire high school years at Jeff.

—*Carol Badran*

The map on the following page is an approximation of the area of Daly City where most of us lived at the time and includes many of the places mentioned in the stories.

AHEAD OF
OUR TIME

Teacher: Dave Peebles

*(White; taught 1966–2004: geography, military history, government,
essential skills/social studies, U.S. history, bilingual U.S. history,
math, world history, team-taught several courses. Coordinated
Title 1 English program in Reading Complex. Librarian for eight
years and mentored new teachers)*

* * *

*Being at Jefferson allowed me to "walk in their shoes" for a moment. I
learned as much from my students as they did from me. They opened
my eyes to the reality beyond the privileged White world I grew up in,
to see the flaws and injustices I was never taught about in school.*

* * *

Dave spent most of his childhood in Daly City's Broadmoor Village. Prior to that, his family lived in the mostly White Sunnydale projects of San Francisco for three years. In time, his father made more money so the family no longer qualified to live in the projects. That's when he bought a house in Broadmoor.

My father was a carpet layer, but his knees were messed up by the time he was in his forties, so he became an auto insurance claims adjuster. My mother worked for the telephone company. After I was born, she stayed home until I started second grade.

It was the 1950s and the children of the early baby boom had started school. The school district where Dave's family lived could not build schools fast enough to house all the new students. He changed schools in fourth grade because his assigned school, Westlake, wasn't finished yet. Dave was sent to "Little Jeff" (Jefferson Elementary) instead. For fifth grade, he moved again to Ben Franklin Elementary, which had just built four new fifth-grade classrooms. Then for sixth grade he went back to his original school, Garden Village, close to home. His classroom was a multipurpose room

which had been divided in half to accommodate two classes. Dave started high school at Westmoor in 1957, the year that it opened, then went to the University of California at Berkeley (Cal).

I started out studying engineering but my schedule was terrible, between the commute from Daly City [pre-rapid transit] and a full-time class load; I had to drive six days a week for twenty-six hours of classes, for a total of seventeen units. It meant studying fifty to sixty hours a week. I realized I was in over my head but my GPA was too low to get into any other school at Cal, so I decided to go to the College of San Mateo [CSM] for the next year and a half. I had a history class with a teacher who was a great storyteller, and I fell in love with history for the first time. After CSM I transferred to San Francisco State University [SFSU], where I got my degree and teaching credential.

To prepare for student-teaching, Dave and his classmates were taken around to schools in various districts, including Oakland and the Jefferson Union High School District.

I was very interested in McClymonds High in Oakland and signed up to student-teach there, but because I still lived in Daly City, I had a twenty-five-mile round-trip every day. I ended up switching with another student teacher so that I could student-teach at Jeff, where there were already some people I liked.

In 1966 Jefferson got money from the new federal Elementary and Secondary Education Act to fund a catch-up literacy program. I was hired to work in that program for two hours a day, in addition to holding two classes in the teachers' dining room. I worked with several teachers—Gary Leahy, Bruce Cunningham, Marci DeAmicas, and Bill Curran. During my first week of observation, John Mongan, the principal, died suddenly. He was a true legend, much loved and admired. Sadly, I never met him. Whenever there was a change in school policy, many teachers would say, "John Mongan wouldn't have done it that way." There is a plaque dedicated to him at Jeff near the old library.

In the middle of student teaching one day, the new principal called me to his office and asked if I wanted a job starting in September 1967. No interview, and he'd never observed my teaching. I said "Yes" and that's how I ended up at Jeff for thirty-eight years. I suspect that others encouraged him to hire me.

Dave's career at Jeff was very different from his childhood.

I grew up in an all-White world. I didn't have any Black friends. When I was at CSM I noticed a White kid who had all these Black friends—they were all basketball players. I'd never seen any interactions like that before. SF State was more diverse. McClymonds, where I was going to teach originally, was ninety-eight percent Black. Jeff was actually more diverse than McClymonds.

When I was in college, I worked at the post office during Christmas. The realtors had redlined the area north of the "Top of the Hill," limiting who could buy a home based on their race. All of San Mateo County was redlined like that. I saw how Frankfort Street was all Black, but I didn't make any connections to redlining at the time.

I'm not sure how much my parents thought about the difference between Jeff and Westmoor, my old high school. But I was the first in my family to go to college and Mom was very proud.

Dave lived at home until he got married in December 1966. He was still student-teaching at the time.

Daly City had lots of old Italian families who had been settled there for a long time. When I first went to Jeff, it was mostly Italians and Irish, some Hispanics and Samoans, several Black students. Jeff had a pretty tough reputation—if you told people who didn't know the school that you taught there, they would be taken aback. When Filipino students came, there was a lot of prejudice toward them at first.

I pretty much got along with everyone. I had very few issues with any of the kids. For a few years there was another teacher there who looked a little like me, and he wasn't popular with students. I'd walk down the hall and kids would grumble. I had to let them know it was me, not the other guy.

One time I was walking and talking with another teacher. We were about eight feet apart. A Black kid walked in between us, just passing through, and the other teacher laid into him for it. I was completely surprised. I hardly realized what had happened. After he lit into the young man, we kept walking, and the incident was dropped. I don't know how the student felt—probably baffled, maybe hurt. I wonder why this incident remained with me. As you age, you look back at things and put them in perspective.

As is the case at most schools, the principal is the key to how a school is run.

Ike McClanahan [African American] was the best principal I ever worked for. Al Sinor [White] was also a great principal—he had all kinds of creative ideas about things to do. And Murray Schneider [White], who was the principal when I was librarian, was very supportive of library programs.

Jefferson had a huge impact on me. The diversity of the student body broadened my horizons. I heard about many of my students' journeys as immigrants, their fears, their dreams. I saw and sympathized with their struggles; I applauded their accomplishments. They talked to me because they knew I cared about them. Being at Jefferson allowed me to "walk in their shoes" for a moment. I learned as much from my students as they did from me. They opened my eyes to the reality beyond the privileged White world I grew up in, to see the flaws and injustices I was never taught about in school. I became much more empathetic. I yearned to travel to some of the places where my students came from . . . and I did.

Dave is not the only one who remembers Jeff as a special place.

It's hard to figure out how Jeff was so special. I do know there were lots of people who went there as students and later returned to work there. Two office staff came back, Fran and Barbara. All the custodians lived close by. Helen, a 1974 graduate, came back to work with students from around the world. She spoke English, Spanish, Portuguese, and Russian, so she was able to help determine their ESL level and appropriate classes. I taught both Joanne and her son. Joanne came back and taught for thirty years. People had a special feeling for the school.

At one point in the nineties, Dave remembers the racial makeup of Jeff as being about forty percent Hispanic, forty percent Filipino, ten percent Black, a few Chinese, a few Brazilians, and very few Whites.

One year there were thirty-two different countries represented by the students. Another year we had a lot of Central American kids—110 kids from El Salvador during their civil war. We'd have kids who were Filipino but were born in Kenya. You couldn't guess the origins of students without being wrong.

We never had any kind of training related to diversity, but eventually had some training on how to teach kids who were English language learners. Prior to that, I taught a class, ESL American history. I'd say something in English, and then the kids in front would go to the kids in back of the class and talk with each other in Spanish. That's how that class went.

Around 1995, I assigned a paper: "What makes Jeff special?" Students had to interview five people about this: two teachers, two students, one support staff. They asked the teachers how and why they came to Jeff, and why they were still teaching there. They also interviewed admin staff and janitors, etc., who had attended Jeff and come back to work there. The kids learned that these staff came back because they felt comfortable at Jeff; it was like a home for some. I assigned this paper because some kids were scared to talk to anyone outside their circle, and it worked out really well, getting them to learn more about others.

In 2006, two years after retiring from Jeff, Dave and his wife learned about Sojourn to the Past, a non-profit program that conducts study trips for high school students to the American Deep South and Washington DC to learn about the Civil Rights Movement of the 1950s–60s. The program attempts to reach students who just didn't connect with any of the history they learned in class.

We'd heard of a teacher at a high school in [nearby] San Bruno who wasn't getting history across to the students—which is typical—so he created Sojourn to the Past.

My wife, who also taught, and I decided to go on one of their trips. It's hard to explain how big an impact this had, even on us. We cried a lot, remembering bad times—the assassinations, the marches when protesters were sprayed with fire hoses and had dogs set on them; the huge anti-war rallies, which were a particular focus for me because the military tried to draft me in 1968. There was so much going on, it was hard to cover it all in class.

We went to Atlanta, all through Alabama and Mississippi, and up through Little Rock. We met the Little Rock Nine women—Elizabeth Eckert, who's in that famous photo in a white dress with the mob after her, and Minnijean Brown. There were about eighty of us on the trip. There was a special group out of New York City, kids from Los Angeles, from Westmoor High, from the peninsula south of San Francisco, and from Ida B. Wells School in San Francisco. One African American girl was legally blind, but she saw more than anyone else. She had epiphanies; I remember looking at her and seeing "lightbulb moments." At one of the stops, she asked me to help her with some exhibits that she couldn't read. Up until that point, I hadn't realized she was blind.

At the end of the trip we wrote letters to ourselves to be sent three or six months later. My wife Linda wrote about amending a relationship with one of her sisters. The trip made that relationship work, and instead of avoiding each other, we are now close. I vowed to get a Jeff teacher to take some of our students on the trip, and one of the history teachers agreed. Unfortunately, it's too expensive to be able to go every year. It's been fifteen years since, and we still get very emotional about that trip.

I have been an active member of a peace group for over twenty years, and we are now publicly exploring racism through a series of race talks at our local library. We began talking about how to respond to racist remarks. Our next scheduled talk is to educate the community about [the proposed bill] H.R.40—reparations for slavery.

Teacher: Willem Beringer

(White; taught French and German, 1968–1993)

* * *

I thought if I could get through to at least one student, my time wasn't wasted. Learning the language wasn't as important as building self-image, which wasn't taught in class. America is so competitive, especially when you come from somewhere else.

* * *

Monsieur Beringer, as I referred to him in high school, was born in Holland (the Netherlands) and was only six years old when Germany invaded his country early in World War II. His family lived about fifteen miles from the port of Rotterdam, which was bombed on May 10, 1940, the day Germany invaded Holland. His house shook and the windows shattered. His family hid under a big table with pillows on the floor to protect them from broken glass. Willem clearly remembers people saying, "We're at war!"

The war shaped me tremendously even though I was just a child. The trauma has lasted all my life. For many years I was afraid to go into tunnels because they reminded me of air-raid shelters.

I remember when the Jews were taken away. I saw the Germans hitting people and spitting at people in the street. The Germans prevented us from getting things we needed. After they bombed us and invaded us, they starved us. We survived by eating whatever we could, including tulip bulbs. The winter of 1944 in Holland was known as "the starvation year," during which thousands of us died.

The war interrupted Willem's education; his school was turned into a German barracks. His parents did their best to teach their children at home, but his father and uncle went into hiding for two years along with a few neighbors to avoid being sent to work in factories, making bullets and weapons for the Germans. The men used a trap door to hide under the house. The family passed food down to them and they would only come out occasionally, very carefully, at night.

7

At the beginning of the war Willem's three-year-old sister was severely burned in an accident and died a few days later.

My mother lost interest in life and was sick for several years. My brother and I had to take care of her because our father was in hiding. There was no medicine. We were given coupons for food, one per person, to take to a central kitchen. The Germans allowed us one loaf of bread a week per household. People traded coupons, depending on what they needed.

Willem and his brother, along with many other Dutch children, were sent away for safety to the northern province of Frisia, where a different language was spoken.

A church group took care of us and I attended an underground school. The teacher was hiding from the Germans and he risked his life by teaching us. We had fifteen grade levels all together, so it was very hard for him and not very good for us. Sometimes people made fun of me because I was trying to learn the local language and I made mistakes. I remembered this when I became a teacher, and I didn't want others to go through what I went through.

At the beginning of the war there were five in my family. At the end of the war I was eleven and returned home as an only child: my brother had died of jaundice because of our poor diet. I had it too, but I survived. My brother's death caused my mother's condition to deteriorate more. She died in 1948 at the age of forty-two.

At the time I thought Germans were the devil, but as I got older, I learned that a lot of German people didn't support the war either. Today I have German friends, even though my family would have lived much longer if not for Germany.

Later, I ended up teaching German.

After the war Willem lived with his father for eight years.

I tried to compensate for my father's sadness by excelling in school. All Dutch students learned French, English, and German—in that order. I finished high school in three years and graduated at seventeen. Not long afterward I got a job with an American company in The Hague. Everyone encouraged me to consider emigrating. America intrigued me—they liberated us from the Germans, which was such a powerful thing to be able to do, and I had seen the generosity of the people. At my school we got "care packages" from

American children who sent us little things like candles, marbles, notepads and erasers. During the post-war years in Holland, food was still scarce. I had never tasted things like peanut butter and chocolate, but at the end of April 1945, American planes flew over Holland and dropped food parcels for us.

By the time I worked in The Hague, my father had remarried, and with him happier I could focus more on myself. My uncle lived in the San Francisco Bay Area and he sponsored me to come over when I was twenty-two.

Upon his arrival in the U.S., Willem lived first with his uncle in Pacifica, south of San Francisco. An American colleague from his old job in Holland wrote a letter of recommendation which led to a clerical job with Standard Oil in San Francisco and Willem's being able to rent his own apartment. At Standard Oil, people noticed his language skills and encouraged him to train as a teacher. He began night school at a branch of San Francisco State University while working full time, then switched to full-time studying and working during vacations. He graduated with a degree in French and German and got his teaching credential in 1968.

When Willem did his student teaching at Lowell High School in San Francisco, he had already interviewed for a position at Jefferson.

Mr. Cereghino, the principal from Jefferson, was impressed because I was European and offered me a job. The starting salary was $6600 per year. I taught three French and two German classes.

At Lowell I had observed that everyone was very motivated, but I felt I would learn more about teaching at Jefferson. The students at Lowell would commit murder for an A. One time I accidentally gave them the wrong assignment—ten pages, and they all did it! At Jefferson, many students didn't even know what an article was [a, an, the], so I realized they would need to learn English grammar along with French and German.

For the first day of school in September 1968 I arrived at Jefferson High wearing a suit. I was surprised when I saw the other teachers... one had just gotten back from Esalen [a retreat/meditation center] and had brought his dog to school. It was a stark contrast from what I was used to in European schools. I had large classes, about thirty-five students per class, which was too many, but I managed.

I didn't know much about Jefferson before I started teaching there. I had heard that it was a ghetto and the students had lots of hardships. Because of my own hardships during my youth, I thought it would be a good fit. I could have taught at another school, but I decided I wanted to go to Jeff.

It wasn't a ghetto—it's terrible to label people like that—it was just lower income. The families were working-class people doing respectable jobs, raising their children as best they could, the same as my parents had. My impression was that it wasn't an academic school, but students are smart and able to learn regardless of their socioeconomic status. I liked the variety and I felt I could be useful; they needed me more. And all the different nationalities and cultures ended up blending well and getting along together, learning from each other.

One time we had a principal who was more interested in sports than academics. I had a few run-ins with him because he took students out of classes to go to a game or decorate the halls. For some time I was the department head. Department heads from other schools, along with administrators, came to Jeff to observe. They were always impressed with my students and how well-behaved they were. Teaching there was the right thing for me. I had a good time; many students told me I was their favorite teacher. They got bored in other classes where the teacher didn't explain things very well.

A lot of students and their families were new immigrants. I had a Greek girl who couldn't speak any English. Her transcript said she had six weeks of French, so she was put in my class. I helped her survive and we became good friends. After three years in my class, she became a top student. I helped her get a scholarship to study in France, and later she returned to Greece and taught at the University of Athens. Now she runs her own school. We're still in touch.

It was the same with some of my other students—Don in my German class was interested in plants. He went to college and eventually opened his own nursery. I always encouraged students to follow their hearts. I thought if I could get through to at least one student, my time wasn't wasted. Learning a language wasn't as important as building self-image, which wasn't taught in class. America is so competitive, especially when you come from somewhere else. Students who were recent immigrants tended to have lower self-esteem.

I would draw a little French flag on their paper when students did well, which they really liked. I also decorated the classroom and played music. At the end of each school year I took my students to a nice French restaurant to give them a different kind of experience and make them feel special.

Willem was fascinated by difference and by the ability to hang on to your own identity when it's under threat.

I went to Thailand many times. It intrigued me because it's the only country in Southeast Asia that has never been occupied by a foreign power, and I'd grown up under a foreign occupation. In Thailand, teachers are highly revered, more so than doctors or lawyers because you're educating young people and molding their minds. I felt a lot of respect from the Thai people. In America, when you make money, people respect you more (than for doing important work). At parties in the sixties and seventies, when I said that I was a teacher, people almost felt sorry for me.

During Willem's time at Jefferson High, one period stands out.

Since things ran smoothly between teachers and students, I never really realized there were race issues. The only time there was a big upheaval was in the early Nineties with the Rodney King incident [the visually recorded beating of a Black man by Los Angeles police]. There was almost a riot at the school. The Blacks and Latinos were angry and united. A big crowd of students assembled in the parking lot and stood up on our cars; my car got lots of dents. The administration closed the front gates so they couldn't come back into school. Most teachers talked about injustice with their classes, but we had to be careful not to inflame feelings further. Some of us were outraged about Rodney King, but race issues were a hot topic that most people wanted to avoid.

Any relationship without respect is not a healthy relationship. You never know what a student is going through, not just because they don't understand the language—things like when I was growing up and my mother was sick or dying. Some of my teachers thought I was stupid, or not paying attention, but I was just preoccupied because my mother was sick. I vowed I would never do this to a child. If a student was going through something I would be gentle. I was surprised other teachers didn't notice when this was going on. One student had a book upside down and read that way—a form of dyslexia. Sometimes a few had no money or food. With shy students, I would try to find out why: were they afraid of feeling stupid, or of being laughed at?

One teacher made Filipino students stand up in the middle of class to tell their story, which made them nervous. A Cambodian girl was crying in my class after she had been forced to swim in the school pool. It turned out she had fled Vietnam with the "boat people" so she was afraid of water. I referred her to the school psychologist. Another referral was for a girl who had been abused by her stepfather; I found out about it because I noticed that she'd start shaking whenever I went near her. It was very important to be aware of students' histories so you could help them.

Willem taught at Jeff for twenty-five years.

Schools were deteriorating over time. At one point I was criticized by other teachers for correcting papers. In the later years I had more problems with some of the faculty than with students. Teachers were more respectful to each other in my earlier years at Jeff.

When we had the big teachers' strike in the late seventies, some teachers showed their uglier side. I didn't support the strike because you don't go into teaching for the money, and other teachers attacked me for this. I think this brought about changes at the school. Many teachers became vindictive, which seemed to rub off on students.

Willem considers himself to be an eternal optimist.

We're all rearranged molecules, and we're all responsible for our own happiness. It's important to realize this. Respect and kindness go together. They give you a sense of contentment. Otherwise, you always want more.

Don't underestimate the intelligence of children—I knew exactly what was happening when I lost my sister, my brother, and my mother. My defense mechanisms really helped me throughout my life.

Some of my happiest days were when I was teaching at Jefferson. Each day was a new day and I was so happy to see my students. They would give me hugs. I was sometimes criticized for that, probably because less popular teachers were jealous. I have fond memories and still hear from former students and colleagues. Many of my students benefitted from my classes and have been successful in life.

Fern

(Black, class of '72, older sister of Adrienne)

* * *

Jefferson allowed me to be me. No one ever told me I couldn't do certain things. I can't imagine what it would have been like going to another school.

* * *

Fern was born in San Francisco, the oldest of two daughters. Her first years were spent in the house her parents owned on a very steep street in a small neighborhood just south of San Francisco, near the Cow Palace. Her parents had moved from the "projects," which were later replaced by Crocker Amazon Park. Neither of her parents was a high school graduate, and they were unique among her mother's relatives in owning their own home.

It was a very insulated community. The only time I had contact with outsiders was when we went to visit relatives or other places. Everyone did things together—go to church, to Brownies. I never felt any different from anyone else. One thing I didn't like was that no one was out playing in the street because the neighborhood was all single-family homes. When we visited relatives living in apartments, I thought that was special because there were so many kids playing outside. At home we played in our backyards, but not on the street.

Fern gradually became more aware of race/ethnicity in elementary school.

I kind of noticed if other kids were the same color as me but didn't notice much else. Race/ethnicity wasn't ever an issue. I had a friend who was Black. I thought, "She looks like me." There was another boy who reminded me of one of my cousins. Nothing was ever brought up at home about race or color.

When I was in second grade, I had a really good Chinese friend who lived nearby. It started raining, so her father came to take her home. She asked if they could give me a ride, but her father wouldn't let me in the car. I went home and told my mother. She hit the roof—not at me; but I still thought I'd done something wrong. My mother explained that my friend's father didn't give me a ride, not because of my color, but because she thought that Asian people didn't like other races. I think she didn't want me to feel badly about my race, so, by putting it on him, she avoided telling me about racial prejudice.

She made my father go to my friend's house to talk with her father. He was there a long time. It turned out that my father and her father had both served in the same unit in World War II. Her father apologized. After that, she and I were good friends for a long time.

Another incident I remember was with a friend who was Black. We played in the schoolyard. From what I understand now, we may have been of different social classes, so the language spoken and how she was being raised were different from at my house. She kept saying the n-word. Later I was playing by myself in our backyard. I yelled the n-word at my doll, and the whole neighborhood heard. My mom called me in and told me never to use that word again, but she didn't explain why. I wish she'd explained things more to me. I had to find out the hard way.

After Fern's sister, Adrienne, was born, the family moved to Daly City, near where the Bay Area Rapid Transit (BART) station is today.

Moving to a new neighborhood and school was a big change. I was in third grade at Woodrow Wilson, a school that was a lot more diverse in terms of non-White races. There was more fighting, more anger, and hostility. I was something of a sheltered child; I still called my parents Mommy and Daddy, so I was often teased and mocked. I didn't want to be there on April Fool's Day—the first day I ever pretended to be sick to get out of going to school. It took me a long time to realize that some kids were not nice people. It didn't have anything to do with race, it was just kids.

One time we did a self-portrait with shadows—we cut them out, so they were the shape of our heads. We drew in our eyes, etc. I painted mine the color that matched my skin, which was brown. My mother didn't like the picture. I can't remember the word she used, but maybe she thought it was too dark. I used that color because it matched my skin.

Fern's mother was from Austin, Texas, and Fern remembers that she was always on the lookout for things that might set Fern apart.

She was extremely sensitive to the differences, where I was oblivious to them.

In fourth grade about sixty to seventy-five percent of us baby boomers were bussed to other schools. I went to Daniel Webster. A lot of people were upset about the bussing, but Woodrow Wilson just didn't have room for us all.

The neighborhood at Daniel Webster was at least ninety-five percent White. My parents were concerned there might be a problem. Everyone kept asking me how I felt about it, but there weren't any issues from what I knew. Maybe that was because they didn't send that many of us there. Most of us who were bussed were Black or Filipino. I hung out with other girls who were mostly White. I never got picked on, even though I had been bussed in. I was really good at sports, and I was smart. I can't think of any teacher acting differently toward me. I participated in everything I could, including traffic monitor, chorus, and orchestra. There was nothing I wouldn't try or couldn't do. If there was anything strange going on, I didn't notice. At that age everything you're taking in is a learning experience; you're not judging it so much.

My sixth-grade teacher, one of the few that wasn't married, was very progressive, on the edge of radical. She had us talk about things we never discussed in other classes—social things around race, like when someone wasn't allowed to go to someone else's house because of color, and if someone was upset about something. I hung out with both boys and girls, and there weren't issues.

A Filipina girl was at Daniel Webster, too. I went to her house to work on a science project together, and later she told me I couldn't visit her again. I was so disappointed.

I had a Black friend who I played outside with. If we had to go to the bathroom, we would go inside her house. Her parents worked during the day, so they told her she could let Black kids come in to use the bathroom, but nobody else. In my mind I still asked, "What's the big difference? Okay, our hair's different, our skin's a different color." That was as far as I could tell was different. I'd been in my friends' houses. We all had kitchens, two parents, etc. Some may have had slightly different foods, etc., but that was all positive to me.

Fern's mother had made sure her daughter was well prepared for mixing socially and getting along with people without compromising what she had been taught was right.

My mother taught me how to behave, and so far it was working, so if someone told me I was wrong, I didn't believe them. I had a good self-image and I was socially acceptable. I wasn't carrying my race as a badge. I was more into what other girls around me were doing and I was learning what to do from them. I didn't realize that a lot of the things I liked were "White things." They were just things the other girls were into.

Things changed for Fern in junior high school.

It was 1967, shortly after the riots in Los Angeles, Chicago, etc. Some people were teaching their children, "This is what's going on in the world, these are the things we want to change." But my mother never mentioned anything, so I wasn't interested. My father worked in the civil service. He'd been in the military, so he was very aware of racial differences, but my parents didn't make a big deal of it, I suspect because they didn't want me to feel like I had any handicaps.

Coming back to my neighborhood for junior high was hard. In seventh grade at Colma, the other Black kids didn't like me at all. It was a 180-degree turn in my life. My identity was thrown out the window. All that time I'd been trying to be like other kids, not realizing I was different. It was really hard for a lot of us, but I didn't know that at the time. I clung to what I knew. At Colma I wanted to hang out with my [White] best friend from third grade, but I couldn't because I was changing classes every hour. People were in cliques and wanted to beat up people in other cliques. I couldn't go to the bathroom for fear of being harassed or jumped. The threat was coming from other Black kids, so it was nothing to do with race.

Eighth graders instigated fights between seventh graders. Some of them told one of my classmates to fight me—it was their way of taking me down a notch, I guess. I wouldn't fight. This girl didn't want to fight either, which kind of kills it. We just stood there and looked at each other. People were watching, but nothing was happening. I guess someone pulled one of us away. I'd never been to a fight before so didn't know what to expect.

I told my parents that kids were picking on me. My father's attitude was to avoid them because they won't be around forever. But my mother said, "You need to learn how to fight. You need to get some of your cousins to put on boxing gloves and teach you how to get knocked down and get up after." I'm a pacifist at heart; there was no way I could hit a person. My teachers always said, "You don't want to fight." I avoided people. I did a lot of running. If I had to, I stood my ground and talked my way out of it. Since I didn't have a huge ego, I knew what I wanted and what I was supposed to be doing. It drove other Black kids crazy because I wasn't changing to fit in. My self-awareness was more than most people's at twelve years old.

I took the bus to Colma—sometimes I couldn't find a seat. There were certain groups of girls I couldn't sit with, not necessarily Black, because I wasn't cool enough. I had to be very careful about where I put myself all day long. It was stressful.

But the teachers were awesome. They wanted me to take everything I could.

Eighth grade wasn't too bad because now no one was older than me. Suddenly boys started noticing girls. Because most people who were picking on me in seventh grade were Black, I never had a Black boyfriend. I was anathema. By eighth grade unless it was a new guy at school, no Black guy would date me. The first time I got a boy's picture was in eighth grade. He was Jewish. I knew there were people who were Jewish but that's all I knew about him. I showed my mom his picture. She didn't say anything. A few weeks later my mom was talking to my aunt and said I had a boyfriend. I showed my aunt the picture, and she acted shocked and laughed. After that, I never showed anyone pictures of my friends. It bothered me a lot. I started putting things together. "I'm this color, he's a different color, people my own color don't like me because I hang out with people of other colors."

Between eighth and ninth grades, Fern discovered drama classes.

That was one of my best summers. I was in a play with people from different ethnic backgrounds. We decided to do Star Trek. It was a time when I learned that my personality and my worth were not based on how I looked.

As soon as I got to Jefferson, the first thing I did was join drama. Since I was always surrounding myself with theatre people, who are the least racist and most open, that may be why I didn't experience as much racial prejudice. We were always representing someone else!

Fern found that Jeff was a good place for her to be, in spite of its reputation.

I remember an adult man, possibly a coach, made an off-hand joke that he'd heard someone from another district say the kids at Jeff were so wild that they were having sex in the bushes. I thought, "Really?" I spent a good portion of my freshman year looking at the bushes! That comment was a reflection on the fact that we had so many minorities. Others were uncomfortable with that, so they thought we were doing these wild crazy things. We had a reputation. Jefferson was comprised of working-class people. I think it made us feel that we weren't better than anyone else. Most of my friends also lived in houses, owned or rented—not in apartments—so I thought we were all the same.

When you start getting into boyfriend/girlfriend, race comes up big time because parents don't like mixed couples, whether or not the parent is a minority. Almost all of us grew up with two parents of the same race, but we were the generation in which things were changing. You went to school with people who weren't the same race. It was inevitable that you'd make friends with someone of another race.

At fifteen I had my first boyfriend, who was White. His family lived in Southern Hills, a wealthier neighborhood. I wanted to visit him, but when his parents found out I was Black, they wouldn't allow it. We saw each other on the side for a bit but grew apart. I later found out that my parents had wanted to buy a house in Southern Hills in 1962, but no one would sell to them because of racial prejudice.

At Jeff there was a group of girls, the Black Student Cultural Organization drill team. For me, that was the biggest thing I noticed—"Hey, they're the same color as me!" In ninth grade I was still trying to figure out where I stood. They'd perform at rallies, but sometimes they'd get militant. One time they sang, "I'm dreaming of a Black Christmas." It was their way of protesting. A [White] teacher sitting next to me said, "Fern, you wouldn't go down and do that, would you?" I thought, "No, I wouldn't, but not for the reason you think." Whenever someone approached me, instead of asking me if I'd like to join, they'd ask, "Why aren't you in this?" But I didn't identify with that at all. I hadn't experienced any overt racism growing up, so I didn't feel a need to join them.

Jeff really helped me to understand that we're all the same. The only time it was different was at homecoming. In the class of '69, my freshman year, it was the classic White jock with the beautiful White homecoming queen. After that it changed and people of different races were queen, etc., so we had better role models. I put it in my brain that "Hey, I can be that, too."

At Jeff I had some Black friends, male and female, but never Black boyfriends. Part of that was because I never got over being treated differently by Black guys. They'd already made up their minds about who I was without getting to know me. When you're teenagers, though, you can't blame them.

If my mother had a problem with my having a non-Black boyfriend, she never mentioned it. My father died when I was sixteen so he never went through that period with me. My mother was very gracious. Since I was doing well academically, she never said anything. Three years later my sister comes up and all her boyfriends were Black. Society was changing, too. A lot of Black men are famous now, really popular. Girls of all races are trying to get their autographs, etc. In my mind there's a disconnect, because when I was growing up people didn't embrace Black people like it's done now. I'm sure there are all these grandparents looking at what's going on now and saying, "Don't be so ethnic," where the kids are excited about "being ethnic," being bold, etc.

I created a "family" at Jeff with my circle of friends. Everyone had a family nickname, like we were relatives. People teased me at first, but I felt there was nothing wrong with that because I wanted them as friends. Jefferson allowed me to be me. No one ever told me I couldn't do certain things. I can't imagine what it would have been like going to another school.

After high school, Fern enrolled at the University of the Pacific (UOP) at Stockton.

I went into the college thing with so little information. I had no idea what I was doing, I had no idea what profession I would pursue. I picked UOP because it was close enough to home. Because I was female, Black, and my father was dead, people started throwing money at me. I just had to show up and sign. I never had to spend a dime while I was in college, which was pretty awesome. But I had to pay it all back.

I'd studied drama and science in high school because that was what my two favorite teachers, Mr. Sinor and Mrs. Mongan, taught. I signed up again for these subjects in college. While in chemistry class, I met a lot of pre-med, pre-dental, pre-veterinary, pre-dietician, and pre-pharmacy students. The ones who were pre-pharm seemed to be the most fun, so that's how I decided to go into that profession. That's how I made all my decisions—if it sounded fun!

I liked Stockton and didn't want to leave. It was smaller then; the campus was in a very safe area. It was my first time away from home. I was my own person. It didn't matter what I was taking, I just wanted to stay.

Fern shares some experiences about racism as an adult.

After Jeff, out in the real world, I ran into racism a lot more. I found out there are people who won't work with you, etc., because of your race. It's not always overt. If a White person knows a Black person, they ask if you know them too, like I'm supposed to know all the Black people in the whole area! One summer I worked on the night crew at a bank. I started at about five p.m. One day at about a quarter to five, before I got there, a Black guy came by the bank. My supervisor saw him outside and told him, "The bank is closed." When I got there, she told me, "Your friends shouldn't come here when the bank is closed or while you're working." I never corrected her. I just said I didn't know who it was and let it go.

My son is half-White, half-Black. When he was born, I really had to start dealing with racism much more than before. Once when he was in the Boy Scouts, selling tickets with another kid, some White man told him that he "didn't do business with [n-words]." My son told us about it. You tell them, "Don't worry about it," but the damage has been done.

In Las Vegas, where I live now, we have power outages in the summer when all the air conditioners are on. I was living with my son's stepdad, who is very White but grew up in a Black neighborhood. He doesn't realize he has White privilege. Once, after a power outage, there was a big explosion at a shopping area a block from our house. My husband says, "I need to see what happened," so he takes my son and goes right up to the police to ask what was going on. My son hung back because he knew he had to be careful. He knew he could be a target. He's very aware that his color will be seen and judged before anything else. I've taught him, as my father taught me, to take the high road when people act like idiots. Think about where a person might be coming from, and if you're not physically hurt, then take the higher road.

Adrienne

(Black, class of '75, Fern's younger sister)

* * *

Every time I went to history class, the teacher showed movies or some-thing about Black people as slaves. She never showed us anything positive that happened for Black people. It was very depressing, so I wouldn't go to class anymore.

* * *

Adrienne was born in San Francisco, the second of two daughters. Her first memories are of living in a neighborhood near the Cow Palace.

I didn't know anybody except my sister and the people at church. Every Sunday our parents dropped us off at an all-White Baptist church and later picked us up. We had to eat oatmeal every Sunday before church. To this day I don't like oatmeal. When my sister was getting baptized, I cried because I was by myself and had no idea what was go-ing on. I thought they were drowning her. Since then I've had a fear of water, which might be why I never learned how to swim.

When I was four years old we moved to Daly City, and I started kindergarten. They'd started building BART [rapid transit] about that time in our new neighborhood, so everyone across the street from it had

21

to move. I skipped school the day of the groundbreaking and ended up on the front page of the newspaper. When Mom saw the paper she said, "I guess everyone will know where you were!"

When we lived on Knowles Avenue [now John Daly Boulevard], I was often at our Mexican neighbors' house. I learned a lot from them about Mexican food and speaking Spanish.

Like many children in Daly City, Adrienne was bussed during elementary school.

Kindergarten was fun. I couldn't stand first grade because the teacher was mean and scary. School was mixed—White, Black, Mexican—the only three categories I knew at the time. Some things we learned were not kosher for today. One thing the first-grade teacher taught us to do as a whole class was to pull our eyes slanted up and say all together, "Chinese," then pull our eyes slanted across and say, "Japanese," then slap our knees and say, "American knees." What a horribly uncaring and racist thing to teach children.

I was bussed to John F. Kennedy school for fourth and fifth grades, then to Margaret Pauline Brown for sixth grade, both in White neighborhoods. My teacher was a White lady who was determined to make sure I succeeded. She took me under her wing. She had me sit in the front row and gave me a sense that I was somebody. She taught me so much. My three best friends [all Black] were also there. One was very shy and would never talk to anyone. Our teacher would ask me to talk to her to see what she wanted. My teacher went out of her way only for me, not my friends. She saw something in me that has since flourished, made me know there was nothing I couldn't accomplish if I put my mind to it, and I am so grateful for that. I believe God gave me that as the basis for the many great accomplishments I have made, putting me in the highest places, including where I am now.

At school Adrienne never learned much about race or ethnicity, but at home it was different.

My mom would tell me stories of things she went through. She didn't trust White people much. One time as a young adult she was standing at a bus stop in Austin, Texas, and this White lady rode by on a horse. The horse stepped on her foot and broke it. The woman just kept on riding. My mom always wanted us to love everybody, but she was a little leery because of what she went through.

Dad grew up in Baltimore, Maryland. He taught me a lot about life but never talked to me about race. Daddy was awesome, but he died when I was twelve.

Mom didn't want us to be prejudiced, but she wanted us to be aware. My sister liking White men didn't make Mom too happy. Her message to us: "Be cautious, be aware." We had to be home by sundown. One time when I was in eighth grade, I was late. I called my mom from my cousin's house to let her know I would be home late. It was dark out. I was scared. I took off my shoes and ran all the way home. I rang the bell a bunch of times, but she didn't answer, so I ran all the way back to my cousin's. I was screaming and crying. I called Mom and asked, "Why didn't you answer?" She replied, casually, "I didn't hear you." She had a way of teaching you a lesson.

Although Adrienne is younger than her sister, she often worried about her in junior high school.

I worried about Fern because she was so little, and Black people didn't like her since she was always around White people. I watched her a lot to make sure she was safe. She had a fight one day, though, and that showed me she could take care of herself. They didn't actually fight; the other girl was following Fern and taunting her, but when Fern turned around and said she'd had it, the other girl could see she wasn't afraid, so she stopped.

Adrienne describes her own time in junior high school, which included the closest she herself ever came to a fight.

At Colma I saw more Black people because they bussed a lot of Blacks there who were different from the Black people I knew. They had learned a lot about Black history. They were loud, cursed a lot, fought a lot. I didn't really understand their anger, but I got a best friend from there who fought a lot but was really sweet. Unfortunately, we were only together for seventh and eighth grades. I really loved some of my Black friends, and I hated that they went on to Serramonte High School without me.

I remember one Black girl at Colma who some kids wanted me to fight. People pushed us into each other, but we didn't do anything, and that was the end of it.

I was everybody's friend—Black, White, Chinese/Asian, all different races. I remember learning Spanish there and one time I made a big mistake. We were all playing volleyball, and one of the Latina girls said something about "manos" [hands]. Someone else asked me what she said. I told her, "I think she called you monkeys [monos]."

Like many younger siblings, Adrienne's arrival at a new school meant there were expectations based on their older sibling(s), but by her junior year she had made her mark.

It was always, "Oh, you're Fern's sister." But that wasn't me. Fern was the smartest person in the world. I was a cheerleader, and I ran track.

Jeff had a big mix of people. I started going to the Black Student Cultural Organization. It was fun performing at rallies with them. I didn't have any conflict with anyone. I still hung out with Black friends.

Every time I went to history class, the teacher showed movies or something about Black people as slaves. She never showed us anything positive that happened for Black people. It was very depressing so I wouldn't go to class anymore. She didn't mind that I stopped going to class. Today the Black people I know tease me because I don't know anything about Black history.

In my junior year I was the head varsity cheerleader, so I mostly hung out with the cheerleaders that year [who were all White]. One of the seniors didn't treat me very nice. The other two were from Brisbane [a mostly White suburb] and they treated me fine. Not only was I head cheerleader, I was also homecoming queen that year. I was so shocked. I didn't know people liked me so much. I thought, "I love you all, but I didn't know you loved me too!" Thank God I experienced it all then, because I ended up graduating after junior year. From going to summer school, I'd earned so many credits they wouldn't let me attend school for my senior year. I had to graduate early. I was very sad to leave.

I pretty much only dated Black guys—that's who I was attracted to. In college I was best friends with a Latino/Mexican guy. I've been friends with all different guys but not attracted to them.

After Jeff, Adrienne enrolled at the University of San Francisco and studied computer science before it became popular. She had a long career in IT, from software engineer to IT manager. She is married with two children, two grandchildren, and is head deaconess at her church, one of many church offices she has held in fifty years.

Adrienne shares some of her family's experiences with racism.

My oldest daughter had a bad time in junior high school in Pleasanton, CA. She was one of only two Black female students—the other

*one was her cousin—but I didn't realize she was having problems. The
teachers must have seen what was happening but didn't do anything.
She herself didn't tell me at the time, and I was pretty disappointed
about what she went through, but she made it. She's a strong girl. I really wish Black teens wouldn't fight against each other.*

*My daughter is a very smart person—on the honor roll, did every-
thing, etc.—but in senior year she stopped going to class. A counselor
told me she didn't need to still be in school. She was done with it, so she
registered for college. She went to Hawaii, got her bachelor's, master's,
and now is working on her doctorate. Once I bought a toy that when
you drop it, it stands right back up. I named it after her.*

*My younger daughter had a problem with someone in junior high.
She told them, "I'll call God down on you," so they left her alone. She
got a wrestling medal. She spent her first year at Amador High and
said, "I want to go to Skyline where there are more Black people," so
we sent her to Skyline. After a few weeks, she said, "Mom, I'm sitting
outside, no one's talking to me. If no one talks to me in a few weeks, I
want to go back to Amador," but I told her she couldn't.*

*She's an actress. She got into drama and went to the same school
the actor Tom Hanks went to. She did well there. She's Black-oriented,
but she's a flower child and loves everyone. After college, she went to
work for Kaiser, where she traveled to many elementary, junior high
and high schools, performing plays to promote health and unity. She
has so much energy it's amazing. She has been blessed with two lovely
sons. I am blessed that her family lives nearby.*

*My husband is very tolerant. He's from Compton, CA. Today he
serves as head deacon at our church. When he was fourteen he was
sent to a private school, then went to Stanford. He's been through a lot.
When we were looking for a house a White coworker told him, "You
could live anywhere; you're Black. You could live in a ghetto." He never
says anything against anyone. He has so many White people at his job
who say things, but he'll just take it. Even now, the White person he
works for is from Texas and told him, "I would rather have a White guy
working for me." My husband is patient, but I would react differently.
His boss has said things that other people have heard, so my husband
could go after him, but he's not like that.*

Adrienne shares some things about her Oakland neighborhood today.

*The first Black person in the neighborhood felt pressured. Other
people living there didn't want her but finally she got a chance to move*

in. She moved here about twenty-seven years ago. It was easier for other Black families after her.

Adrienne's final thoughts about Jeff:

I liked the people at Jeff and my teachers were awesome. I enjoyed cheerleading. I didn't hold any office in the Black Student Union because I didn't know a lot about it. I don't know if I really fit in. I participated in it but didn't know the history. They knew so much more about Black culture than I did. I was disappointed that I had to leave a year early because I had too many credits.

Jacinto (aka Chinto)

(Latino, class of '72)

* * *

When we were growing up, you hardly saw anyone who wasn't White on television. In those days the only non-Whites we saw on screen were Indians, and they were the bad guys; the good guys were White. People get brainwashed. The lack of role models, or negative ones, leads to prejudice.

* * *

Chinto was born in Managua, Nicaragua, the third of five children. The family moved to the U.S. when he was only two and a half, and then moved again to Daly City when he was seven. Chinto's mother was the instigator of the move.

My family came to the U.S. because my dad got into some trouble back home, just running around. My mom came here all by herself, two years before the rest of us. I didn't realize until later that that was why my dad was always angry—he couldn't do what he wanted to do here. My mom wanted to buy a house right away. Dad didn't want to because he wanted to return to Nicaragua. My mom was a small woman but had the heart of a giant. She gave us an opportunity to have better lives.

A major challenge for Chinto during his childhood was that his parents spoke only Spanish.

*Growing up, we had to translate for our parents. It was very dif-
ficult because I didn't always know all the words in English or Spanish.
I did my best. My father used to get mad at me, but he had put himself in
the position of not being able to respond to others. I didn't have a good
rapport with my dad; he just wasn't there for us. He was often angry
and abusive because he couldn't defend himself, primarily because he
couldn't communicate in English, but also because he had been forced
to leave Managua, where his lifestyle was easy.*

Chinto started kindergarten in San Francisco, but his English was
limited at first.

*A lady in our apartment building taught my sister and me English.
By the time I started kindergarten, I could speak a little.*

*I attended St. Joseph's for first and second grades. There were
mostly White kids, a couple of Latino boys, but there was never a problem with how I was treated. I was very fortunate to be at the right place
at the right time with the right people.*

When Chinto's family moved to Daly City, their neighborhood consisted
mostly of Italian families, plus three Irish families and his Nicaraguan
family.

*There were five kids in each household, and we all got along well.
My aunt lived with us and helped raise us. She didn't speak English but
she always cooked enough food for everyone in the neighborhood. Our
home was the gathering place for all the kids. In our culture we were
very open and giving. People noticed. They felt comfortable around us.*

*My aunt spoke to the kids in Spanish. It was amazing. They were
four or five years old and they picked it up so quickly. We played with
one little boy who was half Japanese, half White. One time his dad
came to pick him up and my aunt said something in Spanish. The boy
translated for his dad, and his dad started to cry because he couldn't
believe his son could understand Spanish. He loved that.*

*When I started elementary school at Colma, things went really
well. Everyone just came up to me, asked my name, introduced themselves, and was friendly.*

Chinto's first memory related to race was when he was eight years
old and with neighborhood friends.

*I recall hearing someone say, "Last one up the hill is a [n-word]"
or "Last one up the hill loves. . . ." [a name he didn't recognize]. I'd nev-*

er heard the n-word before and didn't know what it meant. Two years later I was at a corner store, and I heard the same name that I didn't recognize before. I saw the person they had named and realized why the kids had been teasing. Suddenly it hit me how mean and hateful people could be. People might joke around, but I was very fortunate that there was never anything mean or intentional towards me. I didn't like being mean to other kids.

My friend Joe was the only Black guy on our Little League team, so he stood out. He told me later about the jokes people used to make right in front of him. The coach taught at Skyline Junior College, and Joe was disappointed that the coach never defended him or put a stop to the jokes. The next year they split up the team and I took Joe's place. I never experienced the level of racism that he did. Nobody called me a "wetback."

Both of Chinto's parents worked, his father in a warehouse and his mother at a drapery company as a seamstress.

My parents were too involved in earning money to put food on the table to spend much time with us. My eldest brother was five years older than me and he took care of us; we were very close. He was always driven to do well and very dedicated to helping us out. We all got along well. My youngest sister is nine years younger than me.

There was always enough food for us, but it bothered me that my mom always bought things that were discounted even though they had enough money to get better quality stuff. When I was ten, I spoke up when my parents bought me some clothing that had been marked down. I told them they could afford better, and I didn't want to wear something that would embarrass me. They worked hard and could afford more, but they were too money-conscious to spend it.

Our family traveled quite a bit, though. We used to go to Tijuana all the time. We went to Disneyland. I was grateful to live in the Bay Area. God knows what things would have been like for us outside the area and in other states.

Chinto remembers his parents focusing on all their children getting a good education and job, but they didn't address race.

They didn't say who we could or couldn't hang out with. My siblings didn't experience racism, either. Our house was always at the center of things because my aunt babysat for the whole neighborhood. She made homemade tortillas, and after tasting them, the kids wouldn't leave!

When Chinto began intermediate school, he was aware of many more people of color.

It was good, seeing people of different races. There were a lot more Latinos. We were all first generation and most of us were bilingual, with Spanish as our second language. People weren't focused on who other people were. It was just all of us trying to get along.

Chinto reflects on his crushes during his young life.

My first girlfriend was in fourth grade. She was White. The year before, in third grade, I was in a Christmas play. The teacher told me I needed some tights to play an elf. I told her I didn't have any because I'm a guy. She said I had to find some, but she wasn't very helpful—I was surprised she picked me for the play at all because I knew she didn't like me. I went to the class next door and had to tell the whole class that I was in a play and needed some tights. My (later) girlfriend said I could borrow hers. I've never forgotten that.

My next crush was on a Filipina classmate in eighth grade. I don't know how my mom found out that I had a girlfriend, but her friends came over one time and asked me if I had a girlfriend. I said, "Yes," and my mom told her friends that she was Filipina. One of them said, "You're in America now, so you can have a light-skinned blonde girlfriend." This is coming from a woman who had kids out of wedlock. You know how Latinos are—no shame! My mom's friend asked how my girlfriend looked and mom responds, "Oh, she's a lot lighter than he is." My grandmother liked blonde-haired, light-skinned people. Enough! Who cares?!

Another thing that impacts people is television. When we were growing up, you hardly saw anyone who wasn't White on television. In those days the only non-Whites we saw on screen were Indians, and they were the bad guys; the good guys were White. People get brainwashed. The lack of role models, or negative ones, leads to prejudice.

Chinto has positive memories of his high school days at Jefferson High.

It was like the United Nations, and I've always been comfortable with everyone. Everyone got along, especially during those times. I also got along well with kids from Brisbane, who were mostly White and Okies. I did have one White childhood friend who probably was not as comfortable with racial differences as I was. I put up with him. Sure, there were some little problems, but nothing major where people were getting hurt.

When I was a sophomore, one time we were talking about Hank Aaron [famous Black baseball player], who was going to break Babe Ruth's [famous White baseball player] homerun record. There was a new kid from Boston who said, "Are you f-in kidding me? A [n-word] isn't going to break a White guy's record." That was the only time I remember that kind of talk. I was wondering what was going on, the fact he thought the White guy was automatically the best. I remember thinking, "I don't like this person." I didn't want anything to do with someone who had so much hate. It made me wonder what kind of family life he had.

Chinto's closest friends at Jeff were very mixed.

My friends were all different colors. I didn't look at the color of a person's skin. Being in athletics, you're in a team sport in a huddle. I'd call the plays. I saw everybody, but didn't dwell on their skin color or nationality. It was a great experience. We all got along. I struggled with school, but the competition of athletics really got me through things. You always wanted to be the best, to be able to win. That was my motivation to stay on track academically.

Even when we played sports against mostly White schools, I didn't experience any racism among players. Sports allowed you to look at people's talent. You earn the respect of other athletes, so race didn't matter. People focused more on how you played the game. Willie Mays [famous Black baseball player] was my idol. You look at the positives in other people.

Chinto attended the College of San Mateo (CSM) for his first two years of college. While he had a lot of confidence in his football skills at Jeff, he was smaller than most players and wasn't sure if he would be able to play in college against bigger and faster guys.

They had a really good team at CSM. It was very competitive. The coach called me up to see if I was interested in trying out. CSM went to State [championships] the year before, so they had about 120 guys there for spring ball—at Jeff we only had eighteen for our final game. So we were all sitting in the stands and the coach dismissed everyone. He and I went down on the field. I'm on the sidelines and I look up in the stands and see that no one had left. I realized they knew who I was and how I'd broken a bunch of records and made the all-county team.

I didn't think anyone outside our league would know me. I'm not Joe Montana, but it gave me more confidence to pursue football at CSM, and I did pretty well.

After graduating from CSM, Chinto went to Sacramento State College to pursue a teaching credential in physical education.

I really liked living in Sacramento. It was the first time I was on my own. It had nice weather. (I hated the fog of Daly City.) I was lucky to never experience anyone being mean to me the way some of my Black friends did. But during student teaching I was at various high schools on the peninsula, I was back living at home, I didn't have a car and had to take the bus. There were also behavior issues with the students, nothing to do with race, just bullies, and I got tired of it. I got a job at United Parcel Service, where I was earning more than I did as a teacher. There wasn't a problem with race, more about locker room BS. Everyone wants an easier route, better hours. People ask, "Why does he have a better route than me?" I got along with everybody. No problems with the customers—I always kept my clothes on!

Chinto remembers getting together with some friends from Jeff a few years after graduation.

There was a group of us guys who went to Russian River [north of San Francisco] to see another friend who was staying at a resort up there. One of our friends was Black. When he came to the pool, everyone else who was there suddenly cleared out. This was only forty miles from San Francisco. Who were these people? That moment tells you so much.

Chinto's wife Rosie is Latina, born in the U.S.

When I met her parents they said, "He's a nice guy, but he's a little dark." She replied, "But he has a good job with benefits!" Even though her family came from Mexico, they're all blond with blue eyes. They have their moments.

Chinto's final reflections:

The friendships we developed were very special, and what I accomplished—to this day, people ask me what I accomplished, if I can still throw a football. My kids say I live in the past, but it was a real special part of my life. I left my mark there. People I meet at work re-

membered me from high school; they remember that I touched so many people. Being able to still have friendships with so many people from back then is special. Jeff was unique because of the people. You didn't have to go to the Philippines, to Mexico, to Ghana or Zimbabwe. You had everyone right there. It was perfect timing, the best generation. We all got along. I was very blessed because everybody liked me.

Jenny

(Filipina, class of '72)

* * *

I think the biggest lesson we learned at Jefferson was acceptance of the individual . . . what a profound lesson!

* * *

Jenny was born in the Philippines, the youngest of three children, and spent her formative years in Japan before her family emigrated to California.

I look like what I am, Filipina, and so people expect me to speak English with an accent. I don't have an accent, but I have still been asked throughout my life if English is my first language. I've even had people ask me if I speak English at all, or talk past me because they assume I did not speak or understand.

My father was in the U.S. Navy, and when I was four years old my family moved to Japan, from a tropical climate to a very snowy winter in the middle of Japan. I started off in a Japanese Catholic school run by Spanish nuns. It was multi-cultural, made up of various ethnicities, Japanese, White, etc. I didn't feel like "the only one." We were segregated by language—English-speaking and Japanese-speaking—not by race, culture, or creed.

I have great memories of Japan. We lived in a village for a year or so and then moved to the military base. That's where I was introduced

to more of American culture. After four years we left and moved to San Diego, California. That is where my first memory of race relations comes from.

When my parents looked for a house to buy, we were faced with "steering," a form of institutional racism. We weren't allowed to buy a house where there were better schools. Some developments would not sell to people of color; we were steered to a development that had a minority population.

After two years in San Diego, we moved to Daly City. My parents wanted to buy a house in the Westlake area. I remember my mother telling me that—again—no one would show them houses in the area they wanted. They ended up buying in "old" Daly City, where immigrants like us were steered, and I was bussed to school across the freeway. There was a group of us that were bussed. I never asked why I had to go to a different school when there was a school right around the corner from where we lived. The law of the land stated everyone should have equal access to housing, schools, etc. In reality, that was not the practice. It's mind-boggling to me. This influenced how I do my work in real estate to this day.

At my elementary school, Fernando Rivera, most of the kids were White. There were a few kids who made fun of my eyes, saying things like "Ching chong Chinaman." This was confusing. I thought, "I'm not Chinese, so what are you saying?" I had a few friends, but when I was invited to birthday parties I had to be driven there because I didn't live nearby.

Going to Colma for junior high was an improvement. Nobody called anyone out based on their race, color, or creed. I developed some long-term friendships there, with people from various backgrounds from Black and Japanese to Italian and Arab.

Jenny went on to Jefferson High School with most of her friends from Colma.

For high school, I had to take a stance with my mother. She wanted me to go to a Catholic school, but my father said it was okay to choose where I went. I didn't fully understand the implications of my choice, but I had gone to eight different schools already and I didn't want to have to change my friends again. Most of my friends from Colma were going to Jeff, so I wanted to go there, too. If I had gone to another school, my path could have been quite different.

I was pretty comfortable with myself by then. I think when you grow up in an urban area there's a certain level of social comfort with people from various backgrounds, including Blacks, Latins, Japanese,

Italians, Arab, and others. Changing schools so much, you learn how to adjust and survive. The neighborhood we lived in wasn't the best—it had drug dealers; it wasn't the white picket fences and big lawns—but it seemed like people got along and I never felt unsafe. We had a Black family next door. One of my best friends was Japanese American. We often walked to school together.

Events of the seventies were signifcant and transforming. It was an awakening. We were moving from the civil rights movement, to the Vietnam War, to the peace movement, to women's liberation, and we became more aware of how the world looked.

Everybody got along at Jefferson, which probably made it unique. There was real acceptance. I didn't know at the time that many of our teachers deliberately chose to teach in an ethnically diverse community. It wasn't so "White and suburban," nor was it inner-city like Balboa High in San Francisco. I think our teachers were very aware of that, so they made it a point to work with it and celebrate our diversity. I felt encouraged by them. There were certain teachers who really developed our self-confidence and kind of protected us from the world. It wasn't until my adult life that there were incidences I learned about that could have been pretty devastating.

My family's social group was made up of Filipinos we met in Japan. We had all stayed close despite moving around and moving away from each other. But my parents didn't say, "Stick to your own kind, don't trust that other person because of. . . ." As long as I got good grades, they didn't mind who I hung out with. The message was that I was going to college no matter what, and that was my goal.

My close circle didn't look at people in terms of their race. Maybe I was colorblind to it. Our big rival, Westmoor High, was considered the "White" school. They had some people of color, but there was a real division. We were told in various ways that Jefferson wasn't as good as they were at sports, academically, or whatever else. Another school, Serramonte, was established at this time. I think that was a social/educational experiment. They tried to integrate it with both sides of the freeway.

I remember an example of being protected. I was a pep girl and we went to a basketball tournament in [majority White] Auburn, CA, where the other school put us up in people's homes for the night. Two of us—the mascot and I—stayed in a one-bedroom apartment with a student whose mother wasn't around. We slept in the living room. It wasn't wonderful, but as a kid you just go with it. I didn't know until years later that it was a color thing. A teacher who I was close with told me, "You and our mascot were housed with a particular family because you were

*both people of color. Everyone else was placed in beautiful homes."
He said we took it well. There was such a bubble of protection that no
one made a big deal of it. I don't know if you would call it protection or
preservation.*

After high school Jenny enrolled at the University of California at
Davis.

*Davis was a huge culture shock! First of all, I had a White room-
mate who was into Scientology. Her parents were college professors,
and I was from a blue-collar family. I would walk into a lecture hall
with 300 people and there's only maybe five with black hair like mine
or of a different ethnic background. During the summer program, I had
a roommate who was clearly there to get an "MRS" degree! ["Mrs.,"
meaning that the roommate was there to find a husband.]*

*Being a sociology major opened my eyes to many things and de-
veloped my critical thinking skills. I was driven. I was in college and I
would graduate. I became very passionate about Asian American studies, about Asian women's studies. I started to learn about my Filipino
American culture and history in America. One instructor was very significant in teaching me about strong ethnic women. It was all new to me
. . . yes, we can be that strong, it's part of our background. You figure
out where you're going to fit.*

*Later I was roommates with a Japanese American friend, who was
also from Jeff. Partly because of my work schedule we didn't hang out
together on weekends. I remember talking to her about something related to housing. I had already formulated in my head about how to
make money from multi-unit apartment buildings/rentals. I was really
political and socially progressive, but I became a capitalist.*

*I never went out with anyone Filipino until after college. I was
so focused and driven to get my degree. I was also into Black Studies
classes, taking those classes in preference to the conventional White
European courses. When I left Davis, I thought, "Thank God," but, in
retrospect, I see what a great motivating stepping-stone it was. When I
left, I started meeting other people who looked like me.*

*I became more aware and more reflective of race relations. I was
involved with Filipino farm workers, the Japanese internment camps,
and the role of women in minority communities. I recognized and questioned why people of color were not given tenure—I had two long-serv-
ing college instructors, one Japanese and the other Black, who had
never been given status or tenure and had no security. I learned about
institutional racism at Davis.*

Upon graduation from Davis, Jenny moved back to the Bay Area.

I believed I should do something to help people. I was going to volunteer for a year in something related to social services, but a former teacher at Jeff said to me, "Don't ever volunteer; get paid for what you do!" so I worked in the South of Market Head Start program [in San Francisco]. Many of the South of Market people were new immigrants, "fresh off the boat." It may have been where they had friends and relatives or affordable housing. Upon getting settled and getting jobs, some moved to Daly City or the Outer Mission.

It was the seventies; social experiments and liberal causes. Studies said that early childhood education was important for social development. The guy in charge of our team was White, but the rest of the staff was ethnically diverse. I was in it for the kids, the Filipino community, but I discovered that the board members were into it because of the politics. We were being sold out. Head Start was about power and money/funding for some people involved. That was so disheartening.

I applied to graduate school at SF State, thinking I was going to do more sociology, but I switched to interdisciplinary studies with an emphasis in counseling, which seemed more relevant. During graduate school I worked for San Mateo County schools, helping ethnic communities to address issues about jobs, race, and equality. I have an affinity for San Mateo County. It's progressive. It's not perfect, but they're concerned about things like homelessness, education, food, hunger.

After this, race relations became even more prevalent in my life. Proposition 13 [a statewide proposition that fixed property taxes for homeowners] resulted in less money for many social programs. I lost my job but finished my master's degree and got a job at Fresno State as a counselor. It was another awakening. It was a farming community of Mexicans and Blacks, and they were segregated. I and a Black woman were the only two women counselors. Coming from Jefferson, I thought everyone got along. There I learned more about how people viewed race relations, and how important that was. I had a [Mexican] director who said, "You're too radical; we may not renew your contract," but I didn't care. I did do some radical things, which you can do when you're young and don't have any family responsibilities. But then the director's wife [White] asked me to speak to her class. Ethnic minority kids were drawn to me because I was a non-White woman in a position to make a difference. That's when I started to learn about how important role models are.

I was getting summer jobs for my students in Fresno. Someone from San Francisco happened to ask me about a manual I wrote in graduate school. I told him I train counselors and do things related to self-esteem. I ended up creating a job for myself—a program for inner-city youth for the National Football League [NFL]—and left Fresno. The inner-city youth program was really interesting, since it dealt with opportunities with trade unions.

Jenny reflects further on racism.

Do I know what it's like to be a person of color? Yes. Do I know what it's like to be Black? No. Do I know what it's like to be Brown? Yes. Do I know what it's like to be a woman? Yes. And I know what it's like to be refused service because of your color.

*In the seventies my sister-in-law, my sister, and I were in a town outside New Orleans, Louisiana. We went to a restaurant and were waiting to get served. Finally, the waitress comes over and says, "We're not going to serve you because of your color." Looking at my blond, blue-eyed sister-in-law, she said, "We're not going to serve you because of **them**."*

At Davis in my sociology classes, we were already talking about the fact that things start changing when people start intermarrying. If that's happening around the world, that's a good thing. Am I hopeful? I don't think we have a choice but to be hopeful because if we're not, then we might go backward rather than forward.

Jenny's final thoughts:

Getting along and finding your place in the world is not just about color; it's about race, it's about creed, it's about all that. What have we come to today? Black Lives Matter. White fragility. White privilege. My husband [White] and I celebrated our differences and talked about race and culture. A generation ago, we would not have been able to get married because of anti-miscegenation laws. He was proud of the fact that we were married. His parents were thrilled. But I had problems with his son-in-law, who was married to my husband's daughter from a previous marriage. He would make fun of me or say ugly things about race.

In the late nineties we were flying to Colorado and a flight attendant said to my husband, without looking at me, "Does she understand English?" He said, "She's a public speaker. She speaks and understands English perfectly well." I was too shocked to say anything myself; tears came to my eyes. We wrote to the CEO, and the airline gave us two first-class tickets, which we returned. It would be more satisfying if they did some sensitivity or diversity training instead of trying to buy us off.

Our childhood experiences are very significant in race relations, but there are socioeconomics that we need to deal with. Just because you're of a certain color or race or sexuality/orientation doesn't mean that you're privileged or not privileged. I think the biggest lesson we learned at Jefferson was acceptance of the individual. What a profound lesson!

Riley

(White, Jewish, class of '70)

* * *

It's hard for young adults today to understand the stigma attached to having children out of wedlock in the 1950s. It was nothing less than scandalous. And, of course, the child was "illegitimate." I felt less worthy, ashamed.

* * *

Riley was born in San Francisco, an only child with family roots in Daly City.

My mother's grandfather was a founder of the first synagogue in San Mateo County, in what was by then called Daly City. He came from an area of Eastern Europe that is now part of Russia, and he left to escape conscription and pogroms against Jews. He spoke only Yiddish when he arrived in America, but within a few years he became the city solicitor, akin to what a city manager is today. My great-grandparents travelled down through Canada and down to SF. They spoke no English either. My grandmother, Lena, was the only daughter among their twenty-one children. Some of them didn't survive infancy.

When American-born Lena married my Russian immigrant grandfather in 1917, she lost her American citizenship! The US Supreme Court ruled this unconstitutional a few years later and Lena's citizenship was restored.

41

Riley's beginnings were unusual for the times.

I was an accidental birth. My mother was in her early thirties, had never been in a relationship and lived with her very overbearing mother—in today's jargon, it was a dysfunctional family. In 1951 my mother encountered a man at a USO [United Service Organization] dance and conceived me. Her older sister was also at the dance, and she was the only family member who knew what had happened. My aunt believed it was the only time my parents were ever together, and my mother never became involved with anyone else. Somehow my mother concealed the pregnancy until she went into labor! Obviously, her giving birth was an enormous shock to her family. These circumstances shaped my life and still do, even as a man approaching seventy with grandchildren.

I grew up in my grandmother's house with the extended family. My mother's older siblings eloped to escape their mother's grip, but three unmarried siblings also lived with us. Two of them died in their forties. The sole survivor was an uncle seventeen years older than me, more like an older brother. He probably suffered from social anxiety, though it wasn't diagnosed as such at the time. We became very close and remained so until his death at age eighty.

By today's standards we'd be considered lower-middle class. When you grow up with little material wealth, you don't notice it if everyone around you is no better off. I never felt I lacked for anything. I had a loving home. There were no family vacations, and no car until I was eight or so, but it didn't faze me.

As an impressionable seven-year-old, I remember having a conversation with my favorite aunt. She held my hand and told me adamantly, "I want you to make something of yourself. You have the ability to do more than your family has." Her premature death at forty-one, while I was away at college, was devastating.

Riley's grandmother ruled everybody's lives.

She adored me, but not unconditionally. As a parent you love your children dearly, but you raise them to be independent. My grandmother couldn't do that. I think it was because she lost her husband while pregnant with her sixth child. For the rest of her life, she resented being "abandoned," and she tried to raise all her children to remain dependent on her. I was determined to not follow the same path.

Even with a loving family, Riley's life was blighted by his lack of a father.

It's hard for most people today to understand the stigma attached to having children out of wedlock in the 1950s. It was nothing less than scandalous. And, of course, the child was "illegitimate." I felt less worthy, ashamed. In elementary school I made Father's Day cards with everybody else but tossed them in the trash when I left the classroom.

I didn't know anything about my biological father. At six or seven years old I was told that he was dead. I sensed it wasn't true, but I knew not to ask more questions because I didn't want to hurt my mother's feelings. She was very sweet and loving but emotionally fragile. I attribute that to how her own mother controlled her.

The first person I ever shared my story with was my dear friend Richard [Chinese] in high school. I'd gotten in a big fight with my grandmother, who blurted out many hurtful things toward my mother. Each word I spoke to Richard was painful, as if there was a vise on my throat. Shame set me apart from my peers and stayed with me well into adulthood.

In law school I was asked about my father while applying for security clearance for work, and I was determined not to lie. A roommate suggested I contact the Navy, since my parents met at a USO dance and I didn't know where else to start. It was then that I learned that my mother never contacted him to tell him about her pregnancy because she didn't want him to feel obligated—after all, she barely knew him, as far as I know.

It turned out that his name had been on my birth certificate all along, but even after I discovered it, I was less determined to search for him than other people seemed to think I should be. As a father and grandfather, I understand the significant difference between a biological father and a dad who raises and nurtures you. I was curious but otherwise ambivalent.

I never wanted to interfere with any other family he may have had. I can't imagine getting a phone call from someone you'd never known existed. I felt the absence and the loss, but I didn't need to know more about him. As callous as it sounds, he was basically a sperm donor.

Riley didn't grow up with a particularly strong sense of Jewishness, either.

I knew I was Jewish, but we had a fairly secular home. My name isn't at all Jewish! 'Riley' was the nickname of an aunt's husband. It kind of fit the circumstances—unplanned, hidden pregnancy, etc.

I did attend Hebrew school for two years, until my family had a falling-out with the rabbi, who was so strict that he wouldn't be allowed to teach today. My mother didn't have enough money to allow me to continue my Jewish education.

Everyone in my family knew about the Holocaust, but I don't re-member it being discussed at length. Once I asked my grandmother what happened to my grandfather's family. She said he never spoke of them and had no communication with the relatives he left behind. I'm pretty sure that they perished in the Holocaust.

It wasn't until college that a roommate and some friends helped me connect with my roots. I decided I wanted to have a more traditional Jewish family of my own. One Jewish professor in law school became my surrogate father. He had a stern demeanor but a very warm heart, and we remained close until his death a few years ago.

Riley's earliest memories of race/ethnicity are from kindergarten or first grade.

In my earliest days at school in San Francisco, we probably had one African American child in class, maybe one or two Asian children, and Danny, who was of mixed race, although I didn't know that at the time. One day Danny's mother came to volunteer in class—and she was Japanese. I thought, "How can she be Japanese? He doesn't look Japanese." This discovery didn't impact me other than noticing that in some way Danny was different.

When Riley was in the second grade, his family moved to Daly City.

When I got older, I realized the schools I attended were like the United Nations—multi-racial, multi-cultural. My oldest friend was Richard [Chinese]. I remember going up in the hills for a class picnic on the last day of fourth grade. A stranger appeared, probably a White male, standing at a distance. Our teacher asked me to please watch out for Richard. I wondered why she did this, and the only reason I could think of was because he was Chinese. Her saying that struck me as odd then, and still does today.

At home I heard my own family express stereotypes about minority groups—both positive and negative—expressions I would never use. I think it was a reflection of the times. I always questioned things. I was very independent and always a lawyer at heart.

At Colma Junior High School I was intimidated, worried that I wouldn't measure up. I had all the angst and anxiety that middle school-ers often feel. I have no recollection of Colma being more diverse than my elementary schools, although it must have been, as the kids would eventually attend Jeff with me.

Riley arrived at Jefferson High School at a good moment for a young man who craved to expand his horizons and enrich his life.

It was 1966. Jefferson High was the beginning of a whole new world for everyone. I was very excited by my opportunity to make something of myself. I got involved in every extracurricular activity I could. I volunteered in everything I could. It was all part of my journey toward a richer life than my mother and her siblings had experienced.

You spent your days largely with the same people based on whether you were in college prep or vocational classes. In 1968 there were racial incidents, fights after school that may have had racial overtones. I lived a fairly sheltered life with a diverse group who got along well together. My high school friends were like me, striving for a better life than our parents had. We may not have looked alike, but we all had similar goals and all hoped to attend a four-year college. There were many kids I had no contact with because we had no classes together. Several kids in band overlapped with my college prep classes.

My friends were a real cross-section of races and ethnicities. I had dinner countless times at Richard's family's home [Chinese]. I went with them to a family picnic for the employees of the San Francisco Postal Service. There's a photo with about 200 Asian families and one White Jewish kid with glasses.

A close friend, Ken, was Polynesian and Irish but people often thought he was Asian or Indian. His adoptive parents were a Russian-Mexican couple. Another good friend was Helen [Latina].

I often visited the homes of Iris, Sarah, and Deana—three young Black women. It was kind of a counter-stereotype: I was the White guy coming from the single-parent, lower-middle class family, and they all had two parents and a solidly middle-class lifestyle. I didn't focus much on their nice houses, cars, etc. Their lives were just different from mine. I was extremely close with Iris and learned a lot from her about presenting myself more confidently. Years later, she visited me in Oregon and met my family.

Riley didn't have to struggle to get into college; his college came and found him.

It's funny how I ended up at Claremont Men's College [CMC] outside Los Angeles, now known as Claremont-McKenna—a fairly presti-

gious college that I'd never heard of until then. They sent a recruiter to Jeff to find minority kids and encourage them to apply. With affirmative action in the late sixties, colleges and universities were really pushing to increase minority enrollment.

One of the recruiters left a catalog for Claremont Men's College and I asked my friend Iris about it. I took the catalog home and read it and thought, "This school is designed for me!" It had a focus on public affairs, public interest, and government—all the things I was interested in as a teen. I would never have attended CMC had the recruiter not come to Jeff. Besides me, Iris, Sarah, and Helen all ended up attending three of the Claremont Colleges. Of course, I was the only White kid!

In college there were more barriers to racial interaction and harmony. My friend Iris experienced some really difficult social issues with militant students who didn't feel she was "Black enough" for their politics. She eventually transferred out, which shocked me.

My first-year roommate was from El Salvador. Neither he nor his girlfriend had legal status and they were very cautious about making friends. There were definite "battle lines" drawn that I never saw at Jefferson. In high school it was easier to flow between groups of people, at least for those of us in college prep classes where race or ethnicity was largely irrelevant.

Riley's final thoughts:

At Jeff, I was exposed to high schools on the peninsula that were wealthier and Whiter. All their kids went to four-year colleges. I'd run into them, and I remember thinking we were different. We'd show up to a debate or competition with a delegation of fifteen—two or three White guys, Salvadoran, Chinese, Black, etc. We looked different from them, and we felt good about that. And we won some of those competitions!

I had the benefit of exposure to diversity that these suburbanite kids didn't have. That was certainly true of my classmates at Claremont. At Jeff, we may not have had all the resources other schools had, but we were driven. All my friends shared the desire to do better than their parents, for whatever reason. We weren't going to let anything hold us back. And although we worked hard, we had great fun in the process.

Anthony

(Black, class of '72)

* * *

All I remember is him yelling to his mother, "Mom, there's a (n-word) at the door collecting for the paper."...I never told my mom or dad about it.

* * *

Anthony was born in Oakland, California, the second of seven children, and raised in the Excelsior District of San Francisco before moving to Daly City. His parents met in his mother's home state of Texas, where his father was stationed in the army, and moved to California when they were around twenty-one. Anthony's father was a longshoreman before becoming a bus driver; his mother stayed at home raising the family.

Growing up in San Francisco was very different from Daly City. We had a few White neighbors, but they kept to themselves, and we did too. Most of my friends were from my neighborhood and were Black.

At Cleveland Elementary about sixty percent of my class was White. There may have been six or seven other Black kids. They never segregated us—lunch was lunch and recess was recess, and everyone pretty much got along. The teachers were nice, too; they helped if I needed it, and one of them encouraged me to get involved with band and other things. The hardest conflicts that I had were with other Black

47

kids. I don't remember other people of color at the time. If someone had lighter skin than me, I assumed they were White.

At Luther Burbank Junior High, where I started seventh grade, it was pretty much the same because all the kids who went to Cleveland went to Luther Burbank. One of the kids was Middle Eastern. It was the first time I ever heard a name like his and the first time I became aware of a race/ethnicity beyond White and Black. He was a little older than me and hung out with my older brother. He was a little darker and a real nice guy.

Although I played baseball with a mixed group [racially], I can't say that any one of them was my best friend. No one invited anyone else to each other's houses. We played together at school but didn't hang out.

Before they left San Francisco, Anthony had a paper route which took him around the area and led to one unforgettable experience.

When I was in sixth or seventh grade, my older brother and I had a paper route delivering the San Francisco Chronicle. After we delivered it, we had to collect the money from the customers. One time I knocked on a door. A kid answered and called for his mother. All I remember is him yelling, "Mom, there's a [n-word] at the door collecting for the paper." The mother came, paid, and immediately closed the door. I never told my mom or dad about it. That was the first experience with racism that I can remember.

Anthony was halfway through seventh grade when his family moved to Daly City, but he was put into eighth grade, for reasons he never understood.

My parents decided to buy a house in Daly City. I was still in seventh grade, but they started me in eighth grade at Colma [junior high]. I'm not sure why. Colma was a real change. It was still mostly White, but it was very mixed. There were a few Blacks, but there were also Hispanics, Filipinos, etc.

One of the first friends I met was Vic [Filipino]. I was kind of shy so was just standing around the schoolyard. Vic approached and asked if I wanted to play dodgeball. That was how we connected. No one had ever done that before. He was my first friend of another race and we're still good friends to this day. I didn't look at color as much as people's personalities. Vic was a super nice guy and seemed pretty popular. Through him I got to know a lot of his Filipino friends and others. His family treated me like family, which was very nice.

Sylvia [Filipina] was one of the first people I met in class. One time I was standing in front of the class explaining something. A White kid, Denny, said something derogatory, probably about race, but Sylvia stood up for me. Until Colma, teachers were always White, so I had assumed that all of them were White. I never saw any Black teachers before until Mrs. Moss at Colma.

Once I started hanging out with Vic and them, I stuck with that group. We usually didn't have anyone who wasn't Black coming to my house to play or hang out, but when my parents were getting divorced, both Vic and his brother George would come over. They met my mom, but our parents never met. My mom thought they were very nice, especially George because he came over to the house more often.

In Daly City I felt more freedom and no fear walking around. In San Francisco there were no school buses so you'd have to take a public bus, which took you all over the city—that wasn't always a good idea at a young age. Daly City wasn't as big. I had a lot of friends in the neighborhood and I could walk everywhere. It never crossed my mind that I'd be pulled over or anything. I never had any run-ins with the police in San Francisco. In Daly City, the only time I had to deal with them was when my older brother got into trouble. I never had my own dealings with the police until I was much older.

When Anthony started high school at Jefferson, he focused on sports and hung out with people who knew his older brother, but he realized that he needed to forge his own identity.

My brother was a pretty tough guy, getting in trouble, mostly for fighting and stuff like that. I realized that hanging out with the same crowd would be heading for trouble. When I wasn't at school, I'd be at the War Memorial Center. It was my safe haven, playing basketball, volleyball, ping-pong. It was all very competitive. Whoever won could continue playing until someone beat them. When the gym was pretty empty, we'd break out the football. At the War Memorial Center I'd noticed Ken and Robert [Black brothers] shooting hoops, and I'd try to play with them. A lot of the White guys who hung out there were considered pretty tough guys, but I never feared them and we never had any run-ins. We were all more jocks than thugs.

The nice part was that I got to meet a lot of guys who went to Jeff. I didn't play on the baseball or basketball team because I got into wrestling in my sophomore year after discovering I had a bit of a knack for it at the center. Coach Martinez noticed that I was good at sports and asked me if I wanted to join in organized teams.

A group of White upperclassmen—juniors and seniors—subjected Anthony and a Latino friend to some hazing, possibly racially motivated.

During my freshman year, some White guys caught me and my friend coming from the track field after practice. They grabbed us, pulled us down into the gym, and shaved our heads. We resisted but were outnumbered. First they cut off the middle of our hair with clippers so we wouldn't leave while they shaved the other one's head. If we left with it half done it would have looked worse than just having it all shaved. Hazing was new to me. They did it to us because we were freshmen, and we were minorities. You shouldn't do that to people against their will. Afterward, the look on their faces was like, "Who are you going to tell?"

As I became better at sports, I was sort of split between two worlds—my friends from sports who I had a bond with, and then on the weekends I'd hang out with the friends I'd gotten close to at Colma. If there was a social event connected to sports, I'd hang out with those friends—Black, Latino, White. The Brisbane guys always hung out pretty much with all White guys. Even when they'd go up to the War Memorial Center, they were like a clique. There was never any person of color with them.

High school led to dating, and in such a diverse area, some teenagers paired up with people of different races. Anthony was one of them.

One of my first girlfriends went to Westmoor and was White. We went to a dance at Jeff. There was this White guy who bullied a lot of people, and he knew if he could pick on you, he owned you. When he saw me at the dance he purposely stuck his foot out so I fell. I got up and hit him in the chest—he was bigger than I was. He got in my face and said, "Do you know who you're messing with?" A coach pulled us apart. I remember feeling embarrassed, but he never bothered me again. He learned that I was no one to pick on because I would retaliate. I always wondered, though, if he tripped me because I was with a White girl.

The NAACP (National Association for the Advancement of Colored People) made a presentation at school about boycotting sports to protest racism and inequality.

The NAACP representatives met us in the cafeteria. I was getting ready to go to football practice. The meeting was to encourage all of us

*Black athletes to boycott playing sports because they said we were be-
ing used. It was cool that the coaches allowed us to go hear their spiel.
It was interesting, but I still went to practice after the meeting. I wasn't
going to let anybody dictate what I'm going to do and how I will do it.
It was right around the time we were having a big cultural day, Afro-
American Day, where the Black Student Union did presentations at a
rally. Everybody wore dashikis and danced. I enjoyed the beauty of my
heritage but I never wore the clothing.*

Anthony feels he owes many of the positive things he got into at
Jeff to a coach.

*Coach Tom Martinez talked me into playing football and other
sports. He was a mentor. One time I was really upset because someone
had broken in and stolen the new uniforms that the football team was
supposed to be getting, and I was accused behind my back of being involved. My brother may have been, but I had no part in it. It was Coach
Martinez who told me face to face, "Your name came up." I told him I
played for the team, sweated for the team, worked hard for the team. I
would not steal from the team! That was when he told me, "Wherever
you go in life, don't ever walk around with your head down. You need
to walk around like you belong. You have to look like you don't have
anything against someone, so if they have a problem with you, it's their
problem." From that time on, I walked around with that attitude: if you
think my color is intimidating, it's on you.*

*Apart from Coach Martinez, other teachers were nicer to me than a
Black teacher at Jeff. I'm not sure why we didn't get along. I developed
friendships with other teachers, so why wouldn't I be able to with a
Black teacher? It just seemed like we were never able to communicate.*

Anthony's choice of girlfriends sometimes attracted criticism—
some of it muted, some of it explicit.

*For a little while I dated a White girl. I remember a Black cheer-
leader coming up to me and saying, "Anthony, I think you're White-
washed." She seemed offended by my choice of girlfriend. Although my
parents never talked with me about race, my mom pretty much com-
municated without words that Blacks should stick with Blacks; Whites
with Whites. My dad would keep it more to himself if he didn't like
something, but maybe make a snide remark here and there. I've dated
Puerto Ricans. I had a few Latina girlfriends and Filipinas. To me it
was about how you communicate, so color didn't matter.*

After graduation Anthony joined the Marine Corps. Sometimes his uniform protected him from racism, and sometimes it didn't.

This White guy and I served in the same unit at Camp Pendleton. We had leave at the same time so we decided to hang out together. He said we could drive down and stop off in Orange County where he was from, I could meet his parents, and we would spend the night at his house. We were both in uniform when we arrived. His dad answered the door and told me to stay outside. He took his son inside and told him that I couldn't stay at the house. My buddy was embarrassed as hell, but I said it was okay and I would just go back to SF on the bus.

I had to wait two hours for a bus out of this small town. Across the street there was this little bar, so I went inside and ordered a beer. While I'm drinking it, a sheriff walks into the bar and right up to me. It turned out the bartender had called him. The sheriff asks me where I'm going and then tells me he will escort me to the bus station because there were two guys who were going to roll me and take my money when I left the bar. He even waited until I got safely on the bus. This was California, even. It could have gone really bad if the bartender and the sheriff hadn't helped out. All the way home on the bus I couldn't stop thinking about it. As a U.S. Marine in uniform, I couldn't even stop and get a beer in a bar without a hassle.

When we were back at Pendleton, my friend apologized for his dad's behavior. I just said, "Your dad is who he is. I don't know what to tell you."

Out of uniform, Anthony had another experience, one that, unfortunately, will be familiar to most African Americans.

I was driving home from work down highway 101. Two cops pulled me over and wanted to know where I was coming from. It was 3 a.m.— my shift ended at 2:30. They said I was speeding. I explained that I'd just gotten off work. They said I must have been drinking so they made me get out of the car and do a sobriety test. One said, "You didn't do too well on the sobriety test so we're going to take you in and let our supervisor see if you're okay." I said, "What about my car?" The other cop said he would pull it off the road so it would be safe. The first one got up close to me and said, "You're lucky my partner was with me. I'd have left your car right there where it was (on the freeway)." They didn't have any proof of anything but they still took me to jail. When I went to court, the judge asked me if I'd been held for four hours and I said, "Yes." He said, "Well, we'll call it even. Have a nice day."

Anthony's final thoughts.

If I had gone to high school in San Francisco, I'd have gone to Mission High or Balboa, and I think I got a better deal by going to Jeff. Mission would have been more Black, Balboa more diverse, with Polynesians, Samoans, Hawaiians, etc. Jeff was great because it was safe. I was never afraid to go to school. I got along with so many teachers and they all treated me with respect. Hindsight's 20/20, but I think it would have been different in San Francisco. There was more trouble and it would have been harder to stand out because the schools were so big—you could get lost in the mix. At Jeff it was easier to stand out if you were good at something. If I'd stayed in the city, Coach Martinez might not have found me.

Carol Q.

(Latina, class of '73)

* * *

Today, I feel for the Asians and others getting beaten up. We already went through this. Didn't anyone learn anything?

* * *

Carol was born in St. Joseph's Hospital in San Francisco and lived in the city's Excelsior district for her first few years. Her mother was born in Ambato, Ecuador, and came to the U.S. in her late twenties. Carol's father was born in Nicaragua and came to the U.S. as a young man. Her parents met in an English class for adults at Mission High School.

Soon after Carol started kindergarten, she was sent to stay with her father's family in Nicaragua.

I had a terrible case of measles. My family was told I should be in a warmer climate to help me recover, so that's why I went to Nicaragua. My dad took me there and I lived with his sisters. None of them had children, so I was like the little queen. They were very protective of me.

They put me in a private Catholic school. I wasn't used to such strictness—the uniform, the rules; if you didn't obey, you got whacked on the hand. There was also a double standard for boys and girls. Boys could climb trees, but when I climbed a tree to pick some fruit, the nuns smacked my hand and gave me extra homework. I felt like I was under

a microscope all the time. If you did something wrong, you were never allowed to explain; you'd just get punished.

At Catholic school there were only two social classes: poor and rich. A lot of the kids around the neighborhood didn't have shoes. I'd ask my aunts why, and they told me not to talk to them. I noticed the difference between having and not having; my own privilege. My aunts would have a party and go all out. Kids referred to me as 'la Americana' [the American]. I liked to give my clothes to kids who didn't have as many outfits. My mom was a seamstress and always sent me pretty clothes. When I got tired of wearing them, I'd ask her to send me some new dresses, telling her that there was a hole in them! I'd get the new dresses and go sit outside. I'd tell the kids to come to the corner—not to the house—and give them food, my older clothes, etc.

One of my aunts was an English teacher in a poor school. During spring break I'd go to her school and I immediately saw the difference—dirt floors, broken tiles, etc. I'd sit and observe, wondering why everyone didn't have what I had.

I did my first communion in Nicaragua. I wasn't a stranger to it— my mother was very devout. Here in the U.S., the whole class does communion. In Nicaragua, it was just me. I thought I was a princess! There was a couple getting married at the same time; I thought we were having a double wedding and I was marrying Jesus. It made a big impression on me. I felt closer to Jesus, as if he was real, not just a face on a postcard or a name in the Bible. After the communion they had a parade just for me, and we had a big party.

Carol returned to the U.S. for fourth grade and started at Monroe Elementary School in San Francisco. Shortly thereafter, her parents separated.

Because I'd been out of the country, I missed a lot of the breakup trauma that my siblings went through. My mom wanted to bring me back to the U.S. because she was afraid my father's family in Nicaragua would kidnap me. After the legal separation, I changed schools and went to Fairmount for fifth and sixth grade. There was a lot of shame and stigma because my father had abandoned us.

It was hard because I had to learn English again and get used to American schools. My brothers would make fun of me because I had an accent. In school, the kids accepted that I had an accent, but the teachers were less understanding.

There was one teacher who thought I was cheating. In Nicaragua I'd learned to do math in my head. Now an American math teacher handed out a paper and I just put down the answer without showing my work, plus I had an accent. She thought I must be cheating. My mother got called to come in to school, even though she was working and she didn't have time. She asked me if I cheated. I said, "No." Mom told the principal and the teacher to get a piece of paper and put a math problem on it. I did it in my head, correctly. We showed them!

Ever since then, I got a brain-block and I hated math. It wasn't that I felt stupid, but they made me feel stupid. That started my anger about being discriminated against. I had always been taught to give a person a chance, but this teacher didn't trust me because of my accent. She didn't believe I could do the work and she didn't try to find out. Luckily, I had a supportive parent who knew I wouldn't lie or cheat.

Carol doesn't recall her parents talking with her about race.

My dad left when I was ten, so if he ever said anything about race, I don't remember. My mom had Black Cuban friends. She never said anything derogatory about anyone. She was all about trust and character, not about race or ethnicity. Mom wanted to know how a person was brought up, how they treated you. She was always praying. She worked so hard, the swing shift, so she could make dinner for us before she left for work. We were latchkey kids, always having a neighbor or someone looking out for us. We were never really alone, alone.

After Fairmount, Carol attended James Lick Junior High in San Francisco.

I had good experiences at both those schools. They were very diverse. I never felt out of place and the teachers were good. I had fun. Most of the problems were about petty jealousy—maybe someone liked their friend instead of them, etc. It wasn't about race. My best friend in sixth grade was Chinese and had a boyfriend who happened to be Black. I thought he was cute and nice. She saw him on the side, maybe because we were only in sixth grade, but her parents might have had a problem with him. I figured if she liked him, that was it. I liked boys, but I wasn't ready for a boyfriend. We were attracted to someone because of who they were.

Carol's housing situation also changed after her parents separated.

We were still dealing with the separation from my dad. My mom didn't believe in divorce. We lived in my grandfather's house, in the downstairs flat on Army Street [Cesar Chavez Street in San Francisco today]. They were doing a lot of redevelopment on our street, so our house was bought out. Nearby, St. Luke's Hospital was getting bigger, so they needed more land and offered money, which my grandfather took. It turned out to be a good opportunity for us. A cousin of mine close in age had recently lost her mother, so we moved in with her family in Daly City to help take care of her. She became like a sister. While we were living with her, my grandfather bought a house in Daly City, about two blocks away. After a year or so, her father moved out to live with his father, my grandfather, while we kept renting his house and taking care of my cousin. Then he met a woman, got married, and they moved back to his house. It was too much having two families in the same house, so my family moved back in with my grandfather.

I was still commuting to middle school in San Francisco. My sister was at Mission High. We took the 14 Mission bus.

Mission High experienced a major riot which shut down the school and had a direct impact on Carol's sister's plans.

My sister was on the drill team at Mission High. One time she told me to come and see her at practice after school. When I got there, I saw all these people running around. My sister grabbed me and said, "They're going to start a riot." Most of her friends on the drill team were Black, and they said they would escort us out safely. In the hallway, two guys were ready to pounce on us, but two girls from the team told them, "Don't touch them." An older guy opened a locker and took out a rifle and cocked it. My sister and her two friends told us to follow them, which we did. We got out and I heard shooting. I thought I was going to die. It turns out it was the Black Panthers. The school had to be shut down to stop it.

My brothers were having similar problems at Balboa High School, which was having its own issues.

I was going to start ninth grade at Jefferson. My sister had stayed at Mission with her friends so far, but when I started at Jeff, she did too, even though she was a senior. My sister thought Mission was better academically than Jeff, but it was tougher. Jeff was much calmer, which was a factor in her decision. We weren't likely to get caught up in a riot or get shot.

I thought Jeff was the best place in the world. I always had my big sister, which helped, but I always felt safe there. I never felt any racial tension, although I'm sure there was some, maybe behind the scenes. My sister said it was nothing compared to Mission.

For me, Jeff was a stepping-stone to college. My older siblings always encouraged me to be quiet. I was very serious and focused on my studies until I met my future best friend [Latina]. She'd say, "I'm having a party," or "Let's go to a party." She helped put some fun into school. I did afterschool things like softball freshman year, and I joined the gymnastics team. Then she got me to join the Latin Heritage club, where there was a mixture of Mexicans, Nicaraguans, Salvadorans, Peruvians, several mixed—Hispanic and Black. Even though she was a year younger, she knew more people. We didn't get into too much trouble. It was mostly stupid stuff—riding our bikes to some guy's house we had a crush on; then I'd want to get out of there when we saw him.

My new best friend encouraged me to join the journalism club. I learned how to do the school newspaper. They'd let us out early because we had an assignment to go do a story—that was lots of fun.

One episode at Jeff has stayed with Carol. It was not related to race, but to teachers' power and how they can impact a student's self-esteem.

In my senior year, I had Mr. Tate for math. He didn't like my sister when she was in his class. Given the right instruction, I would do fine, but he had no patience. I was stuck on algebra. One day I was almost late to class. The bell rang and my foot was in the door, but he slammed it in my face. I banged on the door, yelling, "Please open the door." He called the assistant principal, who asked me what I was doing. I told him, "I'm a young lady. He closed the door in my face." He had me come to the office to calm down. I told him I wasn't the best student, but I was trying hard and planning to go to college. Later I was in the cafeteria and Mr. Tate came up to me and asked to talk. We went to the teachers' lounge and he apologized. I said, "I'm not the smartest student, but you shouldn't ever embarrass me in front of the class again. You wouldn't want me to embarrass you in front of your colleagues."

After graduation from Jeff, Carol attended City College of San Francisco.

I had to get letters of recommendation to get in the dental program. I needed pre-algebra and strong science. I got three letters from former teachers, including Julia Monares, who worked with Spanish-speaking students. I also give credit to my counselor, Mrs. Erickson. Both of them made a big impact on me. My mom didn't know how to help with this, but she always said I can do anything I put my mind to. She was my pillar of strength.

I got into the program—they only took thirty people each semester, so I felt fortunate. I was the first in my family to go to college, which my sister paid for.

City College had so many resources. It was great for me. I met a lot of people there who are still friends to this day, including a woman from Burma.

Like many people of color, Carol has experienced racism in the workplace.

I became a registered dental assistant and got my license. I was so excited to accomplish what I'd set out to do. I worked in dentistry for twenty years. In that time, the only time I ever felt racism was when a White patient called me a dirty Mexican. We were treating her, the dentist on one side, and me handing him the tools. As soon as the dentist left the room, the patient said, "I don't want you working on me, you dirty Mexican." She said I was lazy, etc. I left the room and went straight to my boss. I told him, "Either you take care of it or I'm quitting." He went and talked to her. "I understand you called my assistant a dirty Mexican. First of all, she's not Mexican. Second..."

I had to go back in there and work on her without stabbing her. She didn't apologize. I'm a professional, so I just did everything perfectly. She walked out and made a follow-up appointment for her crown. When she came back, my boss dealt with her. That situation was disheartening for me because this was in the eighties in downtown San Francisco. My boss was so mad. As soon as she left, everyone in the office said, "Can you believe this woman?"

Carol's final reflections:

Today, I feel for the Asians and others getting beaten up. We already went through this. Didn't anyone learn anything? No one is perfect, but I'm not going to hurt someone because I don't like them. Who am I to judge someone? I have to be right in God's eyes, so I can't judge anyone else.

Russ

(Chinese American, class of '72)

* * *

That was a blatant racist remark, and she didn't even know it. I took offense—you thought the adults knew better. Obviously, they can be guilty of racism and not even know it.

* * *

Russ and his brother were born in San Francisco and raised in Chinatown until moving to Daly City when Russ was five. Both their parents were born in California—his father in San Francisco, his mother in the town of Locke, the oldest rural Chinatown in America, settled in the early 1900s.

Although his parents were American-born, their first language was Chinese.

My parents spoke half Chinese and half English at home. When we had relatives over, the whole family spoke Chinese, but I didn't know what they were saying most of the time. My brother (five years older) learned Chinese later. I never did because I thought, "I'm an American. I should only speak English." I regret it now. My parents offered to send me to a Chinese school in third or fourth grade, but I wasn't interested.

I don't remember much from when we lived in San Francisco except shopping in Chinatown with my mom, and we lived in an alleyway. When we moved to Daly City, we were the only Chinese people in our neighbor-

hood. I was oblivious to the concept of race, even though we had some Hispanic kids and maybe a few Chinese kids at my elementary school, "Little Jeff." Our next-door neighbors were of Greek descent, and the kid across the street was Latino. I played with all of the kids in the neighborhood. My friends would come over to play with slot cars and hang out.

My parents were absolutely no help to me in understanding anything about race. My older brother was no help either. We were close when I was little, but as I got older, things were not as rosy as the families you see on television. My brother felt I was spoiled, even though I was shy and he was outgoing.

Even at "Little Jeff," Russ experienced some racism early on.

Kids who weren't my friends would come up and say, "Hey Chink" or "Chinaman." I didn't know why they were picking on me. I had many White friends at the time, but no one ever stood up for me. I stood up for them sometimes, and then I got my butt kicked. I don't think I ran into any problems in classes, just outside on the playground, but it was nothing blatant. I didn't have any problems with anyone following me home or anything like that. Maybe I'm repressing some of it, but nothing stands out. There was just occasional intimidation and bullying, rarely any actual fighting.

All Asians get the "ching chong Chinaman" thing, not just us Chinese. I wonder now how my dad was able to get by in his day, especially during the war [WW2]—things were really bad then. It must have seemed like anyone with Asian eyes would get taken away to the internment camps.

In junior high school, Russ remembers more racism.

At Colma it was a little bit more stupid and racist. There were a few kids saying that I bombed Pearl Harbor. I'm going, "Wait a minute, that was the Japanese," but they said, "It doesn't matter." I wanted to slap them. We had a Japanese exchange student at school, so I said, "I didn't bomb Pearl Harbor. He did." They said, "Oh, but he's okay." I'm thinking, that doesn't make any sense. You can't reason with them—I didn't even try.

Even some teachers were capable of being very inappropriate.

We were having a discussion on race, talking about the melting pot and what we call people—the Irish, Blacks, etc. The teacher sud-

denly asked me what I was. I was going to say I was Chinese American, since I was born in California, but then she said, "You're a Chinaman!" The whole class laughed, and I was furious. That was a blatant racist remark, and she didn't even know it. I took offense to it—you thought the adults knew better. Obviously, they can be guilty of racism and not even know it.

It was pretty bad that a remark like that came from a teacher. I don't think the other kids even knew it was wrong to say that. I was totally caught off guard and was hoping she wouldn't say anything like that again, but who was going to stop her from doing it?

At Jefferson High School, things were better.

There were a few more Chinese kids, Hispanics, Filipinos. It was a lot more diverse than Colma, and even more than Little Jeff. I didn't have the same problems that I did at Colma—the students were a little smarter in high school.

Russell recalls having crushes on several girls while growing up.

I remember a Jewish girl who I had a crush on, but I was too shy to do anything about it. I thought a Filipina classmate was cute. Most of my attractions were to White women, and I married a White woman. I don't remember being attracted to anyone who was of Chinese descent. The closest one would be the Filipina classmate.

As sometimes happens, when Russ started high school, he and some of his friends drifted apart.

I had most of the same friends from before, but some of them changed. One got kind of a tough guy attitude and distanced himself from me. One of my best friends was a blind [White] kid. I used to help in guiding him around Colma. We stayed friends at Jeff, but he was a bit of a loudmouth. I don't know why I was attracted to hanging out with him. Before I came to Big Jeff, I was kind of a jerk. I guess because I'd been bullied at Colma, I was trying to bully some of the other kids. I was probably acting out, and I'm sorry I did it. There's no excuse for it. Much later in life I ran into someone I'd victimized and I apologized.

At Big Jeff, my friends were mixed—White, a few mixed race, and a few Blacks. I didn't have many Black friends until I was much older. It wasn't that I didn't want to, I just didn't have many while I was in high school. When I was in my twenties and thirties, I had some Black friends

I would go out with and have dinner with. Later I became friends with a few Black people from different hobbies we had in common, specifically racing R/C [remote control] cars. There were two Black guys; we got along just fine.

After graduating from Jeff, Russ went to the College of San Mateo and his life improved.

When I got to college I met my cousin, who was taking the same classes [drafting]. We became best friends, and I would hang out at his house every weekend. I finally came out of my shell, overcame my shyness, and formed my own personality. I met my (then future) wife at my first job and we've been married for over forty years. We had some rough times, but we managed to make it to retirement. I'm a grandfather with a second one on the way and they live quietly in Canada. My kid also married a White woman, so my grandchildren are 3/4 White, 1/4 Chinese.

In general, Russ didn't feel like race was much of a problem for him in high school, not at all in college, and most of the time not at work.

It wasn't a problem at work, except at one place where I worked for ten years. My boss was a racist jerk, but you couldn't tell him otherwise. He came from a wealthy family, just like Trump. He was getting products directly from China, so he needed a Chinese interpreter, and he hated working with her. He would make racist comments and my blood would boil. After five years I realized that's just the way he is, and you can't explain anything to him. One day I was arguing with him about fluorescent lightbulbs. He kept calling them incandescent, and I kept telling him they were fluorescent. This went on for a good fifteen minutes, then he told me I had to go home. I said I had to deliver some parts to our machinist first and, while I was gone, my coworkers finally talked some sense into him.

I'm so glad I left there. Six months after I left, he contacted me and asked me to do some work for him on the side, but I politely told him, "No, thanks." I should have told him, "Hell no!" As much as I hated this guy, I couldn't be rude to him. I guess you could say I was brought up better. He'd make racist comments right in front of me. I think it's one of the pitfalls of being rich, like Trump. When he made racist comments, my coworkers usually didn't say anything, even though we were a mixed group—Black, Chinese, Hispanic, and White. One colleague was Russian.

That particular boss was the only one I remember who was racist toward me.

Even after all this time, racist remarks can come from unexpected people.

Last year I was in New Jersey and went to a Chinese restaurant. I wanted cashew chicken, but they gave me kung pao chicken instead, except that it didn't have kung pao sauce. I told a friend, "I've got this terrible Chinese food in front of me, it's got no kung, no pao." He started repeating it over and over, using a FOB ["fresh off the boat"—new immigrant] accent. It was annoying, but I let it go.

This year, the same friend started saying "no kung, no pao" again in that FOB accent. He kept it up for an entire week and I was getting pissed. At the end of the week, he was talking to someone else on the other side of the table in the FOB accent like a funky Chinaman, and then he said, "I guess I could call (Russ) a Chinaman now." I just blew up and yelled at him, saying, "I'll kick your ass!" He apologized right away. Five minutes later we were talking about normal stuff. All I wanted was for him to talk to me with some respect, like I'm human. After I got home, I sent him a message telling him I can't be his friend any more if he talks like that. He apologized two days later. He was being ignorant at the time, but if he does it again, he's being stupid.

Russ had the last word at a gun range one day.

There were some obviously new Chinese immigrants in a booth next to me. They didn't seem to know how to handle a gun safely. In the booth on the other side of them was a bunch of White guys. One of them said, "Can't drive, can't shoot," referring to the people in between us, the FOBs. Then this White guy looks over and sees me staring at him. I turn toward my target, aim, and fire from twenty-five yards away— almost all of my shots right in the ten-ring. When I went to change out my target, the guy says to me, "Nice grouping," and I said, "I know." I didn't have to say anything else. He got the message—he knew he'd made a big mistake. People don't always look around at their surroundings to see who's in earshot when they say something racist or stupid.

Russ's final reflections about his school days:

High school was kind of a big disappointment, but that was mostly my fault because I was so shy. I never went to the prom or anything. I didn't have any close friends that I stayed in contact with. For some people, it was magical; for others, it was just going through the motions and doing the time. Probably my best memories were at Little Jeff because I was so naïve. I was still a little naïve going through high school, but I thought things were a lot more interesting back in the sixties and early seventies, living in Daly City. The cars were so much cooler back then, too.

Harry

(White, class of '73)

* * *

My dad taught me early that it doesn't matter what color a person's skin is. What matters is what's in their heart, as long as they're a good person.

* * *

Harry was born in a small village called Kandila in the Peloponnese region of Greece. His date of birth is different from the one on his birth certificate because at that time officials wrote the date when a birth was registered, versus the day the baby was born. He was the oldest of three boys.

In December 1961, when he was six, Harry, his brother, and mother immigrated to the U.S. His father was already here, having left Greece by boat on Harry's middle brother's birthday in March 1956. The trip took two weeks. Harry's father's visa dictated the day he had to leave, so he could not be there for the birth of his second son. The family reunited five years later.

We left Athens with three of us on one passport. I was almost seven. We arrived in New York on December 16th. My youngest brother was born in the U.S. four years later.

I had already started school in Greece but remember very little about it. I do remember the house we lived in. My mom's parents, dad's

parents, and other relatives lived nearby. We had a little coffee house on the main street. Our coffee shop had one of the few electrical outlets in the village—electricity had just begun coming into the village in the mid-fifties. Every Friday or Saturday night we had a movie night. We'd set up the movie projector outdoors on the patio from late spring into early autumn. People from the village would buy coffee, drinks, and snacks, and we'd show a film for free.

Coming to the United States posed numerous challenges for Harry and his family.

When I came to the U.S. I spoke zero English; so did my family. On the airplane my mom told me she was thirsty and wanted me to order her some water. I didn't know how to ask for it. I waved to a stewardess to get her attention and made a sign like putting a cup to my mouth. I saw a woman a row behind me drinking something, so I pointed to her, indicating I'll have whatever she's having. The stewardess brought a cup of it, and Mom said, "This isn't water, but it's okay." It was possibly a soda.

We landed in New York during a heavy snowstorm, so we couldn't make our connecting flight to San Francisco. We didn't know what to do. The airline gave us hotel vouchers, and some other Greek Americans helped get us to the hotel and check in. They gave us the key to our room and put us in an elevator. In those days, you needed an elevator operator. The operator was a Black gentleman. Coming from a remote village in southern Greece, we didn't even know Black people existed. My brother and I were scared, so we hid behind Mom while peeking out at him.

It was pretty much smooth sailing after that. A Greek American lady picked us up in the morning. We were put on a bus that took us to the airport and we flew to San Francisco, arriving the next day.

In order to avoid feeling isolated, Harry's family sought out the Greek community soon after their arrival.

My parents immediately became involved in the Greek community because they needed connections. When my mom took us to register at school in 1962, we didn't have enough English. Since my dad had been here six years already, he wrote a note to help get us registered. At the school we learned about another Greek American lady who had children there. They put us in touch with her and she helped us complete the paperwork. We became very close friends. We found a Greek Orthodox church, Holy Trinity, in San Francisco. We went there regularly to try to assimilate into the Greek culture here, which my parents did quickly. We went to Sunday School, etc. It was especially good for my mom, who was more isolated than the rest of us because she was a housewife.

Harry's family settled in Daly City in a house on Brunswick Street.

The house was part of a duplex. The owners lived upstairs, and we rented downstairs. Coming from a tiny village, we'd never seen anything as big as Daly City! Just walking around, it took us months to get to know it. Once we did that, we were comfortable enough to walk to school.

I started school at General Pershing Elementary School in first grade since I was already seven. Every time the class had English, I went off to an ESL [English as a second language] class. My level was basic, so I understood why I had to go to a separate class. We watched a lot of television at home, a lot of cartoons, to try to catch up. School helped because we were forced to speak English every day, and ESL helped with pronunciation. I was at General Pershing for approximately three years. Initially at school I hung out with my brother because our English wasn't good enough to talk to other kids. I was in first grade, and he was in kindergarten half-day. When he wasn't there, I'd play with other kids.

I never got the sense that anyone was making fun of me because I didn't speak English. I do remember one time my third-grade teacher told the class that I and a couple of other kids came from other countries, so don't make fun of us for our English.

In 1964 we moved to East Vista Avenue, which was on the other side of the school boundary, and I had to transfer to Vista Grande Elementary School for fifth and sixth grades. We had Black students, Chinese, Mexicans, Latinos, Russians, etc. in our class, just like it would be later at Jeff. My dad taught me early that it doesn't matter what color a person's skin is. What matters is what's in their heart, as long as they're a good person.

From grammar school on, I felt like it was built into us to accept people. We lived next door to a Black family. On the other side was a Filipino family with about nine kids—they seemed to live very happily in a three-bedroom/one-bath home. We played outside together, baseball, etc., and all got along. We were accepting of people because they were accepting of us.

My mom spoke English with a strong accent because she never had to interact a lot with people outside our community. My dad learned

English because it was necessary for him to work. But accents were fine. There were a lot of immigrants around that time, and that was the way it was.

I'm not sure how old I was, maybe in seventh grade, but I remember waking up with a start and saying to myself, "Oh my God, I just dreamt in English!" To this day I get tingles remembering that. I guess at that point everything kind of switched over from Greek to English.

Junior high school had new revelations for Harry.

At Colma I noticed that there were a lot more people of different ethnicities. We as Greeks felt kind of isolated because there weren't many of us outside our little world of the church and so on. I made some friends, mostly Mexican and Italian, at Colma.

I don't remember any issues with race. When we had PE, all the boys had to shower. That was the first time I ever got undressed in front of other guys. It was a shock! Not that it had anything to do with ethnicity. I don't know how it was for women, but it was embarrassing. You're just starting puberty. The coach casually says, "Okay, go shower." You're thinking, "What? With twelve other guys?! Where's my shower? Can't I just stay sweaty all day?"

There really were no ethnic issues at Colma other than the realization that you had to get along with everyone. You're no better than them, they're no better than you, so why not just get along? The treatment of Black people during that time wasn't good, but we were unaware of that because we were in our little bubble, apart from what we saw on television.

The beginning of high school introduced Harry to school hierarchy.

At orientation in the gym, I was sitting about halfway down and there were handrails behind the top row. Some older White students were standing above us. They were kind of spitting on our heads because we were freshmen. You wipe it once, you wipe it twice, but you don't dare say anything because they'd beat you up.

As far as race at Jeff, being Black, Chinese or Mexican—they were different and that's okay. There's nothing wrong with being different. I felt I was different also, just being Greek. I had some close acquaintances. One good friend was Latino, another Chinese, and another Black. They were good guys. We played football together. We didn't associate outside of school and sports. We got along with everybody because you had to—the Samoans, the Blacks, the Filipinos, the Mexi-

cans, the Russians—everybody. You got along with them because they were just like you. I don't remember any racial fights.

I was on the track team, but I didn't play varsity football because I wanted to play in the band—you can't play ball and march at the same time. I played freshman and sophomore football but got hurt a few times. I tore a muscle in my right hip, sprained ankles, and had my head snapped back. To this day my hands go numb when I ride a bike because I think there was some damage to the back of my neck . . . seriously. I got knocked out once. Playing in band seemed a lot safer than football.

Sometimes I had friends come over—Latino, Chinese, mixed race Mexican/ Japanese—along with White guys. My mother welcomed them all and fed them. After you introduce them, they're polite and she asks, "Are you hungry?" I went to Pete's [Latino] house regularly because he lived on the way to school.

The group of friends I had never got into arguments with anyone. We had outings together. The faculty drove the idea of acceptance into us, regardless of color—Leahy [U.S. history and geography teacher; coach], Larsen [music teacher]. From what I saw they were very fair and accepting. All the coaches had to deal with all kinds of people and races, so they also drove it home: "He's an athlete, so forget what he looks like." On the track team we had a lot of sprinters, long jumpers, etc., who were Black. We always cheered each other on.

After graduation, Harry started at the College of San Mateo, but it was a long drive so he switched to Skyline Junior College. He was thinking of going into physical education, but his family circumstances changed.

After I'd had a couple years of college my dad passed away, so I had to go to work to help pay off the mortgage for my mom. That was fine. I worked at a supermarket for thirty-two years, twenty in produce and twelve as the wine buyer. I retired in 2009. I never had any issues with race there. If you're my customer, I'm going to take care of you.

I was supposed to be retired, but my wife and I discussed it—my retirement fund wasn't huge, and I was still on the young side and wasn't doing much at home, so I went to work in computer sales. We had Black and Asian managers. They put in the work, so they made manager. After five years I had to stop and take care of my mom who had Alzheimer's. It got really bad as she was threatening to kill me at one point, so we had to find a place for her. She was there four years. After she moved out, I got into construction, but it was too much for a sixty-plus year-old guy.

Harry's concluding thoughts:

What made Jeff special was the experiences you had: with your friends, with your teachers, if you got along with them, if they taught you more than what was in the textbooks. We got that from Jeff. You may not like everybody, but you should accept them for who they are. Don't judge. I think we're all guilty of a little prejudgment or prejudice at some level, but once you get to know a person, that goes out the door. There were so many different ethnicities, and you just happened to be one part of it. You weren't standing outside, a White person looking into this ethnic bubble; you were in that ethnic bubble. I think the teachers being so accepting of everybody reinforced that with us.

Akiko

(African American, Japanese, Indian, class of '72)

* * *

I was supposed to transfer to Balboa or Mission High. I didn't want to. Because I'm Black and Japanese, people used to mistake me for being Samoan, Filipino, Mexican, etc. I could see myself getting into so many different fights at Balboa High School because they couldn't tell what I was. Jeff was different, so I stuck around.

* * *

Akiko was born at home in San Francisco, the eleventh of her mother's thirteen children, and the third child of her father. Her mother was an African American dancer/entertainer, and her father a Japanese American merchant seaman from Hawaii. Akiko's maternal relatives have traced their roots in this country.

Through some cousins' cousins we've been able to trace our family back to the slave master. My great-grandfather was a slave born in Georgia, where I now live—I've come back to my roots!

An Irish man named James McMullan served as a military advisor to the colonies during the American Revolution [1775–1783]. His son Hugh had an enslaved woman named Rachel, part Cherokee and part African. She had at least five Black children with Hugh, who also had a White family. At some point Hugh McMullan moved everyone to Texas,

and then another McMullan took a small colony to Brazil after the Civil War because Brazil hadn't outlawed slavery.

My great-grandfather Jasper, one of Rachel's sons, lived until he was ninety-two, and we have the family history that he wrote. We assume that it was the master who taught Jasper to read and write. The White McMullans trusted him and gave him tasks that they wouldn't have entrusted to any of the other enslaved people. His nickname was "Jap," which he kept all his life.

Jasper had eight kids; one of them was my grandfather. My mother—Jasper's granddaughter—was born in 1913 in Fresno, California. We have a complicated family and very large reunions.

The first school Akiko remembers attending was Sheridan Elementary in San Francisco.

I went there briefly—I went to too many schools. I also went to Ortega Elementary. Then my mother got sick when I was in third grade, and I had to go to a foster home with two of my older sisters. My father was still working as a seaman. At the foster home, when I got in trouble they would put me under the table. I remember listening to Captain Kangaroo from under there. They used to beat one of my sisters with a wet backscratcher. It took a while before we were reunited with our mother. We lived in Menlo Park before moving to Daly City.

Akiko comments on the subject of race:

When I was growing up, if you had a drop of Black in you, you were Black. I'm half Japanese, but the other side is half Black, with some Irish and Native American in there. I've never been ashamed of my races. My attitude has always been, "This is who I am." If you ever saw a person mixed Japanese and Black, it was usually the other way around, a Black father and a Japanese mother. When I was at Colma Junior High, two Black girls came up to me and asked if I was a Black Jap. I told them, "Yeah, what about it?" They said, "Oh, we just wanted to know," and that was it.

Once I was with my sister and several Black friends at the school pool at Jeff. There were also some White girls. I saw a swimming cap floating in the water and I asked who it belonged to. It belonged to one of the White girls who had an attitude. After swimming was over, they called us the n-word, so we told the security guard, but he didn't do anything. Afterwards, we were walking home and some of the White girls attacked me. My friends jumped in, and we were all fighting. When we heard sirens, we took off. Those girls didn't bother us any more.

Once, as an adult, one of my big sisters (who is Black, not mixed like me) told me that I don't know what it's like to be Black. I told her that what I go through is worse. A lot of people don't like Black people and a lot don't like Japanese—and I'm both. When a person has Black in them, that's usually just what people see. I saw that people just took me as being Black, but it depended on how I wore my hair. Sometimes they thought I was Black Creole. The racism was out there, but I didn't really feel it. I took more of my Black side because I was proud to be Black. Around that time, James Brown was singing, "Say it loud, I'm Black and I'm proud," so I did! In high school I wanted an Afro so bad that I got an Afro wig because my mother wouldn't allow me to cut my hair.

With Akiko's father away at sea most of the time, her mother was the one who talked to her about race.

My mother would always say you go by the person's character, not by the color of their skin or where they're from, so that's what I've always done. I used to get upset with some White people—just because one Black person did something bad, they'd think all Black people were like that. If a White person did something that another White person didn't like, they wouldn't think all White people were like that.

I think my mother really wanted me to be with someone who was mixed race. My father would talk more with my siblings than with me about race. When he was home he'd tell me about my two sisters in Hawaii. My mother kind of wished that I would meet a Japanese guy, but I told her she should have had me in a place where there were more Japanese folks!

People who had darker skin attracted my attention. I thought they were so pretty. I did think Little Joe on Bonanza [a White character on a television show of that period] was cute, but that's not who I usually went for in real life. When I was working for SF Plastics, I was attracted to my boss, who was Italian, with black hair. He probably could have been Little Joe's brother! My husband is Black.

Jefferson High School was a natural fit for Akiko, but she shouldn't have been there.

I was living in Daly City in ninth grade, so I started at Jeff—but then we moved to Coleridge Street in San Francisco, which meant I was supposed to transfer to Balboa or Mission High. I didn't want to. Because I'm Black and Japanese, people used to mistake me for being Samoan, Filipino, Mexican, etc. I could see myself getting into so many different fights at Balboa because they couldn't tell what I was. Jeff was different, so I stuck around. The assistant principal told me that if I didn't cause any problems, I could stay.

When I started at Jeff, my friend Debbie and I kept in touch but didn't hang around together anymore. There was Tall Curtis, my dance partner. He'd pick me up and we'd go to a club off Broadway in SF where they allowed minors but wouldn't serve you liquor. In the summer before senior year, I hung out with some newer White friends. There was a White girl a year younger than me who lived close by. It was always a diverse group. When you're used to diversity it's hard to be around prejudiced people. One White friend married someone in the military and moved to the South. It was hard for her.

At Jeff I didn't see people fighting because of race, more because of personality. One time there was a fight with another school after a game. I remember Lily [part-Black] saying, "Why are they doing that?" She was talking about the Blacks. I told her it wasn't just Blacks. It was all kinds of kids.

I wanted to go to a Black college. My counselor told me I had enough credits to graduate, but not to get into college, so my last semester of high school was hard—I had to take two math classes to catch up with the requirements. I also needed to take U.S. history. I tried to get out of photography, which I loved, but I stopped going to class because I was concentrating so much on math. The photography teacher had to give me an F because that's what I deserved. My counselor said my grades were some of the worst he'd ever seen. I passed math, but not with flying colors. I wanted to be an X-ray technician, but someone talked me out of that because of exposure to radiation. I didn't know about the precautions that technicians took.

After graduation, Akiko remained in the Bay Area for a while. While living in Berkeley she was in a relationship with her future husband, and became pregnant. They had a baby girl but weren't yet married or living together. In 1980, when their daughter was four years old, Akiko became a born-again Christian.

He and I stopped going out, then almost a year later he called and said, "Let's get married." My only condition was that he didn't try to stop me from going to church. On October 10, 2021, we celebrated forty years.

I got a job at Sumitomo Bank, which was really neat because it was a Japanese bank. I found out I was pregnant with my second child. During that time I had a hernia which was very painful and, combined with the pregnancy, I had to quit work. After giving birth, I had the hernia operation. Not long after that, I got pregnant with my last child.

When we bought our first home, I started doing family day care. I was going to school for child development to finish my associate's degree. I stopped and went back to work at Wells Fargo. We bought a bigger house and started renting out the old house. I became a daycare provider again, differently though. I was actually teaching the kids to read and write before they started kindergarten. I did that until we moved to Georgia.

Akiko put a lot of thought into naming her children.

All my kids have Japanese middle names that pertain to how one should live one's life. For instance, my son's middle name is Yemon, which means "guarding the gate." I told him to make sure he's guarding the right gate! My own name means "bright child."

In 2005, Akiko and her family moved to Stone Mountain, Georgia, the symbolic birthplace of the Ku Klux Klan. Today Stone Mountain is more Black than White.

Yes, it's the same Stone Mountain cited by Martin Luther King, Jr. There are a lot of Confederate flags when we walk up the mountain, but we live in a more diverse neighborhood, more balanced between Black, White and Hispanic. I used to work at a Kroger grocery store which is a minute away from me. When Facebook [FB] came, everyone wanted to be your friend. This one lady, she's a sweetie pie, but I saw her on FB talking about the Confederate flag and I had to unfriend her. The Confederate flag and the U.S. flag don't go together. The Confederacy lost [the Civil War], so there's just one American flag.

My son came out here at eighteen. He had no police record. One time he and some new friends were waiting in the lobby of a theater where another friend was the assistant manager, and his boss told them to wait outside. There was a police officer nearby, watching them. When they went outside, there were some White guys. My son's friend the assistant manager comes out to talk. The policeman comes over and says, "You have to leave or buy a ticket." He didn't say that to the White kids—it was fine for them to hang out, being loud. My son went toward the ticket booth to get a ticket. The policeman said, "Come back here," and my son said, "I'm getting a f-ing ticket," and the cop arrested him for disorderly conduct.

Akiko is very proud of her successful now-adult children, but it's hard for her to see her son getting singled out because of his skin color. She worries about him.

My son was working at a furniture store with a White guy who started calling him names, saying he wanted to fight him, etc. My son secretly recorded him and showed it to the boss, so they didn't work together anymore. The store didn't let the other guy go. They sent him to another store, but they dismissed my son two weeks later.

* * *

Today, what people don't understand when they say, "All lives matter," is that we already know that all lives matter, but Black people are treated differently—like their lives don't matter. When Black lives matter, everyone's life will truly matter.

When we talk about getting rid of the police, we're talking about getting rid of those police who are racist. We're not talking about taking away people's guns, but they don't need guns that are for war.

Sylvia

(Filipina, White, class of '72, older sister of Eddie)

* * *

Some kids from other schools were afraid to come to Jeff. I think it was because they thought we had gangs, but it was just kids hanging out as normal.

* * *

Sylvia was born in San Francisco, the second of six children in a mixed Filipino-White family. She and her older brother Ernie attended a Catholic school where all the other students were of Japanese descent. Shortly afterwards, her family moved to Daly City, where she attended Woodrow Wilson Elementary School from first to third grades.

One of my friends, Gail, was a very tall Black girl, and another was possibly of Italian descent. I was so short that I probably only came up to Gail's waist. Because I was the littlest, they would always protect me—they thought I needed it. One time Gail took me home for lunch. When I met her mom she laughed and said, "You are so little."

Both Sylvia's parents were born in the Philippines and came to San Francisco as teenagers, but Sylvia's mother was half-Filipina, half Irish and Scottish. She was fair-skinned with freckles.

78

My mother's father was a merchant marine, a seafarer. I don't even know what he looked like. The only members of my mom's family that I ever met were her older and youngest brothers. During World War II, my mom hated the Japanese because they occupied the Philippines and killed several of her relatives. They would take them away, and you'd never see them again. When my mom and two of her brothers had a chance, they escaped. I remember looking up at her and seeing a huge scar underneath her jawline. She said it was from shrapnel from all the bombings in the war. She didn't talk a lot about that time.

I wish my parents had taught us Tagalog. I asked my mom why they didn't. She said, "Because we're in America." On my dad's side, we were the only cousins who didn't speak it.

Both my parents were hard-working, which you have to be when you've got six kids. I never, ever saw them argue. My dad tells me I'm just like my mom—very headstrong, very particular about things, hard-working.

Sylvia describes the neighborhood she grew up in.

At the time there were a lot of Caucasians and African Americans. The only other Filipino family I knew were the Franciscos. There was also Diane, who was Japanese and my closest friend before junior high. We'd go to the park; play, whatever.

At Daniel Webster Elementary School where I was bussed, there were mostly White kids. Since it was far away, I didn't have any friends there. I played sports at recess—tether ball, kickball. I was always the littlest one.

Sylvia became more aware at school that people were different.

We all looked different, and I didn't have the same food for lunch as the other kids. I might have rice and chicken and they'd have a bologna sandwich with cheese and chips. We'd always have Filipino food at home and at our relatives' houses. It was my job to make the rice every day. When my mom came home, she'd make adobo or something—always rice, meat and a vegetable. Never hamburgers, but sometimes spaghetti. I never had mashed potatoes until I joined the Marine Corps! I regret not learning how to cook from my mom. She made Filipino desserts from scratch at holidays, and I'd help her grind the coconut, etc., but I never learned how to make them myself. It wasn't that important to me. Now they have fast-food Filipino places, but the food just isn't the same. My mom's been gone for so long, but I still remember the taste of everything she made.

Although Sylvia was teased because of her size, she doesn't recall being bullied.

Maybe I wasn't bullied because, to some people, I didn't look Fili-pino since my skin is lighter and my eyes were only a little slanted. When I was in high school and got a job at the five-and-dime store, the woman who interviewed me said, "You don't have to answer this, but are you Chinese or Japanese?" I thought, "Wrong!", but I didn't think much more about it at the time

There were a lot of new kids when Sylvia got to Colma Junior High.

I noticed there were different races—more Blacks, Hispanics, and others. No one ever bothered me because I didn't give them an op-portunity to. I didn't go out of my way to make friends with anyone in particular. I was on the shy side and hung out with a few friends—three White, one Filipina, one Black.
Colma and Jeff were like a melting pot. Our gang was pretty mixed. I got to know other Filipino families that came to Daly City after us.

Sylvia has little recollection of her parents teaching her anything about race/ethnicity.

I remember my mom telling me to "stick to my own kind." Even though she was half-White, I knew she was referring to Filipinos. I would never tell her I wasn't sticking to my own kind.
If I had a crush on someone, it was all about the person; race/eth-nicity didn't matter. My dad never said anything. He had a lot of friends of different races, the same as my mom, but when it came to getting married, she wanted me to marry someone Filipino. They never said anything bad about anyone, though.

While at Colma, Sylvia met Janet, who was White.

We became best friends and remained so throughout high school. I had only been over to Janet's house a couple of times and even then, I could feel some tension. Janet and my brother started dating. They had to sneak around because of her parents. She wasn't supposed to mingle with us, period. One time when Janet was at my house, her mother drove over to look for her. She didn't even come to the door, just sat out-side honking the horn. Janet's sister was dating a Chinese guy, which was also a big "no-no." My brother and Janet eventually went their separate ways.

In spite of being small and shy, Sylvia was fearless.

I don't remember specific incidents of standing up for anyone, but it was just who I was. If someone did something I thought was wrong, I would do what I thought was right, and stand up for the person.

Some kids from other schools were afraid to come to Jeff. I think it was because they thought we had gangs, but it was just kids hanging out as normal. I remember George [Filipino] got into a big fight one time with Allen [Black]. I don't think it was a race thing though, just that something happened, and they started fighting.

Maybe I made sure I didn't put myself in situations where there might be conflict. A lot of girls hung out in their little cliques. One clique didn't like another. I didn't have cliquey friends. No one ever treated me bad, and I don't remember seeing anyone else being treated bad.

In high school I started taking karate lessons. I remember thinking, I'm going to have to learn how to protect myself because there's not going to be a man beside me to help. My boyfriend at the time, Kevin, didn't know I was taking karate; it wasn't something I thought he'd want to know. The studio was at the Top of the Hill, across from the bank. One day Kevin was going past on the bus. He looked in the window and there I was. When I joined the Marine Corps, I continued taking karate.

Like many young people growing up, Sylvia had a well-kept secret.

I've always been attracted to girls, even when I was little. I remember in third grade I thought this girl was so cute and really nice, but I didn't try to play with her. Right then I realized that most girls didn't have those feelings and, as I got older, I was noticing more girls. But I believed it was wrong, and I noticed a lot of people at school would make fun of a boy who was always playing jump rope with girls. He was the only guy who would jump rope with the girls and he was really good at it. I thought he was kind of like me because he was doing things other boys weren't doing. I wouldn't talk to anyone about it. My parents never talked about gay people or anything; they never said, "Don't be like that." They didn't know I was like that.

There were a couple of boys I thought were cute, but I didn't know if I'd ever be "normal." Even at Colma, because I didn't want to be pointed out, I'd never go out of my way to meet someone I was attracted to. If we were friends, that was fine, and I'd be satisfied with that. I had to be.

In high school there was a girl who I think was trying to reach out to me, but I didn't let it happen. I was too shy. She may not even have been "that way." It may have just been a first attraction for her. We were good friends and spent a lot of time together. This one time she got really really close to me and it scared me too much to act on it. For all I know, it may have been my imagination. She never said anything, and I didn't either. You sort of just pretend like nothing happened. We were friends. She graduated a year ahead of me, started working, got married, and we drifted apart.

After graduation, Sylvia took a civil service test because she didn't think she would be able to go to college.

I figured I needed to get a job. I got one as a stenographer with the Department of Corporations, working with lawyers. I got a job because my mom had passed [killed in a car accident], so I figured I should hang around to see if everyone else in the family was going to be okay. It was pretty good, but not the job of my dreams. What I liked about it was that it was only a block away from Chinatown and I could go there for lunch as a treat. Later, when I was in the Marines, it took me eighteen months to reach the rank of sergeant and make the same pay I was making at the Department of Corporations. And I made sergeant really fast!

From a young age Sylvia had a dream of joining the Marine Corps.

I used to go to the public library and look through an encyclopedia. I got to the M's and saw the Marines. I thought to myself, "This is what I'd like to do." I didn't want to do what everyone else was doing—going to college, to work, etc. I wanted to be different. The Marines was the smallest of the armed forces. From that time on, I wanted to join them.

But the Marine Corps initially turned me down because I was too short. The minimum height for women was five feet. You could get a waiver for four feet, eleven inches, but I was only four feet, ten and a half inches. I was so mad that I wrote to the Commandant of the Marine Corps. I told him I had wanted to join and defend my country since seventh grade. They probably thought I wasn't even going to make it through boot camp.

There weren't many women in the MC at the time. Almost every time I went to a training class I was the only woman. I had to do every-thing twice as good just for them to think I was okay. I always had to be extra sharp, extra smart. I knew that men would always be stronger than women, but I was always going to do the best I could. From growing up I had been taught to keep the house clean, do my chores—things that enhanced my time in the Corps.

When Sylvia joined the Marine Corps, she was engaged to Kevin.

Kevin joined the Navy. We kept in touch and I was really crazy about him, but I didn't love him the way I knew I could. Maybe it was what I had to do. We'd see each other on weekends, go to dinner and dance. We'd have a good time.

When I broke up with him, I never told him why, and I felt so bad. It wasn't because of another woman, but I didn't want to live the rest of my life as a lie. At that point I started meeting other gay people and I realized I wasn't the only one. We would just go and have a good time, dancing, etc. At the same time, we had to be careful because there had been witch-hunts trying to find the gays and kick them out of the Corps.

One night when I was living in the barracks, some straight women broke into this woman's room and beat her badly because she was gay. They called it a "blanket party."

I had a friend who was Black who was murdered. Her nickname was Blackie because her last name was Black. She was a hoot. That night we were all in the lounge playing cards or something. Another friend who lived off-base asked Blackie for a ride home. Blackie took her, but she, Blackie, never returned. The next morning we found out she'd been murdered two blocks from where she dropped off the friend. It had to be because she was gay. She wasn't robbed or anything. We were all questioned and were careful not to say she was gay because we didn't want the focus to be on gay people.

The NIS [Naval Investigative Service]—like the FBI, but military— called me in for questioning. My First Sergeant was with me, which was required. I kept saying, "I don't have to answer that." They asked, "You don't want to answer that because. . . ?" I responded, "We learned this in training, and I don't have to answer anything I don't want to."

I even had a friend get discharged because they thought she was gay—guilt by association. She wasn't, but she didn't say anything.

A lot of things have changed since our day. Some people are so proud they hang the gay flag on their front porch. There are still a lot of haters out there, so I won't do that. Even in the Marines there may have been some women I was attracted to, but I never initiated anything. The people who I went out with, I wasn't attracted to. Kind of weird.

In the mid-Seventies the Marine Corps sent Sylvia to a weeklong counselors' course for drug and alcohol use in Norman, Oklahoma.

They sent a lot of leaders there to learn to spot problems, etc. I stayed at the nearest hotel. One day I went to get something to eat. I walked into a restaurant and was waiting and waiting. Everyone could see I was there. The hostess helped two or three other groups of people. After about thirty minutes, I said, "Excuse me, but I've been standing here for thirty minutes and have been watching you help all these other people." She went to get the manager. I told him the same thing. He said, "We don't serve your kind here." I asked, "What kind is that?" He said, "Well, Indian of course." I started yelling in the restaurant. I felt so bad for the Indians who live in that area.

Sylvia's final reflections on Jeff:

I loved high school. I had a good time. I do regret cutting classes, now that I'm older. I loved the people there. Even though I was shy, I knew a lot of them because of my brother Ernie. You have your tougher kids at all schools, but I chose to hang with good people. Maybe that's what made me so surprised at people in the Marines. To me, I didn't see any racial stuff at Jeff. As far as I was concerned, we were all together. I don't know if it's changed or not. I hope not.

Eddie

(Filipino, White; class of '73, Sylvia's younger brother)

* * *

Her parents realized I liked their daughter, and her mom said, "You're a sweet kid, but if a guy dates my daughter, he has to have blond hair and blue eyes."

* * *

Eddie, a year younger than his sister Sylvia, was born and raised in San Francisco until his family moved to Daly City before he started kindergarten. His parents were from the Philippines.

My [White] grandfather was a longshoreman from Eureka, California, who traveled the world. When he went to Manila, he fell in love with a nurse, my mom's mom. He jumped ship to be with her, trading his permission-to-board-ship papers with someone who wanted to leave the island so that he could stay.

My mom was half Irish and Scottish, so she and her siblings were fair-complected with red hair and freckles. A lot of Filipino people were amazed at how well my mother spoke Tagalog, not realizing she was half Filipina. Dad was Filipino-Chinese. They reminded me in some ways of the television comedy show "I Love Lucy," where my mom was Lucy and my dad was Ricky Ricardo. Dad played the congas and would sing to Mom, like Ricky did. My mom couldn't sing; she was always off-key, so it was funny. We grew up on Rogers and Hammerstein mu-

sicals. All the kids were always singing to musical movies and putting on shows for my mom.

My father worked for Qantas Airlines at San Francisco airport. When he babysat us, he'd bring us to the hangars. We'd see people of all races working together.

Eddie's schools were all within walking distance from home, except for fourth through sixth grades, when he was bussed to Daniel Webster and Fernando Rivera elementary schools. At Woodrow Wilson, which he attended from kindergarten through third grade, Eddie remembers a mixture of all races and ethnicities.

I don't remember standing out as the only Asian. It was a real blend. At Daniel Webster [DW], though, it was predominantly White, but at that age, I wasn't looking for race or ethnicity. Fernando Rivera was similar to DW. I remember taking a bus, but I also rode my bike and walked there. I'd walk through areas with people coming out of their houses, walking their dogs, etc. who were predominantly White, but I wasn't really thinking about it.

At Daniel Webster I was more fearful that I wouldn't know anyone and wondered how others might think of me. I'm a talker and make friends with everyone. I make sure I say "Hi."

When I went on to Colma Junior High, I don't remember racial tensions, but there was an art teacher who people said was gay. Being raised near San Francisco, you don't think anything negative about a guy liking guys or a girl liking girls. I thought of someone being gay like just another nationality.

At Colma we had every ethnic background you could think of in our group—Blacks, Hispanics, Whites, Asians. I always considered them family. My friend Anthony [Black] used to talk about the projects where he had lived, and sometimes there were problems. My mom told him if he ever needed a place to stay, he could stay with us. Anthony and Ronnie were the Black part of our family.

In junior high school, Eddie fell for a girl who was to have a big impact on his life.

My sister brought a [White] friend, Janet, home with her. I looked up and saw this starry-eyed angelic girl. She ended up liking one of my best friends and they went together off and on. I was always the kid in the background, fantasizing. When they broke up, I started talking to her more. She said that phrase every guy hates: "I love you like a brother." *My heart sank. I'm in the brother zone, not even the friend zone! So I kept my distance. She went out with another guy who wasn't good for her; me being the "brother," she always cried on my shoulder. She finally broke up with him. We started talking more. I got out of the brother zone, then into the friend zone, and worked my way up. We started going out.*

At first, we didn't want anyone to know about us because she was my sister's best friend. We always met where we were going—dances, movies, bowling. I was too young to have a car. I said, "Let me pick you up and go to a dance." She responded, "We can't, because my mom doesn't like us girls dating." Some time went by. I spent time at their place and befriended her parents, who thought at first I was just a kid who hung out with her. Then they realized I liked their daughter. Her mom told me, "You're a sweet kid, but if a guy dates my daughter, he has to have blond hair and blue eyes." That's when it hit me. I knew there were racial problems all over the place, but this really affected me. I talked about it with Janet. We cried and hugged. It didn't end the relationship but made it more passionate, doing things behind her parents' backs.

That was the only time I experienced prejudice in Daly City. I didn't see anything else related to racism until high school. I liked a White girl, and her folks brought it to my attention that I wasn't a White guy.

Outgoing and popular, Eddie was likely to enjoy his time in high school.

I had friends all over the place—the Road, the brains, the jocks, etc. Even though we had the rah-rahs, stoners, and nerds, I didn't look at it that way. If I needed help or wanted to talk to anybody, no matter who they were, I could just go over and say, "Hey, I need your help." No big deal. I loved everyone. I was class president from fifth grade to my senior year of high school. The last few years at Jeff, I didn't really have to run because people said, "Eddie's our president," because I was for so long.

We had a Filipino Club at Jeff. We'd have a festival and everyone would come over to our house to make lumpia with my mom.

My favorite teacher was Mr. Yamaguchi, not because he was Asian but because we had martial arts in common. Another favorite teacher was my [White] math teacher. We called him a penguin because from behind he kind of waddled.

The group I hung around with was older. I remember sitting down with a White pompom girl who was two years older. I was having girl-

friend problems, she was having boyfriend problems. We just talked about our problems, cried on each other's shoulders, but didn't look at each other as anything other than friends. One of my dearest friends was White; another one I loved, Janice, was Black.

I remember an older student who fell in love with a teacher. They eventually married. He was White and she wasn't. Everyone knew what was going on and heard the rumors. I never thought of anything beyond teacher and student, versus being mixed race.

Eddie doesn't remember his parents talking to him about race, but his grandmother had something to say to him and his White girlfriend.

I don't remember my dad or mom saying anything to us about any race, nothing like "Don't hang out with those people," etc. My dad worked as a barber on the side and brought everyone home, including Chinese, Korean, Japanese, even Black. He was also a musician, and his band always had several different races. I remember a skirmish between a Filipino and Chinese gang and my dad got caught up in it—something related to his band. He didn't say anything about it being related to race.

One time I went to my grandmother's house with Janet. Right in front of her, my grandmother, who comes from the [Philippine] islands, looks at me and says, "Couldn't you find someone Filipino?" She wanted us to stay within "our tribe." It didn't shock me, even though she married a White guy herself. I don't think she said it (that I should find a Filipina) out of prejudice; she's just thinking about what's familiar. When people come from war, they want everything to stay in their own little bubble.

After high school, Janet and I talked about marriage, about eloping. We made a plan. She went to Europe every other summer. We were going to meet in London, get married and come home together as husband and wife.

Six months before we were going to do it, she called and told me she couldn't go through with it because her mom would hate her and she'd be kicked out of the family. That ended our relationship. We're friends now.

Eddie also remains in touch with many friends from high school.

Those were my happiest days, when my mom was alive. She was the glue that held our family together. She died in a car accident when I was a junior. My mom loved Janet; she'd always tell her, "I can't wait 'til you two get married and have my grandkids." Janet really loved her, too. When my mom died, Janet was by my side all the time and told her parents, "Screw you. I love this guy and he just lost his mother." Janet's parents even came to our house to give condolences. We went to the cemetery together. Janet came to me and grabbed my hand. There are times when the one you love needs you, so you do what you need to.

One of my dearest friends right now is of Chinese descent, raised in Daly City, where her family had a little Chinese restaurant. Her parents are from China. She'd tell me all these stories that happened to her at Jeff. I'd be in disbelief. Because she was Chinese, people called her names and bullied her. At reunions [after graduation] she'd point people out who had said racist things to her. It was so hard for me to believe, but hearing stories like that from someone who is dear to your heart, I knew she wouldn't make it up. She's still affected by things people said. I remember her dad, too. Because the Japanese treated the Chinese so badly, he had issues with Japanese people. He'd witnessed so many terrible things during the war.

Eddie joined the Air Force after graduating from Jeff.

I didn't plan on college because I was too in love; I found a way to be near her. If you're in the top ten in your training, you get to go where you want. I was, so I chose London—I wanted to be in close proximity to Janet, who was spending time in Europe. When she called it off, I stayed in the Air Force and tried to be the best I could.

I saw a lot of things that opened my eyes (to racism)—shocking things. I trained in Biloxi, Mississippi, in the early seventies. There were signs that said, "Blacks only; Whites only." Being neither White nor Black, I didn't know where I was supposed to go. Could I drink out of both fountains?

My drill instructor [DI] was an old Marine who cross-trained with the Air Force. A White guy had problems with Blacks, and a Black guy from the west coast had problems with Whites. The DI puts them together and says, "You guys hate each other too much. You gotta learn to live together." They ended up being friends. The DI knew they'd be able to work it out. They had to, because if you serve together you have to trust each other. If you're pointing your rifle in the same direction I am, you're family; you have my back, I have your back. That's the way it needs to be.

As an adult, Eddie learned that his sister Sylvia was gay.

We knew all my sister's boyfriends and she went out with several guys. It never dawned on me that she was gay. A couple of them asked her to marry them, and she just said she wasn't ready. When she finally wanted to come out and tell me, Ernie [older brother], Syl and I were all in the military all over the world. We met in a nightclub. I asked her, "What's up?" She said she had something to tell me. She sat me down and was all nervous. I asked her if she was pregnant. She said, "No," then said she was gay. I said, "And what? You're getting married to a girl?" She said, "I like women." I said, "I do too, but don't steal mine!"

After I got out of the Air Force, I went back to school at San Jose State. The people I dealt with were predominantly Hispanic. I had three part-time jobs. I met my future wife, and then I got a job offer I couldn't refuse in Las Vegas.

Eddie still lives in Las Vegas today.

I always tell my nieces, nephews, and my boy, stories about when we were growing up. It was such a different time. They don't believe the things we used to do. We'd go up San Bruno Mountain to camp for the weekend; we'd sleep down at Thornton Beach. It wasn't dangerous. There was no need to worry. We walked around with a push lawnmower offering to cut grass for twenty-five cents. We could go into any yard, grab a garden hose, and take a drink from it. Someone might come out and ask, "Are you okay?" and offer us a piece of pie. Can you imagine that now?

At my son's, nieces,' and nephews' high schools in the 2010s, they had cliques. My son only hung out with Filipinos and Asians, though his partner is Hispanic—they met in seventh grade and he's twenty-five now. It never seemed like anyone was bothering anyone, but people stuck to "their own."

When the nieces and nephews hang out together now, it's like my old school gang, very mixed: Whites, Asians, Blacks, Hispanics. I brought up my boy as a single parent. I can honestly say I never spanked him. I always explained to him if he did something wrong. My son was always the responsible one when he hung around his cousins. When they party now, he's the designated driver. We all do family things, camping, etc. We instill in them, no matter what happens in the world, family is family. Nothing is tighter than family. The older the kids got, the more sense we made to them.

Teacher: Jeannine Hodge

(White; taught social studies, civics, sociology, psychology, Wilderness School, and "American Problems," 1964—1987.)

* * *

These kids—Black, White, Asian—most of them had been together since kindergarten or first grade. This subject ("American Problems") was not new to them. Integration was not new to them, as it was to the larger culture.

* * *

Jeannine was born and raised in western Washington state. She describes her early years.

We lived way out in the boonies. Our house didn't have electricity until I was in second grade, and I went to a one-room country schoolhouse in first grade. That one-room school was the best year of education I ever had because I could observe everything being taught to all the grades. The nearest city was ten to fifteen miles away, and it was all White except for one Black man whom everyone referred to as the "shoeshine boy" because that's what he did. There was one block in town where women wouldn't walk because it was where drunks and roughnecks hung out. That's where the shoeshine stand was. One Chinese family had a restaurant that they never came out of. There were also some Indians [indigenous to this land].

After the Japanese bombed Pearl Harbor [in December 1941] we moved to Seattle because my father worked for the Boeing airline company. A few lovely Black ladies lived next door to me. They would send me to the corner store and give me an extra nickel to buy an ice cream or penny candy.

In second grade, in Seattle, I went to a very integrated school. I remember when the police came into our class and took some of the Asian students away [to internment camps because of Pearl Harbor]. I couldn't figure out why they took some of them, but not all; they looked so

91

much alike. The Japanese girl they took away and the Chinese girl I walked home with were my best friends. I went home crying. When my dad came home my parents both talked to me about what was going on, even though I was only in second grade. They told me that everyone in this country was totally focused on one thing—winning the war. Even something small like saving the tinfoil on gum wrappers was helpful as it could be rolled up into a ball to melt down for the war effort.

Before the end of the war a Boeing Air assembly plant opened in my old hometown, so we moved back to the boondocks. There were 136 of us in my graduating class. Many of us had been together since grade school.

Jeannine shared why she left her hometown and how she ended up in San Francisco.

When I was four years old I used to play on an abandoned railroad track. I'd stand on those tracks and look beyond and say, "I know there's somewhere else out there. I want to go there." It was far in the future—twenty-five years ahead of me, since I was only four. When I was older I used to listen to Wolfman Jack on the radio—out there in the sticks we had to hold the tinfoil antenna [to get radio reception]. He'd talk about California.

My timing was great, moving to SF in the early sixties. People would ask, "What are you going to do this weekend?" We'd answer, "We're going to hitchhike to Big Sur." It was all safe.

I had done a couple of years of junior college in my hometown, then went away for a weekend. I bummed around in Yakima [Washington state] for a little bit, then went back home to my parents. I got married and my husband and I both wanted to come to California. He was working for Cal Trans, so we had a choice, and I knew it was San Francisco.

I went to work for a bank in the financial district. At Christmas I wanted to go visit my family and I asked for time off. They said no, so I quit. I thought I'd go back to school. I applied to SF State and that's where I got my teaching credential. I student-taught at Jeff in '64 and got hired right away.

I graduated from SF State mid-year, and the Jefferson Union High School District hired me to be a long-term sub. Every morning I'd get a call to teach at any one of the schools in the district. I taught at all of them. Jeff was by far my favorite because of the diversity, the freedom and friendliness, the openness. It was a very tolerant place.

That year, 1964, was the last year the state of California gave out general teaching credentials, so I could teach anything. I taught social studies, civics, sociology, psychology, and American Problems. I also spent a lot of time in the Reading Clinic and the Wilderness School.

"American Problems" was a social studies requirement for seniors that focused on current events but was not part of the established curriculum. Jeannine had people come to talk to the classes about what was going on—local Black leaders and preachers.

What I remember is that these kids—Black, White, Asian—most of them had been together since kindergarten or first grade, so this [subject] was not new to them. Integration was not new to them, as it was to the larger culture.

Prior to her student teaching, Jeannine knew nothing about Jefferson.

It was an incredible school. There wasn't any kind of support or guidance from administration about working with Jeff's [diverse] population at all. It was sink or swim! The support came from one another. There were some really smart, well-educated people teaching there, a lot of Berkeley graduates; Harvard too. I was blown away by the faculty. I used to love sitting in the lounge and listening to them arguing with each other about almost anything, including politics, civil rights, Vietnam; whatever were the current events. I would sit there like a little bump on a log and absorb everything that was being said. I was impressed to be there among them—me, a kid from the boondocks.

I remember Ike McClanahan [one of the few Black teachers]. There was something special about him. He grew up picking cotton in Bakersfield. Then he became a policeman, then he became a teacher, and then a principal. I felt like he was still one of us. He would always listen, and even if he didn't agree, he was open. He was one of the ones who engaged in faculty-room debates.

I loved Jeff's students because they were so diverse, from all different countries and backgrounds. They were very open and free. I thought they were fascinating. I learned as much as I taught. You could present a problem to a class and get twenty-five different responses because there were so many different cultures.

I remember being in a class of seniors when I realized that they were all intently staring at me, not because of what I was teaching. I asked, "What are you staring at?" They said, "Your eyes." "My eyes?" "Yeah, they're blue."

Jeannine was in school, in the company of a student, when she learned that Martin Luther King, Jr. had been assassinated.

I remember so vividly when MLK was killed. I was in the Reading Complex, standing right in front of a young Black man who had been a student aide. We were face to face the minute that news came. I saw his eyes turn to hatred in that precise moment. It was like everything turned, everything changed in an instant. I have no memory of him after that. Everything changed with all my students from that moment on. My previous feeling of ease was impaired. The comfort level was just not the same, and I'm sure that was true of society at large.

I know there were [racial] incidents [at school after King's assassination], but I don't remember. I don't know whether I didn't want to pay attention or focus on it.

Jeannine taught in the Wilderness School for some of her time at Jeff.

The Wilderness School was funded under the Elementary and Secondary Education Act of 1965, which provided extra money from the federal government. Some teachers at Jeff used part of this money to set up reading clinics and part for the Wilderness School, which focused on non-academic subjects, life skills and such, for students who had poor attendance and were more likely to drop out. It was intended to get kids out of the urban environment, teach them some self-reliance, and get them away from drugs. There was enough money to go on camping trips for one or two weeks. We did challenging things like rock-climbing and white-water river rafting. As part of that program, I also had to get some training myself. I went to Outward Bound a couple of times, learned to rock climb and rappel, and did white-water rafting.

I was one of the only women in the Wilderness School. It was also an era when we were doing sensitivity training. We'd sit in a circle in small groups and talk about things you wouldn't normally discuss in a classroom. We teachers talked among ourselves and eventually worked in small groups with the students about specific situations they were dealing with. It was very satisfying to be part of that. It was somewhat racially mixed, but not as much as the school was. There were more males than females. One time the guys had all gotten together and taken the boys off on some trip. So I got Ms. Jansen and we organized a trip to Big Sur for the girls. When we got to our campsite, a bus arrived, a Big Sur bus—a bunch of hippies who lived on an old school bus and would go from campsite to campsite. They pulled up and all the kids disappeared into the bus. They all survived and came back.

My years at Jeff were the most interesting, the most exciting, the most adventurous, the most life-altering years of my life. Before I started teaching there, I was working for a bank, an 8-to-5 job I could almost do in my sleep with the same people every day. Going back to college at an older age, I knew what I was interested in, and I would participate more in classes, choosing my education, not just being spoon-fed whatever the college wanted to teach.

When I started teaching, I was old enough to have the confidence to walk into a classroom believing I had something worth sharing with students, something that could benefit them. In the credentialing program I had been taught "You go, you give, you teach." Not only did I share and teach, but I got so much back from the students, big time. What was life-altering at Jeff were the things I learned about my students and about myself. The diversity made it so vital and alive. There was always a new student from somewhere else. It was always evolving, never stagnant. I'm sure it would have been much more boring if I'd taught somewhere else. I was so lucky.

Teacher: Dave Smith

(White; taught U.S. history, world history,
social studies, 1965–2010.)

* * *

I'd always heard, "You don't go up there (Jefferson) by yourself," and
"Be prepared for trouble if you go." But I fell in love with the people and
the place.

* * *

Dave was born at Yale University Hospital in Connecticut, attended by the famous pediatrician Dr. Benjamin Spock. Several moves took Dave's family to San Mateo, California, when he was very young; he considers San Mateo ("a real suburban bedroom community") to be his hometown. His parents divorced when he was in fifth grade, and, later, his sister went to live with their father while Dave stayed with their mother.

I'd grown up on kind of the wrong side of the tracks before living for a few years in a more upper income area of San Mateo. There were two distinct groups—the wealthy kids, and the kids from the rest of the city, which was more of a mixture, east of Bayshore Freeway where I grew up. My best friend in junior high school was Chinese and I visited him often in the more diverse part of town where he lived.

But, mostly, I grew up in a White bubble and wasn't really aware
of prejudice until I got older. At San Mateo
High I did have friends who were Asian
and Black, and there was a fairly liberal
teacher who taught government. She talk-
ed to us about current events and got us to
read James Baldwin and Ralph Ellison, so
my awareness was growing.

San Mateo had one big advantage.

My high school was pretty academic.
About thirty-five of us from my graduat-
ing class went to UCB [the University of
California at Berkeley]. We were compet-

96

ing for admission with schools like Lowell, one of the best high schools in San Francisco.

If there was one college campus that was the epicenter of the sixties in the United States, Berkeley was it.

I lived in Berkeley for four years as well as Oakland during my last year. I changed a lot during that time. It was during the Free Speech movement of the sixties, when students pushed back against the attempt to restrict on-campus political activities, and many of the faculty took our side. As I learned more, I became more and more liberal, and am still that way today. I wasn't a leader, but I took part in many marches and demonstrations. The one I remember most vividly is marching from Berkeley to the Oakland Army Terminal, which was the embarkation point for guys who were drafted to go to Vietnam. At the border of Oakland there were about 100 police in riot gear waiting for us, along with a crowd of anti-marchers. The leaders of the march decided it wasn't safe to continue, so we turned and went in a different direction. I was also at Sproul Hall [the administration building at Berkeley] when the police arrested about 600 students who had occupied it. I watched the speeches for a while, but I left before I could get arrested.

In Daly City, when I started teaching, the Serramonte area was re-stricted to Whites only, so I picketed. Throughout my time in teaching, I was very active in the teachers' union and was a union representative for a while.

After graduating from Berkeley in 1964, Dave got his teaching cre-dential.

I went to a job fair and was interviewed there. I'd been thinking about going to Oceana High School, south of San Francisco in the coastal town of Pacifica, because I knew some people there. While I was waiting to hear from Oceana, I got called in for an interview at Jeff. I was offered that job on the spot and I took it. This was in 1965 and I taught at Jeff steadily until 2010.

Jeff always had a reputation as a tough school. From growing up in San Mateo, I'd always heard, "You don't go up there by yourself," and "Be prepared for trouble if you go." But I fell in love with the people and the place. Originally, my goal was to teach at college level, but I got attached very quickly to the school and the kids.

Dave moved to San Francisco and lived for two years in the Fillmore district, which was then a predominantly Black neighborhood. His apartment was on the fringes of the Haight-Ashbury district, famous for hippies and the Summer of Love, as well as a lot of drug use.

I lived in a big apartment building. Aside from being burgled a few times, it was okay. I never got in any physical confrontations while there. I was so into teaching that I didn't get to know my neighbors well. During that time, I had a diverse group of friends through teaching.

No multi-cultural training was provided when Dave began teaching at Jeff, although he recalls some attempts in the early seventies to increase teachers' sensitivity to the diverse student population.

There were trips to Esalen, a retreat center south of San Francisco, founded in the early sixties to support alternative methods for exploring human consciousness. The idea was to try to change people's attitudes, etc. I think teachers are generally sophisticated enough that no one at Jeff made any overt racial comments around others, at least none that I ever heard. There were, however, different philosophies of teaching. One teacher lamented loudly that you could no longer hit kids! My philosophy of teaching was almost 180 degrees the opposite.

I very rarely had problems in class. I think the kids knew I really liked and respected them, so they respected me. In my first few years someone threw something, a battery I think, at my head when I was at the blackboard. I told them that no one would leave until I knew who did it. The students said I couldn't keep them there, and I said I'd give it my best shot. One of the "leaders" finally went to someone and made him tell me that he did it so everyone could go home. That was one of the worst incidents that I had in almost forty years of teaching.

Jefferson was a fascinating place to work.

That's why I changed my plan to teach college. The principal, John Mongan, hired all kinds of very sharp, very interesting people, which resulted in fascinating conversations in the faculty lounge. Although almost all of us were pretty strongly liberal, it was a hotbed of conversation with many different points of view—about Vietnam, the civil rights movement, all of it. I made many good friends, some of whom I still have to this day. Many of us became leaders, department heads, and mentors to new teachers. But by my last few years at Jeff, almost nobody used the faculty lounge except for making photocopies.

Like many teachers who stay at one school for a long time, Dave expanded the subjects he taught.

I spent a good part of my career in social studies. In 1975 I started working as the coordinator of the Reading Complex [a federally funded program to support students who were struggling with literacy]. Working in such small groups allowed us to get a lot closer to the students, and we'd end up helping them with whatever other problems were going on in their lives. After that I went back into the classroom and taught remedial and advanced placement [AP] classes most of the time. The AP students were expected to go on to four-year colleges, but some went to community college first, often for financial reasons. Some of the remedial students were really talented in the arts or sports, even if this wasn't reflected in their grades. One thing I appreciated about the kids at Jeff is they didn't have feelings of entitlement. They knew they had to work hard to prove themselves.

Dave does remember occasional fights.

I broke up a fair number of fights, sometimes by getting right in the middle of them. Boys fought, sometimes girls fought—teenage hormones, mostly, although a few kids were really disturbed and ended up in jail. One time a kid threw a punch, missed his target and clipped me instead. I just pretended it didn't happen since I knew it wasn't intentional.

Dave reflects on why Jeff was the way it was.

A lot of the school was shaped by a few strong, very talented and very sharp people. Al Sinor [chemistry teacher and later principal] was a Renaissance man who could do almost anything. Dave Peebles was my alter ego with whom I periodically traded jobs. He became my closest friend in teaching and we're still very close. Rudie Tretten became head of the counselors. He was very bright and taught at college level after Jeff. Karen Fellom was a very caring and creative English teacher.

Another teacher was also very talented but he was, unfortunately, a victim of the teachers' strike in '79. He was the principal at another high school and was ordered to arrest any striking teachers. He refused to do so, and they fired him on the spot. Another one of our teachers was more controversial but he was named among the best teachers in the state. He ran his room as a "crash pad" where kids could go and get away from whatever they needed to get away from, if they were stoned or just upset; they could sit on sofas at the back even if they weren't part of his class. He also testified in court about certain books which were branded obscene, but he never thought they deserved a ban.

In 1969 Dave got married and moved with his wife to the Outer Sunset of San Francisco, about a block from the beach.

The Sunset was predominantly Caucasian when we moved there, but now it's more mixed, with many people of Asian origin. After living there for decades, my wife became more and more incapacitated by multiple sclerosis. In 2010 she took a fall on her scooter and broke her hip in three places. She never really walked again and was in a wheelchair for the last several years of her life. Five years after her accident we moved to Daly City, and she died four years later.

I've had connections with Daly City since 1965. I'm currently in a senior assisted living facility there, although I've had minimal need of assistance.

Dave's final reflections:

Jeff has been multi-cultural for a long time. In my early days, there were lots of Italians. Over time the Latinos and Asians—Filipinos, mostly—increased. Kids form groups, and one of the bases for the groups is having similar backgrounds. I think most kids would say they had one or more friends from other backgrounds, though. ESL students tended to stay as a group, but those who were more fluent in English mixed more.

I felt Jeff was special from the very beginning, and almost everyone who taught there felt the same way. It slowly changed over time in that the feeling that "we're a group" disappeared. John Mongan, my favorite principal, encouraged diversity and brought in a variety of people. After he died, there were new principals who were more about "keeping the lid on." The teachers who remained were unhappy about those changes. After the first teachers' strike in the late seventies, there were principals who were seen as anti-teacher.

They weren't bringing in any controversial new people and there was a deliberate attempt, in my opinion, to pull the "problem" teachers, like those active in the union, and send them to other schools— spread them out so they wouldn't be as strong. It backfired because many of them ended up being leaders in the other schools. They strengthened the union wherever they went.

Joe

(Black, class of '72)

* * *

We'd walk around near a real estate office with signs that read "Jim Crow must go." Most people's response to us was, "Why don't you go back to Africa?"

* * *

Joe's parents came to California from Alabama during the "Great Migration" of Black Americans in the late 1940s. His father was an electrician, his mother a homemaker. Joe was born in San Francisco, the fifth of seven children, and grew up in the Bayview-Hunters Point projects and the Fillmore District of San Francisco before moving to Daly City.

His family was very close and very religious. Various aunts and uncles stayed with them on and off, so his home life was always full of extended family. When Joe was seven, his parents bought a house in Daly City.

Our neighborhood had some African Americans, along with Whites, Mexicans, and Filipinos. At home, everything was about religion. Family friends and a lot of people in the church came from the South, like my parents did. During the summer, relatives came up from Mississippi and Alabama to get away from the sweltering heat.

My family used to go with our church on small-scale pickets in Serramonte, a newer development in Daly City where they wouldn't let any Blacks live. Our pastor was a little guy who breathed fire into everything he did. He had elders like my Daddy and a few other deacons who could spin Bible verses and stories with the best of them. We'd walk around near a real estate office with signs that read "Jim Crow must go." Most people's response to us was, "Why don't you go back to Africa?"

Joe's family lived half a block from Marchbank Park, and three blocks from his neighborhood elementary school. Joe was the first in his family to be bussed to an elementary school in Westlake, an all-White neighborhood.

Westlake was a culture shock, straight up. It was the first time I'd been around that many White kids. I got along well, even though most of them were afraid of me. I was athletic and people liked that. . .the big kickball games, etc. Some were real cool with me. I guess I made a big impression because I've had some of the girls and guys look me up on Facebook and we're now friends. One of the girls contacted me and told me she used to have a crush on me!

Joe knew that there was something not quite right about having to take a bus to a school far away when there was one so close to home. He admits to occasionally having bullied some "nerdy" kids in order to impress girls.

One time after school I met a kid I'd bullied, a real quiet guy who never got into any trouble, but something happened in kickball and I told him to meet me to fight. He was there, and he clocked me upside the head before I even got a punch off! That was all it took for me to end the bullying. I never forgot that lesson and avoided fights after that.

For junior high school, Joe walked almost two miles a day to get to Colma.

It was really cool that Colma was so diverse. I was very into basketball, and also played little league [PAL] baseball in Westlake, so I still saw some of my friends from there. I was the only Black player on the PAL team. Two of my best friends who were Jewish saw what I went through, because they also experienced discrimination. One of them, Todd, kept others from picking on me.

Our team's coach was a college professor and had a son who also played ball. The coach took us to a Stanford football game one time. On the drive there, an Italian kid from another school asked the coach, in front of me, "What did God say when he made the [n-word]?" The coach asked, "What?" The kid answered, "I burned one." Everyone in the car laughed except me. Once we got out of the car, my friend Todd stood up for me. He grabbed the kid by the collar and told him, "You may have on a white shirt but that doesn't make you any better than anyone else." The guy never made any more jokes around me after that.

But that happened outside school. At Colma I never heard anyone use the n-word. My neighborhood was very diverse. I used to always go across the street to a White family's house because I was into cars and they had a fancy truck, so we just shared interests.

I had a paper route delivering newspapers to people on Junipero Serra Boulevard, near where Bay Area Rapid Transit is today. A lot of the customers were White, but they didn't seem to have any issues with race.

In junior high school my basketball teammate from PAL league called me to find out what time practice was. His brother got on the phone and said, "Who's this? You sound like a [n-word]." My friend got back on the phone and apologized. There were times when I felt like I had to be better than some of the White guys on the team in order to start. The PAL coaches tried to pit me against some of the White guys. There was this White guy who was supposed to be the fastest on the team. After I joined the team they encouraged us to race against each other. I won.

One of Joe's favorite memories is when he graduated from junior high school and his mom took him to a Giants baseball game.

During that time, my idol was the San Francisco Giants' third baseman Jimmy Ray Hart [JRH], who ended up having a big impact on me. JRH hit a home run and I caught it on one bounce! I couldn't wait to get home to show it to everyone. As freshmen, me and a few buddies used to go to Giants games and sneak into the players' parking lot to try to get autographs. The cops would always go after the Black kids, so our plan was that the two White friends would run in the opposite direction when JRH came out so the cops would chase them, and I would be able to get his autograph.

Their plan worked so well that—far beyond getting the autograph—Joe had a conversation with JRH, who learned that Joe lived in Daly City, and offered him a ride home. So there was Joe, waving to his friends as he arrived home in JRH's car!

As he was dropping me off, he invited me to the Giants' clubhouse the next day. I was so excited! He said he would pick me up at 9:30 the next morning. I got up early and waited outside, starting at 6:30 so I wouldn't miss him. Since I had told everyone about it, by 9:30 the whole neighborhood was outside waiting, thinking I had made it all up because JRH hadn't showed up, but I kept waiting. My parents felt sorry for me and told me to come inside for breakfast. Just as I was going into the house, I heard a car honking, and it was JRH!

When we got to the clubhouse the first person I saw was Willie Mays, who I heard cussing. I was shocked, thinking, "Not Willie Mays, oh my God!" I was introduced to several players, a dream come true. During batting practice, I got to sit in the dugout. JRH gave me a ticket to the game and I got to sit with all the players' families. I did this for three days in a row.

Later, Joe became the batboy for the Giants, which he did for five years. During high school Joe played baseball and missed some of his own baseball games because of his batboy job.

My school coach knew I was a batboy, but he didn't like it. He used to joke about how I wore my socks outside my pants, the way the Giants players wore them. I don't think he liked me very much. If I missed a game or two, he started the second-string player in my position in the next game I was at.

At Jeff, Joe was quiet, but he stood out on the basketball court and the baseball field. His closest friends were people he played sports with: a few Black, a few White, and one Latino. Joe remembers experiencing some racism from his own teammates.

*We had two basketball players from Brisbane [a mostly White area] who weren't in my grade. I felt these players didn't get along with Blacks. One time one of them made a joke about Pontiac. "The word Pontiac, if you spell it out, is **P**oor **O**ld N[-word] **T**hinks **I**t's **A** Cadillac." When I heard that, I walked away without saying a word. It hurt, but I had to shrug it off. They said it to see my reaction. Then I got the old cliché, "No offense, but . . . ." It was a trip because we were teammates. There weren't any other Blacks there when they said it. Years later I saw them at a reunion. They were all happy to see me. It felt like the guys liked me okay, but their racism was so strong they'd say stuff* *anyway.*

One time after basketball season was over, a Brisbane teammate's family held a party at their house.

It was me, another Black player, and a White player in my car. Another Black teammate drove behind us in his car with a Hispanic friend. When we came out on Bayshore Avenue, I could see the Brisbane cops following me. We got pulled over. While I was waiting for the cops to come up to the car, I was talking with my friends in the car. Suddenly a cop banged a shotgun against the car. He told us to get out, all of us. He pointed the shotgun at my stomach. He searched us but never even looked at my license or registration. Finally I asked, "Why did you stop us?" "Because you have a stolen car," which wasn't true. He searched the car but didn't find anything. Eventually he let us go. I was so terrified that when I got home I woke my parents. Dad told me, "You're getting bigger now and you have to be careful."

Up until age eighteen, Joe went to church regularly.

My first girlfriend was the preacher's daughter. There were a few Black girls at Jeff I kind of liked, but I ended up dating a White girl. A Black girl approached me when she saw me walking this girlfriend home and said, "I bet you give her your money, too." After that, my girlfriend was kind of scared of Black girls. My dating White girls caused others to notice. There were times when I got "looks." It just wasn't done. I remember the police trying to pick on me a couple of times.

In 1972, when Joe graduated from high school, his parents moved away and left the house with Joe and his sisters. Joe went to Skyline College for a few semesters, where he played basketball. He didn't think the team was going anywhere, so he left. He still went to Giants games regularly.

I should have stayed with the Giants. One of the guys who became batboy after me is one of the main guys in the front office today.

Three years after graduating from Jeff, Joe joined the U.S. Army and served for seven years. He did his basic training at Fort Ord in Monterey County, California, and was sent to Fort Belvoir in Virginia to learn the skills of a mechanic/generator technician, to work with the big generators that run hospitals.

In the military, I learned that this is not a democratic society. Sel-

dom will things be fair for you. There are so many set rules, a code of justice—military justice, which is not the same as civil justice or democratic justice. They make sure you learn that when you join.

When you first get off the bus at basic training, everyone has to run a mile. Whoever pushes the hardest is chosen for squad leader. But everyone is fresh off the street. They may be able to run fast but have no leadership skills. You have a barracks full of guys from all over the country in the same building—no one knew each other but they quickly became clannish. Everyone stuck with their race. In the beginning I had a White and a Black drill sergeant. This immediately threw out the segregation and showed that everyone had to have everyone's back. I felt good about that. This is where I realized I needed structure to discipline myself.

After basic training I went home and showed my family my bald head. Then I was shipped to South Korea, where I was for twelve months. It was a culture shock. The Korean people were not very timid. They knew how to fight, but in general were very welcoming, and gave you the benefit of the doubt, at least with people under thirty.

In the military there's big-time systemic racism, just like the racism that's here in the U.S. with the police. If you're Black, the first thing the military police want to see is your identification. If you're not in the system, they want to put you in it. If you went to any clubs off the base, you might get pulled over and they'd mess with you. It didn't matter if you were on the base or not. You rarely saw any Black officers.

Later, when I was in Panama, I had a Black officer who was from the same city as my mom and dad in Alabama. You salute every time you see an officer and they'd salute back. Sometimes White soldiers wouldn't salute Black officers, which was very disrespectful. The Black officers would let it slide. But I could be punished and put on restrictions if I didn't salute.

I got out of the military because of what happened when I was in Panama. I had my own squad—six guys, four squads to a platoon. The squad leader has to make sure they all know how to march, etc., so there's a lot of pressure on you.

We had a new [White] second lieutenant. I didn't want to be involved with him but I had no choice. A second lieutenant only spends six months in officer training school. I'd been in for seven years, and this guy was trying to tell me how to run my troops. I told him to follow the chain of command if he had a problem with me. He was a hothead—he called me "son," and I got in his face. We ended up in front of our commanding officer [CO], and the lieutenant lied. I didn't get to tell my side

*of the story. The CO didn't give me a chance, even though I had wit-
nesses. They took money out of my paycheck, and I was on restriction
for a month—get up, go to work, stay on the compound the whole time.*

*In 1977, when President Carter gave the Panama Canal back to
Panama, I got to shake Jimmy Carter's hand. Panama was the first
place I'd been that didn't have four seasons. It would rain so hard and
two hours later the ground would be dry. I saw howler monkeys, fruit
bats, and vampire bats with two-and-a-half-foot wingspans. I loved
Panama, but I didn't like the fact that people with only book-training,
and very little of it, outranked me.*

After the military, during Clinton's presidency in the nineties, Joe
got caught up in the era of crack cocaine and went through a difficult
period.

*I was with someone I'd sold drugs to before, but the guy had be-
come an informant. With the new laws, I ended up going to prison—five
years and six months in prison for selling $100 of cocaine to an under-
cover cop. My original sentence was for ten years.*

*Blacks did crack cocaine, Whites did powder. If a Black person got
caught with crack, they'd get as much as forty years; if a White person
got caught with powder cocaine, they would get five years.*

*Prison was terrible. Everything was segregated; a White and a
Black person couldn't live in the same cell. The correctional officers
instigated the racial stuff. The Norteños [northern Mexicans] fought
and hung with the Blacks; the Whites and Sureños [southern Mexicans]
hung together. There were more Hispanics in prison than any other
race in California at that time. If the southern and northern Mexicans
ever came together, they'd run everything.*

*I was a loner. I'd exercise and stay out of people's way. If there was
a riot or something, if I wasn't with the Blacks and I went with anyone
else, they'd kill me, straight up. There was always something going on
because you've got all this testosterone and everyone has to be bigger,
badder than everyone else—the Crips, the Bloods, the Aryan brothers,
even Muslim gangs.*

*I got paid minimum wage, $5.50 an hour, while in prison, and end-
ed up with $7000 when I got out.*

After serving his time, Joe bounced back. He moved to the valley
near Modesto, closer to where his parents lived.

Today I've been clean and sober for twelve years. I'm married to a

White woman whom I met during the days I was doing drugs. She's been clean and sober for over fifteen years.

Although my wife's parents accepted me, I remember what happened the first time I met her dad. After a few hours, he pulled me to the side, sat me down, and asked what I had in store for his daughter. I told him I'd known her for years, so I wanted to move to Ohio where she was living. Things went well, but after it snowed a lot that winter her father decided to move the family to Modesto, where his son was living. I was working for a company out of California, so it was easy for me to make the move to nearby Merced.

Joe's final thoughts about Jefferson:

I thought Jefferson was special. I didn't want to leave. What made it special was the people I knew. Everybody was fair. You had the popular students, the jocks, the nerds, the stoners, but everyone got along. I miss those times. I used to go over to the houses of some other guys, and I wondered about how they grew up. My family was very religious, and my dad was a workaholic, so there wasn't much room for me to bring friends home. I liked the teachers, too. I wasn't one of the top students, but the school touched my heart.

Irma

(Latina, class of '72)

* * *

When I went looking for jobs, I'd be wanting to submit my application, and there'd also be a White girl applying. The White girls would always get picked, but not one of us. I was thinking, "What's the difference between them and us?"

* * *

Irma was born in San Francisco to first-generation American parents of Mexican origin. Her mother was born in El Paso, Texas, and her father in San Francisco. Irma was much younger than her three siblings, who were already in school when she came along, and both parents worked—there was no one at home to take care of the new baby. For this reason, when Irma was four months old, she was taken to live in Ciudad Juarez, Mexico, with her aunt and grandmother, who raised her until she was seven.

I thought my aunt was my mom. I grew up with two cousins. One biological cousin was left at an orphanage, the other's parents were divorced, and my uncle ended up taking him to live with my grandparents too.

I was raised by my aunt Maria de Jesus Vallejo Villa, my mom's younger sister, whom I called Mommy even though I knew later that she

was not my mother. I started school at the age of five. They didn't have kindergarten, so it was considered like first grade.

When I was seven, my parents came to Mexico to take me back to California. I was scared and missed my aunt very much. I recall my aunt saying as we both cried, "I will come and visit when I can. Your father wants you back home to live with them." I cried in the car all the way from Ciudad Juarez to Daly City. My aunt and I cried when we talked on the phone after I left. We would call each other almost every weekend to stay in touch.

My parents introduced me to my siblings: "This is your brother; they are your sisters." In time I bonded more with my father than my mother. He passed away about eight months after I graduated from high school. My older sister and brother were already married with kids, so my relationship with them developed mostly through babysitting for them. My other sister was in her last year of high school and would shortly be leaving and getting married herself.

Soon after, my aunt came to the U.S., I went to stay with her for a short time at an uncle's house in San Francisco because my father could see that I was totally bonded with her. When my parents enrolled me at Colma Elementary School in Daly City, right across the street, my aunt came to live with us. All the neighbors were White. The neighbor to the right of us, her family and siblings were all so nice. They were Italian. She taught me how to ride a bike. I used to go to her house and play. We were really close. She was very down to earth. Her family was so loving but loud when talking to each other. I always thought they were arguing. In their conversations some words sounded like Spanish, but they were Italian. I recall asking, "Do your parents ever argue?" She said, "All the time." I asked my parents if they argued. They said when they did, they'd take it outside of the house. They'd go for a drive and come back happy. All this was very weird to me as I did not grow up in Mexico with loud yelling.

My aunt was a performer who got very involved in the community down in San Jose. She recruited my cousins and me to perform, especially for holidays. When I was around ten years old, I always had to dress up as the boy "Charro" in the Mexican hat dance, because I was tall and skinny and the only one that fit in the outfit. Once I performed at San Quentin Prison, which was very scary. When I took my hat off to throw it on the ground, the inmates went crazy, yelling, "She's a girl!" That was the most inter-racial place I had seen at that time.

When Irma began school at Colma, she was put in kindergarten, even though she was already seven years old—the tallest girl and the oldest kindergartener.

I should have been in second grade, but I didn't speak any English. In the U.S., school was so different and seemed very easy-going; the teachers were much less strict than in Mexico and the teaching was aimed at kindergarten level. I already had learned a lot of the work in Spanish, so it wasn't hard for me. I just couldn't speak English. I don't remember anyone ever making fun of me for that. I remember being bored—all they did in kindergarten was play and take naps, more like daycare. Naps were not allowed in Mexico. You only had five minutes to go to the bathroom, so if you were late coming back, you'd have to stand in the corner, and you might even have an accident and pee your pants. School in Mexico was no joke. They were very strict. We used to get hit on our hands with rulers and get our ears pulled if we were bad! Oh man, and guess who got a taste of all of that? "Me!"

I don't remember anyone at Colma speaking Spanish to me. They used to send the work home with me and my parents would help me out. I refused to go to a babysitter, so I'd be at home by myself after school when my aunt was not available. My parents would just tell me to make sure to go to school and come home. My mom got home at three and sometimes helped me with my homework. My brother and sister didn't speak much Spanish. Neither did my father. Sesame Street helped me a lot with English and I started to catch up.

After a little while I was so bored in school, I told my mom I couldn't take it anymore. If they had left me in Mexico I would have been going into second grade. After second grade, I skipped third grade and went to fourth. I was supposed to skip another grade after fifth, but I no longer wanted to because I had friends. When I graduated from high school I was nineteen instead of eighteen.

Today I notice some people complaining that kids aren't getting as far in school because English-speaking kids are in the same class with others who don't speak English, or barely. I think there should be special classes so everybody can work at the right level.

When I started at Colma, I knew Chinto [Latino], Ron [Black], and Frank [Italian] from grammar school. I didn't associate with too many people until I got into sixth grade. I was more of a loner, even after I became fluent in English. Ron's mom was a teacher and I used to talk to her. I never had her as a teacher, but she substituted a lot.

There was a White girl who lived a couple of houses down from me. She supposedly was a wild little girl. I remember everybody was scared of her. She'd get in fights. Somebody asked me if I was scared of her and I said, "Why should I be?" I approached her one time and asked her why she was so aggressive. She told me, "I don't know, I just

*feel like people don't like me and they talk about me." Her sister was
more mellow.*

Irma doesn't have any memories of discussing race or ethnicity at
home.

*I don't recall ever having any kind of race issues until years later,
when I started working. My parents never really talked about it, but
they were very open to people of other races. It was never an issue at
home or when I was at Colma.*

*I don't remember the first time I saw a Black person. I was very
dark myself, and my friend Chinto was very dark, as well as Ron, but I
didn't really pay attention. I was very aware and curious about other
races and ethnicities. My friends were mostly White, Filipino, Latino,
and Black. I can remember being attracted to a White boy in sixth
grade, and later to other races/ethnicities—Filipino, Latino, Black.*

*Every summer I'd go back to Mexico to stay with my grandpar-
ents, until they moved to California. In the summer when I was about
fourteen, I went to a [Mexican] meat market that had a lot of Chinese
people and they were all speaking Spanish. I was amazed. They told
me, "A lot of Chinese people speak Spanish."*

*My parents always had parties and people over to their house.
They had Puerto Rican, American Indian, Portuguese, Italian friends
over, and played salsa, Mexican ballads, etc. I've always loved music.
I would sit on the stairs while my brother and sister had parties—they
wouldn't let me join in, so I sat on the stairs and listened. Since my
siblings were eight to twelve years older than me, I heard a lot of music
from the forties and fifties, rock and roll, and Motown.*

Like most people in junior high school at the time and without the
internet, Irma doesn't remember much about what was going on in the
rest of the country.

*I recall the television broadcast about Martin Luther King being
killed, but I mostly remember the marches. I heard more about them on
the news than anything. I don't recall any of us going on marches or anything like that. My most memorable thing was President Kennedy being
shot and everybody crying. I also recall when the Zodiac Killer was out.
My parents said I couldn't go trick or treating, and I'm like, "Why?"*

When Irma got to high school at Jeff, she was used to being around
people of different races and ethnicities.

Since I was around other races and ethnicities throughout my growing up and school years, I had no different feelings. I don't recall ever running into any problems related to race.

I remember not wanting to go to PE and go swimming because I never knew how to swim. The teacher said I'd flunk if I didn't go in the pool, and then I wouldn't graduate. I made a deal with her that if I jumped in the deep end, I'd get an automatic A. I got my A! They provided the swimsuits, the caps, everything. But we had to buy our own gym clothes.

My closest friendships and relationships during high school were very good. It was after I graduated that I noticed people being more prejudiced and showing favoritism, mostly when applying for jobs and when shopping at malls and in restaurants.

Irma's father passed away just after she graduated from Jeff, so she didn't go to college but went straight into the workforce to earn money and help her mother.

I took a six-week course to learn computer skills. It was in Westlake, a primarily middle-class White area. In this class there were a couple of Latina, a couple of Black, and some White girls. They would start us on the typing. Whenever we [Blacks and Latinas] raised our hands to ask a question, they would ignore us and choose the White person that raised their hand. I remember thinking, "What?" During the breaks we [the non-White kids] would look at each other like, "Whatever." We'd mind our own business to get through the course. At breaks, people hung out with their own race.

When I went looking for jobs, I'd be wanting to submit my application, and there'd also be a White girl applying. The White girls would always get picked, but not one of us. I was thinking, "What's the difference between them and us?"

I started working for a law firm as a legal secretary and there was a nice security guard who was Black. He used to take me out to lunch sometimes. We'd go to a restaurant and people would stare at us. I'd be thinking, "Why are they doing that?" He would notice it and say, "Don't pay attention to it," but it really bothered me. One of the White guys who worked in the office asked me, "Irma, do you only go with Latin guys?" I asked, "Why?" He answered, "Because I asked you to go out one time and you didn't want to go with me." He wanted to invite me to a party, so I said, "Let's go!"

I had one bad experience with an attorney I had to help at the last minute with a document. He was yelling at me and telling me I wasn't doing it correctly. I did not appreciate his rudeness and attitude, so I told him to do it himself. Later that day the founder and attorney of the firm passed by my desk and nodded at me, up and down. I thought I'd get fired, but the next day the rude attorney apologized to me, and the founder told me that his behavior had been totally unacceptable. I've been with that firm for twenty years now.

Irma's final reflections:

What made Jeff special for me is that I had such awesome friends of all races and ethnicities. Everyone was friendly and we all got along together and respected each other. Everyone was accepted for who they were. There were a few who felt different, but overall, everyone was great! I have great memories and always hold them dearly.

Gary P.

(White, class of '70)

* * *

At Jeff, the band people were kind of different. There was a real mix of people. We all got along well. We were all kind of "band nerds."

* * *

Gary was born in San Francisco, the third of four children. Both his parents were from Missouri, where they grew up across the creek from each other, with a farm on each side of the creek.

Both families had five children and some of them married each other. When Pearl Harbor was bombed, Dad signed up for the Navy, and he was in the war for the duration. They wanted to send him to the occupation in Japan, but he didn't want to go. Married men got a few extra "points," so my parents got married and he didn't have to go to Japan. He was honorably discharged to San Francisco.

During that time my mom and aunt were building escort carriers in Bremerton, Washington. Mom wanted to be a journalist. She had worked on the paper in their small Missouri town. With the war effort, her sister went to Bremerton to make money, and my mom followed.

My parents owned a house on Curtis Street in San Francisco which is now part of Daly City. They sold the house to move to Brisbane.

Gary was two years old when his family moved, and he lived in Brisbane for the next fifty-five years. He has fond memories of his childhood.

It was great growing up in Brisbane—very undeveloped at the time. It was a swamp; you could catch frogs and snakes all day long. Everyone felt safe. No one locked their doors. Everyone was midwestern Okies, mostly from Missouri and Kansas. Later on, we got a family of Samoans, then a Filipino family. There were a few Hispanics.

Our biggest trips growing up were a road trip to visit family in Missouri and taking the Greyhound bus to the dentist in San Francisco. Dad never took us to too many places. It was hard to leave Brisbane if you didn't have a car.

When I was growing up, there was no off-ramp to Brisbane, so there was only a roundabout way to get there. Once they developed the dump—San Francisco dumped their garbage there—they put in an off-ramp. That's when Brisbane started to go downhill. It became desirable property and got overbuilt.

On the other hand, Gary was aware that life in Brisbane was not perfect.

I think probably most people from Brisbane had some degree of racism. When my father was in the Navy, they had segregation. When we got out in the world, though, things changed. I think my father probably used the n-word, but his best friend was a Mexican guy. We'd go over to his house in SF and he and my dad would fix things. Dad worked for a company that ran the parking and car rental concession for the Palace Hotel on Market Street. When he retired, he recommended a Black guy to take his place. We were surprised, but that's what he did. Later he'd go down and help the guy if there was a problem. I don't know if he helped him because he had recommended him, or because he just wanted to help him out. Maybe he softened up a little.

Mom was very quiet. We were all kind of quiet because we knew better than to speak up; we were raised to be "seen but not heard." That applied to wives, too.

Since Brisbane's schools only went to eighth grade, Gary and his siblings, and all their classmates, were bussed over to Jefferson High School. Both of Gary's sisters played in the band. His older brother played in the jazz band.

Before I started at Jeff, my sister told me to join the band, which ended up being the only thing I really did there. She said to watch out, pay attention to my surroundings; Daly City wasn't Brisbane. She knew I was a dumb, skinny freshman. I probably looked like I was nine years old. My brother didn't really tell me anything.

Brisbane had some tough kids, and it was pandemonium on the school bus every day. I pretty much minded my own business. Because of band, I had to take the late bus home, so it was dark, but most people on it were band kids. At Jeff I hung out with Joe [Filipino], Ray, Gerald, Don, and Martin [all White]. Ray has been my best friend since kindergarten.

One of my first experiences at Jeff was getting robbed after I got off the bus. A couple of big Black guys came up on either side of me and told me to give them whatever money I had, which wasn't much. I don't think they went to Jeff because I never saw them again.

I felt pretty comfortable at Jeff. I knew where to go and where not to go. You didn't stray off campus. You had to be careful on The Road -- if someone was high, they might reach out and punch you, which happened to me once, even though some of the stoners were my friends. I heard people say the only safe bathroom was the one in the gym, but I don't remember having any problems.

The band people at Jeff were kind of different. There was a real mix of people and we all got along well. We were all "band nerds." I don't remember any problems, but Mr. Larson [teacher/conductor] would never have let anyone get away with anything.

I remember some tensions early on between Blacks and Whites after the Watts riots, but they didn't involve me. My cousin from Kansas joined the National Guard because he was afraid of being sent to Vietnam. The first thing he had to do was go to Watts. He had a bad first experience with Black people.

The Vietnam war was still going on when Gary graduated from Jeff.

I was worried about being sent to Vietnam. People were getting drafted and we were all sweating it out. There was a lottery system—you got a number and it just depended on how many spots they needed to fill. My number was mid-level, so it wasn't likely I'd get drafted soon. My friend Ray and I took the postal exam, and I got a job with the post office. It was part-time, so I could go to junior college. But part-time ended up being seven days a week sometimes. There wasn't any FedEx or UPS, so there was always work. I saved some money, got a car and a house in Brisbane, and started enjoying myself.

After Jeff, Gary says he was "right back in the Brisbane bubble."

As an adult, my first real interaction with people of different ethnicities was when I took a three-month leave of absence from the post office in 1976. A buddy and I took off on our motorcycles and rode the perimeter of the U.S. We camped out and stayed with people we met along the way. We rode over 12,000 miles that summer. We spent time in the deep south, New England, and on the Great Plains, hanging out with folks from all walks of life. It was a good summer.

I had an older Black neighbor who was very nice. Everyone treated her like everyone else because she was a nice person—she may tell you a different story, though. There were only a few Black people around. We used to pal around with a Black guy who moved into the new development with his [White] wife. There was a Black preacher who always wore a top hat. I don't know where his church was. He would go up and down Main Street, preaching.

Every year the rodeo would come to the Cow Palace and all hell would break loose in the bars in Brisbane—this was forty years ago. The trouble with Brisbane until recently was that there were more bars than churches! There were a lot of fights among White rodeo people; all the crazy ones from Texas, Montana, etc. Brisbane used to have "Western Days" every year, a real Okie thing. There'd be a parade, guys would dress up as cowboys and go around town with guns, women were dressed up as Miss Kitty [the saloonkeeper from the sixties TV show Gunsmoke]. Things got out of hand, so they don't have them anymore.

Gary and his wife have been married for thirty-two years and live in the Sierra Foothills, where they moved after he retired. They have four children including two from his wife's first marriage.

Our kids had friends of different races. People didn't form groups based on race—there weren't enough of any race to hang out together in groups. They didn't group together based on culture either because it was basically White culture. Our youngest's long-term girlfriend is Chinese. Our oldest is married to a Latina. [Gary's wife adds, "Latinx."]

Where we live now there is no diversity, but that was not a deliberate choice. My wife's job moved to Rancho Cordova, and there were tax reasons that limited our choices to two counties. Out here it's probably

95% White. The fastest growing ethnic group in the area is from India, because of tech jobs and medical jobs.

One of our best friends here is a White guy married to a Black woman. They're great people. If someone is a jerk, I don't care if they're White or Black, I avoid them.

Gary's final reflections:

I didn't think Jeff was that special. I did learn quickly where to go, where not to go, and that kind of thing. I was more of a wallflower, not a joiner. Most of my focus was on band. But it was a learning experience, being around people of different ethnicities/races/cultures. Their stories about their lives were completely different from my stories—my life was pretty boring compared to other kids. If people were nice, I could be comfortable around anybody.

Ginny

(Hawaiian, Filipina/Portuguese; class of '74)

* * *

My dad always taught us to respect and treat each other as equals. He kept saying, "We're all one but we all come from different backgrounds and ethnicities, so should learn from each other."

* * *

Ginny was born in the little town of Paia on the Hawaiian island of Maui; at the time Hawaii was still a U.S. territory, not a state. When she was four years old her family moved to San Francisco, where her younger sister was born.

Dad had come to San Francisco from Hawaii by himself for one year to establish himself before he brought Mom and me over. When I started kindergarten, the school required us to wear dog tags with names and phone numbers as a way to identify us. We lived in SF until 1962, when we bought a house and moved to Daly City, right below San Bruno Mountain and above Colma Elementary school.

Ginny shares some family history.

On my mother's side, my grandmother's family of nine came from the town of Santo Domingo, province of Ilocos Sur, Philippines. My grandparents went abroad to work on a sugarcane plantation on Maui,

121

and the Philippines would only allow their three youngest children to travel out with them. My mother was fourteen at the time. My father's mother's family was from Portugal and came to Hawaii years before my mother's family. My father's mother wasn't married yet when she, her parents, and two siblings sailed out from Portugal to Hawaii. My father's father came to Hawaii from the Philippines in the early 1900's. My father was the youngest of their eight children.

The two sides of my family worked in the cane fields and lived in different camps on the cane plantation. There was a Portuguese section where my father's family resided, a Filipino section where my mother's family lived, and a Japanese section. My mom went to St. Anthony's School, while my dad graduated from Maui High. It was funny how my parents met. My mother was a roller-skating waitress. My dad was driving for the Coca-Cola company, delivering all over the island. He met my mom at Tasty Crust Restaurant in Wailuku, which is still in business today—I eat there all the time when we go home to visit. They kept seeing each other at the restaurant, and he'd keep coming back, always parking in the section she worked. He asked her out, and although she initially said no, he kept asking and she finally agreed. They married in 1955 and moved to the small town of Paia where I was born.

Soon after, my mom's parents, her younger sister, and older brother returned to the Philippines, but my mom stayed behind, working at the restaurant. Dad's grandparents returned to Portugal after mom and dad were married. The last remaining sugar mill on Maui finally closed a few years before the COVID-19 pandemic.

Dad spoke only English because he was born and raised on Maui. Mom's side spoke both English and Ilocano, a Filipino dialect, which was only spoken at home. Outside the home they spoke only English in order to respect people who did not understand Ilocano. Dad's family name was originally Cordero, but it was changed accidentally when he joined the U.S. Army. My grandfather tried to get it corrected, but the army said it was too difficult to change it back, so we became Corden instead of Cordero. This made things difficult. When my grandfather's mother died at age 104 in the Philippines, it was really hard for the family to find my grandfather in Hawaii. Eventually they tracked him down through the army. Otherwise he wouldn't have been told about his mother's death.

While Ginny's Filipino grandparents had no problems migrating to the U.S. in the 1950s, things have become more difficult since then.

When I was grown up and married, my parents adopted a ten-year-old cousin who was living in the Philippines. They wanted to bring him over here. Unfortunately, he never got to come because it's much harder to come now than before. He is still in the Philippines, now a grown man, raising his own family and carrying on our family name, Corden.

After Ginny had started elementary school in San Francisco, her family bought a house and moved to Daly City.

I went to John F. Kennedy for second through sixth grades. I was supposed to go to Colma, but they'd divided up the neighborhood so one part would go to one school and the other part to another.

At JFK, there were several different ethnic groups. It never bothered me—we got along well. It was nice to know people of different backgrounds. I remember there were a lot of Mexicans, so we did Mexican activities in school. There were a few Chinese, a few Japanese, a good share of Whites, and not many Blacks. When I got to Colma Junior High, there was more of a mixture—more Blacks, Asians, and Whites, but not as many Mexicans.

There were a few other Portuguese and Filipino families on our block, as well as Irish, Italian, Mexican, German, and Black. There was only one Black family in our neighborhood. Teri was the first Black girl I met growing up.

On Hillside Boulevard there were farms on the mountainside. A lot of the Mexican children came from that area because their parents worked on the farms. There was also a ranch on the edge of the cemetery which my backyard faced, where people would go to ride horses. On the right side of the street was a pet cemetery, and on the left there were other cemeteries. I don't know where the Mexican kids went to school after JFK since I never saw them again. I remember a few of them saying they would be going to Woodrow Wilson and another school up at the top of the hill. I thought it was strange because it was far away.

Ginny's parents instilled strong values in their children, and Ginny was always allowed to mix with a variety of people.

Coming from Hawaii, my father and grandparents always made us believe we were all one, there weren't differences between people, even coming from different ethnic backgrounds, and we should learn from each other. We all respected each other and treated each other equally. When I first met someone from India, I wasn't sure where they were from. My parents explained to me more about other countries, like India. I don't remember any racism toward me or anyone else. I was always taught not to judge anyone because, no matter what, everyone is

*their own [person]. My dad always taught us to treat others as equals.
He kept saying, "We're all one, but we all come from different backgrounds and ethnicities so should learn from each other." This was
totally different from San Francisco, which was so ethnically divided:
Chinatown, Japantown, North Beach [Italian], Fillmore and Hunters
Point [Black]. There was a sense that if you weren't from that part of
town, you should stay away to avoid trouble.*

*As years passed, the ethnic mix changed in my neighborhood. One
of my best friends growing up was Black. She lived across the street,
and we were good friends until we left high school. My parents welcomed her like part of the family. I had another good friend who was
Mexican who lived around the corner. My family never blinked about
my friends, and they would invite them to eat with us. My mother always
cooked traditional Filipino food because she didn't know how to cook
American food. I never knew what spaghetti was or other Italian food
until I met my husband.*

Nevertheless, Ginny felt that high school was a big change.

*I think everyone had different ideas about how things should be.
I witnessed bullying, but don't remember it being racial—upperclassmen would pick on freshmen, etc. Maybe I didn't recognize it and didn't
understand why they were doing it. I wondered if they just wanted attention or to have more power over people of different backgrounds.
It wasn't just one background, though. There were certain groups that
didn't like other groups. From what I remember, the groups were mixed
racially and ethnically, so it wasn't a racial issue.*

*Westmoor High School [which was mostly White] was our rival. I
remember when they came for football games, the field was blocked off
by the security staff so people couldn't cross on foot, to keep everyone
apart and prevent fights. We had police blocking off the entrance and
checking everyone's ID. Westmoor's team was driven all the way onto
the field. We were even in the newspaper, where they claimed that we
[Jeff] started all the trouble, throwing things, etc.*

*But Jeff wasn't like Westmoor. We had a variety of races and na-
tionalities and, as far as I remember, everyone got along really well.
I had friends from all different backgrounds and we respected each
other. I didn't feel the same problem with the other high schools who
came to our school, only with Westmoor.*

*I was very proud to be at Jeff because of the different backgrounds of
the students. I was proud to be the mascot [the Jefferson Indian]. Sometimes I go back and look at my yearbooks and remember the good times.*

I graduated early, in January instead of June, but was able to join the ceremony on stage in June. There's a little group of us from the Class of '74 that started doing Zoom meetings together when the pandemic hit. We're still together today.

After Jeff, Ginny enrolled in a part-time nursing program at the College of San Mateo (CSM) while working.

After graduation, I worked part-time for MacDonald's clothing store in the Serramonte shopping center and attended a nursing program at night at CSM. Then my dad got sick, so I stopped working to help take care of him for a while. After five years of dating, I married my husband. I went on to work for an optometrist, then in 1979 I got scouted by Kaiser and started working there. I graduated as an optician and managed the optometry department at Kaiser Redwood City and Santa Clara until 2009. I retired early because they were changing pension plans and I would have lost money if I had stayed. My husband and I decided to enjoy ourselves while we were healthy—unlike my father, who had a massive stroke three months after he retired, but lived for another twenty years.

I took care of my dad until he passed away in 2015, and then my mother passed away in August 2020. We were able to keep both of them at home with us until the end. I had promised my parents that I'd do everything in my power to take care of them, and I was able to keep that promise. It was more work than when I was working, but it was well worth it. I have a lot of good memories. After my dad died, I had five more years to bond with my mom.

While Ginny doesn't have many memories of being judged because of her race, there are two things that stand out.

My husband's family is Italian, German, and Dutch. When he was growing up, his aunt lived in Little Italy [North Beach]. I didn't have any problem with Bob's parents when we were dating, but with the older generation [in their seventies and eighties], I felt uncomfortable and unwelcome because I wasn't Italian or White. Over time, I grew on them and they got to know my family. They realized that even though we have different backgrounds, we're not different, and they accepted me.

I traveled a lot when I worked for Kaiser. Once I went to Marin County with a colleague who was Chinese. We went to a restaurant for breakfast one morning in San Rafael, and there were only White people there. Everyone stared us up and down as if to say, "What are you do-

ing here?" We were so uncomfortable that we decided to leave. That was in 2001. That's probably the first time I ever felt like that. The way they looked at us gave me goosebumps all over.

My husband would sometimes suggest that we take a ride up to Marin. I'd decline, because I kept remembering that time and I didn't want to be around that kind of prejudice.

I'd sometimes ask my husband, "So what made you want to date me, was it my nationality, or what?" He said, "Because you were you." My parents never put limits on who we hung out with or dated. The Hawaiian way was to always welcome people into your home with open arms. There was never anyone my dad said could not come into our house. You can do whatever you like, but all they cared about is that you treat everyone with respect.

Ginny's final reflections:

Jeff was special—it was the best school. I had a great time. What I liked about it was there were a lot of different ethnic backgrounds, we got along really well, and were all treated with respect. I was able to learn about other people, how they lived, what they ate, their beliefs. All I'd known was the Filipino and Hawaiian way. I didn't know about Jewish people, Baptists, etc. I was raised as a Catholic, so when I went with friends to a Baptist or Chinese church, or a Jewish temple, I learned new things and really enjoyed it.

This rubbed off on my two sons—my oldest son's wife is Mexican and German, and my youngest son is marrying a woman who is Guatemalan and Nicaraguan. My dad used to say that we're really all one, so we're all connected, all related.

Don

(White, class of '73)

* * *

Jeff was a very friendly, easy-going high school. What was interesting was having so many different friends from so many different nationalities and ethnic groups. It was very rich as far as diversity. The lack of racial tension was probably unusual.

* * *

Don was born in San Francisco, the fourth of five children, and grew up in Daly City.

My father's side came to America from Germany in the 1800s. Dad's mom was from Switzerland, but her mom was born in Germany. Mom's side goes back to the 1600s, with mostly English, Scottish, and Irish background. Our Christmas traditions were mostly German— German cookies, Christmas trees, all from my dad's side.

My dad's parents were born in SF. Both of them lived through the 1906 earthquake as children. My grandmother vividly described the fires and the loud booms from buildings being dynamited to stop the fire. My great-grandfather was born in Illinois but moved to California with his parents.

My father grew up in San Francisco. My grandfather had a business in Daly City, where they were building like crazy, so my parents

127

bought a house. It was a very friendly neighborhood. Everyone knew each other, and everyone had kids. You could play in the streets.

My mom was born in Kansas. Her mother, my grandmother, got divorced when my mom was three or four, and my mom never saw her dad again. My maternal grandmother moved to San Francisco and worked in the hospital where my dad delivered X-ray solutions [chemicals for "developing" X-rays, just like in photography]. My grandmother played matchmaker. She told my dad what he wanted to hear—how my mom loved to fish and do all kinds of sporty stuff. My mom never fished a day in her life! They hit it off anyway and married after a brief courtship. At twenty-six years old, he was ready for that. My mom was nineteen. She didn't have any siblings, so she wanted a big family.

Don's neighborhood was mostly White, but his first two schools were not.

We lived off of Hillside Blvd. When I went to kindergarten it was racially mixed, mostly White, but some Asians, a few Blacks, and Hispanics. We were all just kids, so we never thought anything about it. I never heard my dad say the n-word. My older brother didn't hear it either, but he did hear our dad use another derogatory word. It was nothing blatant or anything like that. No one in my family grew up to be prejudiced.

I went to kindergarten at Vista Grande, then to Holy Angels Catholic school for first through fourth grades. From fifth grade on, it was public schools—George Washington, Colma, and finally Jeff.

The kids on my block that I hung out with were mostly White. I didn't go to a lot of other people's houses, and we didn't have a bunch of people coming to our house, either, but that wasn't unusual; kids, especially boys, played outside rather than inside. I had a lot of Asian friends, although not at Holy Angels, where it was pretty much all White. But from fifth grade on, I had a lot of friends of different races.

George Washington was very mixed. That was my first experience with Black kids. We used to play German dodgeball—you could catch the ball and then it was your turn to throw it at others. There was one light-skinned Black boy who could throw the ball really hard, picking people off. He wasn't a mean kid but just was much more developed than everyone else. At one point, he was in my class and the teacher wanted us to do a play. We had to record it [voices only], and then acted it out. I played Oliver Twist. I was one of the tallest kids. This Black guy was much shorter and played Fagan. All the kids had a big laugh about it.

In sixth grade, I was kind of dorky, but could run really fast in softball even though I was pretty useless at throwing, and batting. One time I was going through the motions of hitting the ball and this Black kid says, "What's the matter with you? Hit the damn ball!" I was embarrassed and kind of mad at him, so I swung really hard and hit the ball way into the outfield. He congratulated me and said, "See, I told you." That episode made me realize that I just wasn't applying myself. Things flipped. By the time we got to high school, instead of being the last person to be picked, I was the captain and picking others.

At GW and Colma, I was getting in fights with White kids that I didn't start. I was quiet and soft-spoken, but I was taller than most kids. In fifth and sixth grades, some of my friends and I would walk to school instead of taking the bus because we were bored waiting for it, and also to try to stay out of trouble.

I remember thinking there was going to be a revolution after Martin Luther King, Jr. was assassinated. My friends and I talked about it because people were pretty riled up; Black kids at Colma were so angry. People were doing the Black Power thing. You'd watch television and see race riots. I was concerned about what was going to happen, and we talked about it at home. By then, my brother was graduating from Jeff. He went on to San Francisco State, where they had some riots. Then he transferred to University of California at Berkeley, where he got gassed by the police at demonstrations and had guns pointed at him. He just wanted to go to school, but it was hard to avoid the problems.

At Colma I hung out with a Chinese kid, Ray, one of the smart, dorky kids. About four years ago, he contacted me and we became Facebook friends. He told me that I made a big difference because I was nice to him when a lot of other kids were not. I guess I didn't see that. We'd just hang out and talk about science and different things.

I had another friend who came from Hong Kong. When he first got here, he thought the Golden Gate Bridge was made of gold, and that everybody in America was rich. He told me about Mao Zedong and said how he could do miraculous things, like swim the Yangzi [Yangtze] River and jump thirty feet in the air. I told him I didn't think so. We talked about all kinds of religious stuff—original sin. I didn't think people had to be baptized and I didn't think there was a hell.

Another Chinese friend, Sammy, made his own firecrackers. We'd blow them up on the way home in sandy lots. We got cigarettes from somewhere and puffed on them until someone told us you were supposed to breathe them into your lungs. I tried it, coughed, and thought it was a really stupid thing to do, so I never smoked again.

I was sort of a teacher's pet in eighth grade. I really liked this teacher named Mr. Gridley. I was already taller than him. He was an interesting character because from the first day we walked in there, we didn't open a book. All he did was talk to us—about when he was in Korea; blood and guts. He was raging. We thought, "What did we get ourselves into?" After that, he was just a normal teacher. I liked to talk, and sometimes got in trouble for that. One time he sent me outside to sit for a while, which I didn't like. Then a few other kids were sent out one by one. It turns out the teacher was doing an experiment, so he needed us out of the room.

Don felt that his older siblings paved the way for him at Jeff.

One teacher always called me Doug, my brother's name—he was seven years older than me. My older brother and sister always got straight A's, so I was expected to get good grades, which I did.

I didn't really observe any racial incidents while at Jeff. I played football freshman year and did track. It was quite a mixed group. I had all different friends—Italian, Greek, Mexican, Irish, Japanese, Chinese, Filipino, Hispanic—lots of guys from South America, and a couple of Black girls from my classes. Everybody seemed to get along. I didn't hear anyone saying anything derogatory and I didn't notice teachers treating others differently. It was more like smart kids and dumb kids. If anything, if someone thought someone else was gay, there might be comments. One kid made a comment about a teacher being gay, and a coach stood up for the teacher. He said, "Some people are like that. Just worry about yourself." I think there was more stigma for being homosexual than for being Black. My brother was gay, and my sister, too, but they didn't come out until years later. It wasn't accepted so much back then.

In football, I didn't know what I was doing. I was just running around tackling people, so they put me on the defensive line. When I was a sophomore, we worked out with some of the coaches for the juniors and seniors for practice. I didn't like it. We had to run up this hill at the back of the school and yell, "Kill!" as we were running up it. That really turned me off. The coaches singled out two White kids who were on the small side and said they weren't macho enough. There was another thing where we had to tackle each other head-on. Everybody was getting the wind knocked out of them. I thought it was stupid and degrading and started having nightmares of not being able to move my legs, not being able to run. I quit football.

Another thing was we didn't have anyone who could kick field goals, yet we had all these Hispanic guys who played soccer and could kick a ball a mile. They were never recruited for football.

After that, I just did track. With track, I sunk or swam on my own. I wasn't impressed with the coaches, so I did warmups on my own before everyone came out. The coaches let me do my thing. Later, when I did track in college, I learned that if I had done more endurance running earlier I could have been much better. Speed I had, but endurance was what was needed, and the Jeff coaches didn't teach that.

When I was a senior, our team won the annual physical fitness contest that involved sit-ups, pushups, standing broad jump, pullups, and the 300-yard shuttle run. Every year the trophies were displayed in the coach's office, but not that year for some reason. We were told we'd get them at the awards assembly. All the team members were Hispanic except me and a Filipino guy. We also placed third in the Western United States in the Marines Physical Fitness contest. If we had placed second, we'd have gone to Washington DC. At the awards assembly our coach was supposed to give us our school trophies. The Marines awarded us our third-place medals and left. We stayed on the gym floor waiting for the coach to come out with the trophies he'd promised us. He never came out. People started laughing because we were just standing there. The guys turned to me and asked, "What should we do, Don?" I said, "Let's go find Coach." We went downstairs to find him, but he'd already left. I never found out what that was about.

That year I was given the Bank of America plaque for liberal arts. I'd gotten straight A's in English, German, and literature. I'm sure my German teacher, Mr. Beringer, had something to do with it. I graduated with a 3.7 GPA but didn't do that well on my SATs, mostly because Jeff was not an academic school.

After graduating from Jeff, Don went to Skyline Junior College.

It was almost like going to Jeff as far as its racial mix, but I wasn't academically prepared for college. I was kind of shell-shocked. I really had to kick it in gear. I hadn't realized how inadequate our classes were at Jeff. I'd see what people took at other high schools—they were like college classes.

One year in, I decided I wanted to take horticulture, so I transferred to the College of San Mateo, which was Whiter. Then I transferred to Cal Poly San Luis Obispo.

I had a college girlfriend from San Ramon [CA] who asked me, "Where did you go to school?" I said, "Jeff, in Daly City," and she said, "Really? That's a really tough school." I told her I never saw any fights or anything. She said, "Yeah, but there's all those gangs." I replied, "At Jefferson? There's no gangs." She said, "Yeah, they wear sweatshirts and put a jacket over it." I told her that we did that because we're freezing our butts off in the fog, not because of gangs! Jeff's reputation was known far and wide, but we didn't deserve it.

After college, I worked with undocumented people in the Bay Area. They'd just make up a Social Security number and would get hired. Some of them could speak English, some couldn't. I took some Spanish classes to be able to communicate better with them. We got by. Sometimes we'd communicate by drawing pictures in the dirt. I had a really good experience with those guys. Most were serious and worked very hard, saved their pay, and sent money home. When you work side by side with someone, loading and unloading trucks and doing all kinds of stuff, it's hard to think of them as bad. You find out about their family, where they came from. Most of them were from rural Mexico. The ones from the city were rowdier and would drink, but you didn't have to worry about them working hard. The older guys would get on their cases if they slacked off. It's a lot different from the White-guy work ethic. You always got your money's worth.

Don's final thoughts:

Jeff was a very friendly, easy-going high school. That part was great. I had a lot of friends. What was interesting was having so many friends from so many different nationalities and ethnic groups. It was very rich as far as diversity. The lack of racial tension was probably unusual. I just didn't have any issues, didn't really have any problems.

Ron M.

(Black, class of '72)

* * *

From growing up in a multi-racial area, it felt like we (Blacks, Latinos, Asians, etc.) were all included in the world. Then, after MLK's assassination, it was really magnified that we were still considered second-class citizens. My family was middle-class and educated, so we had believed that things were improving with race relations, especially compared to Texas, where my parents came from.

* * *

Ron's parents were both college graduates from Texas who met and married in San Francisco. His father had his own machine shop, and his mother was the first Black teacher in the local school district. She taught there for thirty-five years.

The family moved to Daly City when Ron was three years old.

There were no Blacks in Daly City in the fifties. My mom told us that the real estate agents didn't want to sell us the house, which cost $16,000. They tried to steer us to Lakeview or Hunters Point in San Francisco, but my parents were determined—our family was going to have the American Dream, a house of our own, not an apartment.

I grew up on Woodrow Street, about a block from Marchbank Park, and three blocks from Jefferson High School. The neighborhood was very mixed, Filipinos, Chinese, Latinos, Blacks, and Whites [Italian].

We all played together, skateboarded, rode bikes, and went to each other's homes for dinners and sleepovers. We were like family.

There were some Black kids on the other side of Mission Street who called us "Oreos"—Black on the outside, White on the inside—because my mom was a teacher and we never had to go without. They knew we were doing okay. We had nicer clothes and stuff that they didn't have.

I was bussed to Daniel Webster for fifth grade, and Fernando Rivera for sixth grade. I walked to my other schools, except at Colma [Junior High] I rode with my mom since she worked there. In elementary school I hung out with the same people from the neighborhood, but the school was majority White. I got along fine with everyone. I didn't experience any racism growing up in the early years.

Ron feels lucky that he had a "perfect" childhood. The outside world didn't intrude until later.

My mom and dad were happily married until my father passed away, and I had a perfect childhood, full of fun. My older brother was the first Black person in Daly City to get a scholarship to go to University of Santa Clara for baseball. He played for the St. Louis Cardinals' Triple A organization for a while.

Things changed after the killings of John F. Kennedy and Martin Luther King, Jr. I was at Daniel Webster when the announcement came about JFK, but it was after Dr. King's death that things really deteriorated. From growing up in a multi-racial area, it felt like we [Blacks, Latinos, Asians, etc.] were all included in the world. Then, after MLK's assassination, it was really magnified that we were still considered second-class citizens. My family was middle-class and educated, so we had believed that things were improving with race relations, especially compared to Texas, where my parents came from.

Summer trips back to his parents' hometown gave Ron a very different perspective.

We drove to Texas every summer until I was twelve. It was a different world. A restaurant in New Mexico refused to serve us. In my mom's hometown, outside of Dallas, we couldn't ride around in the car with any other race. The washateria [laundromat] had "Whites Only" signs in the front with the good washing machines, and Blacks in the back. We couldn't eat inside at the Dairy Queen; we had to order at the window. But at the end of the summer we got to leave all that behind and go back to liberal California, and Daly City, where we didn't see color—we saw friends.

My parents taught us to be respectful from an early age. We always got "the talk" that Black folks were treated differently, so we had to conduct ourselves carefully, especially in Texas. If you talked or acted decent, you didn't get treated as horribly.

Ron had a good time at school, but it was challenging to be the child of one of the faculty.

Everyone knew my mom, and my brother was at school before me. Everyone would say, "Oh, you're Mrs. Moss's son." The hardest thing for me at Colma was my mom teaching there. I could never cut school or act up in class. If I did, they'd send me to my mom's room instead of to the principal's office. It was humiliating. There was also some favoritism for my mother's sake.

Ron had a learning disability.

My mom and dad always said, "What you learn they can't take from you." My brother was a straight-A student, but I had dyslexia and attention deficit disorder [ADD], although there was no such diagnosis at the time. Everyone just thought I couldn't read. I couldn't retain information, either, and had a hard time spelling. I'd get words or letters mixed up. I couldn't distinguish between D and B. I tried to hide the stigma by becoming the class clown. I developed an excellent memory. Numbers were much easier. In sixth or seventh grade I got sent to a reading clinic. I try to read as much as possible now.

Outside of school, Ron enjoyed growing up in Daly City.

We'd go to the War Memorial [Community Center] or Marchbank Park, play sports, go out with our friends. This was why my parents moved us to Daly City: we were having too much fun to think about stealing or taking drugs. We weren't into gangs. We did start the "Fog Town Boys," but that was more about how we dressed. It wasn't about getting into trouble. My cousins who grew up in Hunters Point were smoking weed, etc. Some people sniffed glue in Daly City, but no heavy drugs.

It didn't matter what house you went to, they treated you like family. That meant if you did something wrong, you either got your butt whipped then and there, or you got dragged to your own house.

If I'd grown up in Hunters Point, I bet I would have turned out a lot different.

The police in Daly City were all White except one Black, Officer Glass. No one did anything wrong. We knew every inch of Daly City on our side of town.

Life didn't change much for Ron when he went on to Jefferson High with his "gang," the Fog Town Boys.

We were not a gang like you think of today, just a group of guys, really—a multi-racial group: Black, Filipino, Latino, White.

I wrestled at Jeff, played junior varsity football, and did track. The wrestling team was undefeated in '72. I have no memory of racism from playing at other schools. When we played Terra Nova [south of DC in Pacifica] we'd get the stares, the atmosphere—you always feel it when someone doesn't like you—but we always dominated them and didn't have any trouble. In Daly City I never heard the n-word or got pulled over. It wasn't like nowadays; today it's crazy. Or maybe I was too naïve to see it back then, but I think I'd remember.

I don't remember any teachers being racist. We only had one Black teacher at Jeff. My father was a machinist, so I was learning the trade and was the Black teacher's aide during senior year. We had some teachers who got high, some teachers who were stoners and hippies.

The only teacher I couldn't stand was my algebra teacher because he was too strict. I have not used algebra since the day I left his class. I used trigonometry and geometry, but never algebra.

We moved to South San Francisco in my final year, but I was able to stay at Jeff to graduate. Westborough, our new neighborhood, was very nice, up on the hill overlooking the airport. It was also a good mixture of every race.

After graduation, Ron married young and went to work at Wells Fargo Bank.

I married a Latina girl from California. We were together for thirty years and had four beautiful half-Mexican, half-Black children. I was the first one in my family to marry outside my race. One of my daughters married a Filipino man, so my grandchildren are even more mixed.

After I got married, I started working at WF Bank. I had my first kid in '76, and still lived in South San Francisco. I worked for Wells Fargo for ten years. Then I got into some trouble, but instead of going to jail I went to college, and graduated in '85 from the College of

San Mateo with an associate degree in machine tool technology. If my parents had not had money to hire a lawyer, there would have been a different outcome. A kid from the projects who had a public defender wouldn't be telling this story.

Later in life, retired, divorced and with both parents gone, Ron moved to Texas, near where his sister lives.

Three years ago I moved to my mom's hometown in Texas. Before she passed, my mom told me not to do it because she was afraid I'd get killed. I'm only five foot five inches tall, so I learned how to protect myself years ago. I'm licensed to carry a gun, but I have to keep quiet and not react to situations; I use my intelligence to maneuver around them. If you have thin skin, you shouldn't live in Texas. If you're not careful, you'll end up in the jailhouse.

Confederate flags and Trump flags are everywhere. Nobody has worn a mask during the COVID pandemic. They'll call you "boy" or the n-word in a heartbeat, especially the older White generation—even my neighbors.

There are only two Blacks on my street. Everyone else, out of thirty houses, is White. I love gardening and I'm outside a lot. I have a big rose garden out front, and a vegetable garden out back. Every time I go out and cut my lawn, everybody else comes out and cuts theirs. They don't want my yard to look better than theirs.

The lady who lives on my left is a Trump supporter, but we're still friendly. I cut her lawn because we share part of it. Anyone my age and older seems to be racist, but the younger ones will invite you to share a beer or a joint. It also depends on how they were raised.

My sister and my cousins live in a Black community nearby. The houses are falling down and all the roads have potholes. It's the same city council for the whole town, but they don't give a damn about the Black neighborhoods. My sister tried to get on the City Council. She ran into all kinds of problems—people telling her, "This is not your place. Don't come here trying to change stuff." Dallas or San Antonio is more liberal, like San Francisco, but the outlying areas are a whole other story.

Ron's final thoughts about his growing up:

Daly City was very multi-cultural and very down to earth. It was a great place to grow up and have a family. You were included. Nobody worried about you unless you did something to them, not because of your race. People there accepted you for who you were, not what you looked like. If you were responsible, kept your property up, didn't cause any trouble, and respected others, nobody bothered you, no one called you any names.

There is still a group that calls itself the "Fog Town Boys" today, mostly Filipino, but we were the originals.

Elaine

(White, class of '72)

* * *

After Linda (my sister) got jumped, my mom told us that everybody has a different path. Sometimes their path makes them angry, like our father, but it might not be who they really are. They're lashing out, reacting to their circumstances.

* * *

Both of Elaine's parents, and all of their five children, were San Francisco natives. Elaine, the youngest (with a twin brother), spent her early years in the Glen Park neighborhood. Her parents separated when she was two and eventually divorced.

My mother grew up very sheltered, an only child who spent a lot of time alone. Her parents had a pharmacy. She went to Lowell High School, which was one of the best schools in the city. Unfortunately, she fell for a "bad boy" and ended up marrying him—my father, who was abusive to her. After he left, he just wasn't around for us.

As a twin, Elaine was particularly close to her brother Bill.

Bill and I were always extremely protective of each other. Bill was less confident than I was, more of a follower. He was very "old school," didn't take chances, was too shy to talk to girls he liked, and didn't let

*me kiss anyone until I was sixteen! All of us are very close to this day.
I respected my brothers a lot and they looked out for me. Bill and I, as
the youngest, grew up without a father, apart from a short time with
our stepfather. I really did feel I came from a "broken home." It embarrassed me. I never talked about it to anyone because I felt "less than."*

Life in Glen Park was very diverse.

*Our best friends across the street were Black. We used to go over
there a lot and eat with them. Our next-door neighbors were Latino,
and other neighbors across the street were from India. I remember their
food always smelled good. There was a Jewish family on the block. The
first time I really noticed color was when a Nicaraguan family moved in
next door. They had accents, so I asked them where they were from. The
neighborhood felt very safe, and we played outside all the time.*

*When I was ten, my mother remarried and we moved to Daly City.
We lived across the street from Marchbank Park, and my brother and
I were bussed to Fernando Rivera Elementary School in Westlake, an
all-White neighborhood.*

*The people who lived in Westlake looked different from my peers
surrounding me on the bus. Westlake was a predominantly White area,
which I wasn't used to. I never felt White, but I didn't think much about
it until my sister's first day of school at Colma Intermediate—Linda was
a year older than me. She got jumped by a Black girl while waiting for
the bus. The girl who jumped her didn't know Linda had gone to Den-
man Junior High, a tough school. Seven other kids all ganged up on
her. She fought back all by herself. When the bus came, the driver drove
her home because he was afraid for her. He told my mom there were
race issues at Colma, but my mom rejected that idea.*

*Whenever there was a problem, my mom would sit us all down for a
family meeting. Doing the right thing was drilled into us. After Linda got
jumped, my mom told us that everybody has a different path. Sometimes
their path makes them angry, like our father, but it might not be who
they really are. They're lashing out, reacting to their circumstances.*

*In Daly City I made friends with Diane, who was half-Japanese.
Larry [a very smart White classmate] lived on the other side of the street.
The academic kids didn't come out to play. Diane and I went down to
Marchbank Park to listen to the congas. There was a Black friend who
lived nearby. All the kids were always hanging out outside, but her fam-
ily never allowed her to come out. They were strict and protective of her.*

*Even though we'd moved to Daly City, my older sister and brother
went to Balboa High School in San Francisco. Balboa had a reputation*

as a tough school, but my brother was a star baseball pitcher, and my sister was comfortable staying there because our brother was there. When I was in seventh grade, my stepfather left, so my older brother kept us on the straight and narrow. There was a lot of sex and drugs around, but nobody we knew was into that, as far as I knew.

At Colma Junior High, Elaine didn't notice race that much, but she did notice class differences.

The houses near Colma were nicer, and people who lived there had nicer clothes than us. I became aware that we were poor. Near the park where I lived, it was Filipino, African American, White, Ukrainian, even French families who spoke French. There were more single parents, so it was a very comfortable place for us to be. Lausanne Street near Colma was very White, traditional, and wealthy. There was also a lot more cement—not many gardens.

I never noticed any issues with race until Martin Luther King, Jr. was killed. Then I saw a big difference. When he was shot, Ken [a Black friend] called our house telling us, "You guys be careful, don't go out. There's going to be a big riot today." His mother told us to stay off Mission Street because people were out on the streets, throwing things and trying to overturn cars—they were outraged by the assassination. We spent a lot of time at Ken's house. My oldest brother was really good friends with his brother, Eddie.

Starting high school at Jefferson made a big impact on Elaine.

1968 was a big time in our lives—Huey Newton, Angela Davis, the Black Panthers—a lot of militant stuff, and our Black Drill Team at Jeff was very active. It was a real time of learning for all of us. I was cautious if I was around someone who wasn't familiar, but I never felt scared. I thought the people from Brisbane [a very White town] who were bussed to our school were very insulated.

The Black students at Jeff had a bathroom upstairs that no one else went into. It was on the top floor by Mr. Sinor's class [chemistry teacher]. Downstairs near the cafeteria was the stoners' bathroom. We even had crash pads up by the woodshop where people who'd taken "Reds" ["downers," sedatives taken recreationally at the time] could stay until they came back to normality.

Other schools we played in sports feared us because Jeff had a reputation for being tough. Sometimes it was obvious they looked down on us, and this made Jeff students angry. When Westmoor [mostly White rival school] played at Jeff one time, there was a riot. Later, my older brother married a girl from Westmoor, and she told us that she was on their bus when kids from our school were trying to push it over, which was untrue.

At the same time as the militant era, it was the hippie era—peace and love. If our school counselor saw that we weren't serious about education, he focused on encouraging us to get through and graduate. He just wanted to talk—"How are you?" It wasn't until my junior year that I got serious about studying, so I had to take all the bonehead classes when I started college.

I'm grateful to have gone through all of it up close in person. I think it prepared me for life much more than someone growing up in other states. Later, when I was working in the corporate world and I was often the only woman in meetings, I wasn't intimidated. I didn't avoid controversy, I could problem-solve, and deal with men who thought it was fine to come on to me in that setting. A dear friend of mine who grew up in Minnesota used to ask me how I could hold my own in all-male groups. I think that came from my mother. She was very encouraging: "You don't need a man in your life. You need to be able to take care of yourself." She wasn't judgmental and would never impose her opinion unless you asked for it.

Upon graduation from Jeff, Elaine went to San Francisco State to become a teacher, but she didn't remain in teaching for long.

In 1978, after Proposition 13 [a property tax initiative that took money away from social programs and schools], I lost my teaching job and went into general aviation, starting in administaration and working my way up. My manager was African American and raised in North Carolina. He and I used to fly around the country on business. Traveling with him in the south was an eye-opener. We'd check into a hotel in separate rooms, but checking in together and going to dinner was scary. There were endless stares. He described his hardships since marrying a White woman in the sixties and raising two daughters in the south. He had many experiences of being refused at hotels, not only in the south [Florida and North Carolina] but also in Salt Lake City, Utah. This was in the early eighties. He told me many, many shocking stories.

Where I grew up, I was a guest in many homes—Black, Asian, Filipino, Creole, Hispanic—and they were always welcome at our home as well. It was our norm. Later I started hearing about stuff, especially from people who grew up in the Bay Area, whose experiences were very different from mine. After school one day, a good friend of mine who was Black wanted to go to lunch. I told her we should get some soul food. She said she would pick it up for us and bring it back because they didn't want White people in the restaurant.

Elaine's final reflections on her time at Jefferson High:

What's really interesting is that so many of us have such a strong allegiance to Jeff. Most people don't have that connection. One of our classmates, Chinto, organizes an annual barbeque to keep the flame alive. A lot of people still go, all these years later.

I have very warm memories. Academically, our school was weak; socially, it was 100%. Preparation for life, for reality, it was 100%. It taught me about compassion, judgment, and trust—who I could and couldn't trust. It taught me about the differences in families, what goes on behind closed doors. It was an open book for me in terms of experiencing other cultures. It was a fast-forward preparation for growing up. I felt much more prepared for life than people I met from other schools. Our teachers were so involved in our lives.

In our mixed culture at Jeff, we didn't discriminate. Today, my immediate family is made up of Portuguese, Puerto Ricans, Chinese, Thais, Blacks, and Caucasions. In our family, we pride ourselves on the diversity we exemplify.

Clarke

(White, class of '72)

* * *

Being around so many different races was helpful. Even though I had some bad experiences, I never held others of the same race account- able. Some of the worst experiences I had during high school were with White people, but not in our class.

* * *

Clarke was born in San Francisco at St. Joseph's Hospital but grew up in Brisbane. Both his parents were from the South, his mother from Texas and his father from Oklahoma. They met before World War II and married in 1946. Most of their relatives still live in those states, al- though Clarke's grandparents came out to California. His grandmother lived with the family before she died.

I was the youngest boy in the neighborhood, which had a lot of kids of all different ages, so sometimes I'd be the "experiment." Anything that could happen, would happen to me. We lived on the hillside next to a canyon, with a lot of nature around us. We climbed trees; we hung out in the canyons. It was a fun time.

From kindergarten on, I mostly had the same friends. Four of us still live in the neighborhood today, which is unusual. I've traveled around the world and lived in different states, but ended up back here. My dad said it best before he passed away. He had been living in North-

144

ern California and I was driving us back into Brisbane on a beautiful spring day, with grass that glistened from the moisture that burned off from the fog. As we turned into Brisbane he looked up and said, "I could have searched the world over and never found a better place to raise my family."

Clarke reflects on Brisbane's racial makeup.

It was mostly White, and it was a pretty racist town. Most of the families came from the South and a lot of them just didn't like people of color. I think it must have been taught at home. My parents were never like that. We were taught to always treat others as you want to be treated, the golden rule: don't judge a book by its cover.

A girl across the street had black hair and dark skin. Maybe she was mixed race, maybe Native American or Islander—I never thought about it at the time. She was my buddy. She was tough. Some boys would say stupid stuff and she'd beat them up. Her family ended up moving away.

Some people would use a derogatory term for Black people, but I didn't know why. I didn't even see anyone around who was Black. My brothers and I would say to them, "What are you even talking about?" We didn't comprehend it. It was like hearing stupid dirty jokes for the first time—what are they talking about?

Brisbane was an interesting place to grow up, with rednecks, hippies, closeted gay people, and then you had people who were open-minded and accepted everyone. That's how I was raised. It was about 16% Hispanic in the 1950s. Very few Asians. Realtors wouldn't sell to Black people back then. One friend's father was New York Irish, loud and gregarious, and his mother was Native [Indigenous] Mexican, very dark-complected and quiet. A Samoan family with a son who was my age moved in. In kindergarten I went up to him and said, "Hi," and he started crying because he was scared. I felt badly for him. We became lifelong friends. I was the only White kid his family would let in the house. His dad was a Marine and he liked to sit and talk with me about things like real estate or politics. My friend and I couldn't figure out why he liked talking to me. The demographics of Brisbane have changed tremendously over the years. It has become a melting pot of ethnic groups and cultures.

For elementary and junior high, Brisbane kids attended local schools. Clarke heard a lot of stories about Jefferson High, about race riots and tensions between Blacks and Whites in 1965 and 1966. He wondered if that would happen when he got there.

At Jeff, there were some race issues when my older brother started in 1966, and less when my next brother started in 1967. They were both into sports—basketball, baseball, and football. They had teammates who were Black, and they didn't experience racial tensions. I wondered if I'd have to go into sports when I got there; I sucked at them! I was kind of a nerd, into birds and science.

Freshman year was kind of bizarre. I didn't really have any friends, other than the ones from Brisbane, but we all went our different ways when we got to Jeff. I didn't really connect with anyone. I was quiet. I was supposed to try out for baseball, but I didn't because I was afraid of getting hit by a fast pitch.

Once while I was watching baseball by myself, a group of Black guys approached and asked for the time, and then one of them ripped my watch off my wrist. When I asked him to return it, he hit me on the head with the butt of a knife and they took off running. They weren't from Jeff. That experience made me angry but didn't really affect me in terms of being around Blacks because I didn't know who these guys were. I hadn't had any problems with any Black people before. It did change my attitude in that I felt I needed to be a little tougher. I ended up going out for football and that helped.

As a sophomore the only issue I had related to race was with a Black guy who kept pushing a basketball through a chain hoop so it would drop on my shoulder and hit me. I said, "Okay, you've had your fun, don't do it again." He did it again, so I grabbed him by his head, and squeezed his chin really hard. I meant to warn him not to do it again. He jumped up ready to fight, so I put up my knuckles. He swung at me and I punched him several times. It broke up the practice. The next thing I know, a Black varsity player is flying through the air from the other end and knocks us apart. The kid, the instigator, was crying. The next day he and a group of Black guys followed me from class to class. It got irritating after the third class, so I turned and said to the instigator, "You guys want to do something?" He said, "No, we're cool." It was weird because it was really between me and that one guy, but suddenly these others are following me around. After that there weren't any problems.

I started hanging out with Ken [Black], who became my closest friend in high school. His brother and one of my brothers also hung out. We'd go to each other's houses and churches. My mom and dad really liked him. We didn't go drinking but would sometimes take blankets and sneak into the drive-in movies.

A lot of guys would tell racist jokes. My brother would say stuff like that with his friends, but he wasn't raised that way. He might say to a friend who was Mexican, "Hey, Mexican," but he was joking. It was weird to me. They'd say the same thing to Chinese guys—call them Chinaman—but they didn't think it was derogatory. I never said stuff like that; it's hurtful.

One time a Chinese friend and I were working at a summer job. He had so much anxiety from being called "Chinaman." One day he decided to take out his frustration and started punching me. I understood where he was coming from but wasn't going to be his punching bag. I made him stop and told him he couldn't take it out on me. I knew he felt very isolated and alone.

When I was playing sports, some of the White guys and some of the Black guys would talk smack to each other on team buses, always the same guys. Just silly stuff, not racial: "When you were born, your mother said, "What a treasure," and your dad said, "Let's bury him.""

Clarke wasn't impressed with some of his classes at Jeff.

My whole freshman year was weird. We had no books for English class. We'd sit around talking about life and current events—the Vietnam war, the draft, the Tet Offensive—rather than learning grammar. At the end of the quarter a paper was passed around where we put down the grade we thought we deserved. I put a C+. I thought that was fair since we didn't do anything in class. What a bozo. Everyone else put an A, even people who didn't show up every day.

In math class we had a student teacher with long hair and a beard who took over the class. He taught us to play hearts, spades, and pinochle.

I had another student teacher for history. He was like a bulldog with a crewcut. One day he asked me to help him get some papers out of his car. We go out to the parking lot and on the front seat there's all these papers, along with a half-full bottle of Jim Beam. He grabs the bottle, opens it, and says, "Want some?" I'm a freshman and I don't drink, so I say, "No." He takes a few swigs, puts the cork in, and we go back to class. One of the Daly City [White] kids is mouthing off. The student teacher says to him, "Shut up." He's drunk. The kid says, "I can say what I want." The student teacher reaches over, grabs him by his leather coat, yanks him out of his chair and slams him against the wall. He tells the kid, "I told you to shut the f--- up." Everyone in class must have been thinking, "This guy's nuts!"

One time, out of the blue, my science teacher tells me he wanted to talk with my parents on a Saturday. I said, "Well, come over, I guess." He came over and I never knew what it was about. I never really con-

*nected with him. I was quiet. I used to space out in class if I wasn't in-
terested; I'd just sort of go to my own place in my head. I did this from
second grade on.*

*My humanities teacher also used to come over to our house and
talk with my dad about construction stuff. He'd come with his wife, and
they'd have coffee with my parents. He was one of my favorite teachers.
His classes were interactive and fun, so I was more engaged. I showed
a side of myself that I never let out—more humor. He quit teaching a
year later and started building houses.*

*Based on my freshman year, I would later joke that for every dollar
of property taxes paid, normally you get a dollar worth of education,
but at Jeff you got a dime's worth.*

Being at Jeff was challenging for Clarke.

*I always felt like a square peg trying to fit into a round hole. I
felt uncomfortable because I was never in the "in-crowd," but I didn't
want to be. My own insecurities made me feel alone. A good portion
of high school was painful, going through hormonal changes; I didn't
have any direction. I tried to live up to my older brothers in sports, but
that wasn't what I wanted. You want to be independent and have your
own life. My goal was to get the hell out of everywhere: home, school,
Brisbane. At the time I didn't want to go to college.*

*I had a lot of conflicts with my father. During high school I helped
him build an apartment building and he tried to teach me how to square
a wall using Pythagoras' theorem. I didn't take trigonometry; I had no
idea. He draws it out on a piece of paper and starts explaining. I didn't
know what he was talking about: "You're trying to tell me a triangle
is a square?" I'm thinking, everyone is trying to screw with me. . .my
brothers, now my dad. I walked off the job.*

*By the time our class was graduating, though, I felt we were really
together. As freshmen I think there were still some racial issues, with all
these big changes going on—that year, 1968, was the year when Robert
Kennedy and Martin Luther King, Jr. got shot—but it was very different
when we were seniors. It felt like our class had evolved. I think it's part
of the reason a lot of us still get together.*

Clarke joined the Air Force after high school. He remembers getting a letter from a classmate.

*When the letter came, I was in tech school in Illinois. It was a deso-
late place, with extreme heat and cold. Tech school was four and a half*

months, much longer than basic training. You got to see who people really were, and some of the people from the south were very prejudiced. It wasn't just them; White guys from New York were just as racist, and they were all brutal with language. I was only seventeen. To read a letter from a former classmate was comforting, taking me home—a classic case of not knowing what you had until it's gone.

From there I went to work with the Air Force precision flying team. In 1973 I was sent to Southeast Asia—Thailand, near Laos and Cambodia—for several months. It was intense, with bombing going on 24/7. Gunships would fly over the Ho Chi Minh Trail and wreak all kinds of havoc. It was a war zone, but I really liked the culture. The rickshaws— three-wheel bicycles. The drivers were the poorest people in the country. I befriended a driver. I loved the guy. I'd give him money, but he wouldn't take it from me unless he took me on a ride.

Some Blacks I served with were racist, too. Twice I got called "honky" when I was just sitting minding my own business. I don't even think this way, but they're thinking that way toward me? It was puzzling.

After leaving the military Clarke turned down a job at Travis Air Force base, where he'd been stationed, to go back to school.

All of a sudden I got hungry for learning. I knew there was some stuff I'd missed. I enrolled at the College of San Mateo, where I played football and studied electronics. I had three job offers, so I went to work instead of transferring to Cal Poly at San Luis Obispo to continue studying. I excelled at electronics but didn't agree with management. After two and a half years I walked out and started managing a small company in Hayward which I turned around. I put my heart and soul into it.

I got married in 1983 to a Samoan woman from Brisbane. We separated the first day we were married! This is where I'm a slow learner, because we stayed married for twenty-five years. We had our good times but it was a tumultuous marriage. We finally divorced in 2008.

I'd moved out of Brisbane in 1983 and moved back in 1990. I dated an African American, then a Latina. They were both crazier than my ex-wife was. I was convinced something was wrong with me, attracting loony women. I quit dating. I figured if I was attracted to someone, something was wrong; my gauges were broken. I even told my dad's significant other, "If I ever find someone I'm really interested in, I want to bring her up here and you tell me honestly if she's okay or not."

One day in 2006, I was minding my own business, eating a steak. I saw a woman who looked familiar. She smiled at me. I thought she was very attractive. I told her, "I know I've met you somewhere before." It wasn't just a line. We started talking, and I told myself, "Don't ask her out." She asked me out! I took her to my dad's and within five minutes his girlfriend gave me the thumbs-up. We've been together since then. She's from Samoa originally. She had four kids and now grandkids. One of the grandkids kind of became my kid. She'd stay over and wake up screaming in the middle of the night, and I'd pick her up and comfort her. We're raising that little girl and her sister now.

In 1993 I ran for Brisbane City Council, later mayor. I served twenty-three years total. I put my heart into that work. People could be so passionate and anxious about an issue that they wouldn't be clear in what they said, and they'd come across as being nuts. By being respectful and listening patiently, I was able to get things done for them. You have to filter out who is telling crazy stories and who's legitimate. Everything I went through in life, including with my ex-wife, helped me to develop patience. I wouldn't be who I am now if everything else in my life hadn't happened, both the positive and the negative.

Clarke's final reflections:

I learned some things at Jeff that have been beneficial for adult life, such as observation skills and how to listen if someone really wanted to talk—not to offer advice, but just listen to what they had to say. Also, teamwork and camaraderie through sports.

Being around so many different races was helpful. Even though I had some bad experiences, I never held others of the same race accountable. Some of the worst experiences I had during high school were with White people, but not in our class.

Barbara

(Latina, class of '75; worked at Jeff in administration from 1983–2022, younger sibling of Ron G.)

* * *

I felt discrimination my whole life. I went to parochial school and felt like an outcast.

* * *

Barbara grew up in Daly City with two older siblings and has lived there for most of her life. Today she lives around the corner from Jefferson High School in the house in which she grew up. She worked at Jeff from 1983, until she retired in June, 2022. For five years after her graduation she lived in Pacifica, but ended up moving back to Daly City.

For elementary school, Barbara attended a parochial school, Our Lady of Perpetual Help (OLPH). She distinctly remembers feeling discrimination her whole life, beginning at OLPH, yet she can't pinpoint any specific incidents.

In my neighborhood I was friends with all the kids. It was very mixed; we all hung out and got along. The kids who went to public school were fine, but at parochial school almost everyone was either of Italian or Irish descent. I could have "passed" because of my light skin, but my name was Gonzales. I can't explain it, I just felt that I was different. I would invite a kid to my house, but the parents wouldn't let

151

them come. There was another girl with a Hispanic last name, and we sometimes talked about feeling different, so it wasn't just me. In the third grade I had an African American friend and I know that she felt it, too. She always seemed angry and fought with other kids.

My Latina friend and I were together the whole time at OLPH. There was one other Latina girl and the three of us hung out together. Sometimes at recess we'd hang out with her older sister. There was only one class per grade and about thirty kids per class. We stayed with the same kids the whole eight years, except for the African American girl, who was only there for one year.

While it's hard for Barbara to recall specific incidents, she felt it from the get-go at OLPH. This came up a few times as she shared her story.

I absolutely did feel that the nuns treated me differently. Maybe in the third grade the nun was also the same way toward the African American girl in our class. There were things that a lot of people wouldn't be aware of, but it seemed like we were always the last ones in line, the last to be called on in class. Things that most people wouldn't necessarily notice. It was a horrible feeling.

Barbara doesn't remember her parents telling her anything about race or ethnicity.

I know it was hard for my mom after she was widowed when I was seven years old. She had a heavy accent and was raising three children on her own. She would take me shopping with her, etc., and I would have to translate for her even when I was pretty young. We never really talked about it.

All parents were required to volunteer each year at OLPH. Because Barbara's mother worked full-time, she had limited availability. When she did help, it was usually in the cafeteria. Her heavy Spanish accent stood out among the other mothers.

Barbara's older brother Ron. who was already at Jeff was due to graduate before Barbara started. Their mother really wanted Barbara to continue at a parochial high school, but Barbara begged to go to Jeff. She wanted a more "normal" experience and was so happy when her mother gave in. Only two other students from OLPH went to Jeff; the rest went on to parochial high schools.

Starting at Jeff was a significant and positive change for Barbara.

It was new, exciting, and fun. I liked it because we changed classes every hour. I met so many people. My brother was four years older than me and I used to go to see him on the wrestling team while I was still at OLPH. His friends would come to our house on weekends. Some of his friends were a year younger than him—they kept an eye on me when I got to Jeff. He had friends of all different ethnicities. I didn't feel any segregation at Jeff. It was a melting pot and I felt really different from how I felt at Catholic school. It was the same for every teacher there, too; I didn't feel like any teacher had anything against anyone. They were so nice. It was a completely different atmosphere.

There was one English teacher [White] at Jeff whom Barbara remembers as being very strict with many of her students.

She really liked my brother Ron, so when she found out I was his sister, she was nicer to me. She called my name, looked over her glasses as she pulled them down, and asked me if I was Ron's sister. Sometimes I remember her behaving certain ways with other students, not as friendly, but I wonder if that was just the way she was. She did say to me on more than once occasion, criticizing: "You should be more like your brother." But she was never bad to me.

Barbara has vague memories of a couple of times at Jeff when a few of the Black and White students may have had an issue and met after school to fight it out, but these incidents were rare and brief. There weren't long-term conflicts during her high school years, and Barbara had an open attitude toward race, with friends of all ethnicities.

Barbara had not intended to work at Jeff.

It was an accident that I went to work there. My old business teacher walked by when I was outside my house one day. I had been home with the kids for six years and had been planning to go back to work for the county. I wanted to brush up on my typing skills, so I asked the teacher if I could stop by and pick up a typing book. The next day I got a call from the principal, who said, "Miss Patton told me you were looking for a job. We have an opening. The deadline is today. We need to have you come in and complete the paperwork." I found out the job was three and three-quarters of an hour a day. With three little kids, I wasn't interested, but my husband thought it was great. After two years I went to full-time and worked in administration. I was always thinking of finding something else, but having summers off with my kids worked out well.

As an employee, one year I worked as a paraprofessional with kids who had lower reading skills. I helped five or six kids with writing and spelling. Sometimes I observed that the [White] class teacher seemed to pick on this one [Latino] student in my group. I thought he was behaving fine, the same as others. When it came time to grading, I would give all the students the grade I thought they deserved. I knew the quality of their work since I worked so closely with them. With this particular student, the teacher wanted to give him a grade that was lower than I thought the student deserved. I told the teacher, "I want to tell you something and I hope you don't take this the wrong way. I know I'm newer here, but I saw that a couple of times you picked on him when I didn't see him doing anything wrong. As professional as you try to be, it seems like you don't like him—you have something against this kid. You're going to give him whatever grade you're going to give him, but I don't agree with you."

The way the teacher picked on him brought back the feelings I had when I was at OLPH. His behavior wasn't professional. I don't think this teacher was there when we were students at Jeff. I knew it was unjust, and I couldn't let it pass when it came time for the grades. The teacher asked me, "Do you feel strongly about this?" I told him, "Yes. I can show you his folder." In the end the teacher trusted my opinion and gave him the grade I recommended. His attitude was disappointing, but at least he changed the grade.

During Barbara's thirty years of working at Jeff, she saw the school develop different personalities as the population of students changed.

I remember gang rivalry in the mid-to-late eighties—all Latinos— the Norteños and Sureños, and similar identifiably Latino gang names. One gang wore red and the other wore blue. Since members recognized each other by the colors they wore, everyone at school had to stop wearing baseball hats in order to stay safe. It was pretty bad for a while. Some gang members came from the city once. The principal and security tried to keep the kids apart. It wasn't enough; they had to call the police.

In reflecting on Barbara's time at Jefferson, especially as a student, she shares her final thoughts.

It doesn't take that much for everybody to get along, just a little bit of kindness and respect for the person next to you, regardless of color or race. At the time I was a student, I don't think people were really thinking about race, at least not at school. It was more about: "Where's the party? Where's the band playing?" Everyone just got along. I don't think the kids today have as much school spirit as they did in previous years.

Ron G.

(Latino, class of '71, older sibling of Barbara)

* * *

My mother spoke English with a heavy accent. I remember people asking her, "What'd you say?" I recognized at an early age that people were biased against accents, and I wanted to fit in. I heard all the disdainful names people called others, like "you Mexican" or "spic."

* * *

Ron's father's family had deep roots in California and the Southwest. When he researched the family tree, he found them in what is now the United States, but was then Spanish territory, all the way back in the 1500s. Many generations lived in what later became New Mexico. Ron's paternal grandparents moved to Denver, Colorado, where his father "got tired of the snow," so he moved on to California. Ron's mother was a first-generation Spanish-speaking American who came by herself from El Salvador.

Ron was born in San Francisco and moved as a baby to Daly City, near the Top of the Hill. When Ron was seven, the family moved again, to West Cavour Street, one block from Jefferson High School.

The first school Ron attended, General Pershing Elementary School, was fully integrated in kindergarten; his elementary school was much less so.

I went to Our Lady of Perpetual Help [OLPH—the same parochial school attended by his sister, Barbara] from first through eighth grade.

The kids were primarily Irish, Italian, and some Filipino, but there were only a few of us Hispanics and I became more aware of my ethnicity. My mother spoke English with a heavy accent. I remember people asking her, "What'd you say?" I recognized at an early age that people were biased against accents, and I wanted to fit in. I heard all the disdainful names people called others, like "you Mexican" or "spic." I always understood everything my mom said, so it was hard to see how others couldn't understand her. She read the Chronicle every day. She had a lot of common sense, including good business sense. She was very kind-hearted and helped other immigrants. She believed in paying it forward. I'm very proud of her.

My earliest memory of being a Hispanic family was when we went to the Excelsior district in San Francisco where we owned a triplex. It was rented out to all Latino tenants, and my father would take me along when he collected the rent. That's where my plan to own rental properties began. I understood the value of rental income.

My family was very social, and we hosted or went to a lot of parties. Most of my parents' friends were Hispanic, but there were also a few White people and fewer Blacks.

Ron didn't get off to a good start academically, partly because his parents were always working and couldn't help him with his homework. The nuns at OLPH sent him to summer school, which he enjoyed. In fifth grade he went to summer school at Colma and excelled there. It was more mixed than OLPH.

When Ron was ten, his father died of a heart attack.

My uncle told me, "You know, Ronnie, you have to help your mother now; you have to be a man." By the time I was eleven I had realized there was no silver spoon in my mouth. I got two paper routes. I ran into one of my best friends from kindergarten who also had a paper route, and he introduced me to a lot of people from Colma [Junior High]. When we became teenagers we went to parties together near Marchbank Park. It was where I learned how to dance. There were a lot of Black people and I'd dance with Black girls. Everyone was friendly. One girl had been in my kindergarten class and our older brothers were friends. I got to know a few of the other Black families from my old neighborhood.

When Ron was in sixth and seventh grades he hung out at the War Memorial Center whenever he could, playing basketball and other games. Ron remembers it as a mixture of various people just playing.

It was supervised and a fun place to go; some of my best memories as a kid are from there. Sometimes there were dances on a Friday night. I met girls but didn't have crushes on anyone until eighth grade—more of a friendship. You feel something inside and are attracted to someone but nothing too intimate . . . just a kiss on the lips and holding hands.

Ron's older brother, Bob, was very popular.

He had so many friends. They'd come over to our house all the time. Before my father died, we took a trip to Tijuana, and my brother's friend [White] went with us. We slept in the back of our station wagon. I woke up and saw all these Mexican people around. It was a whole new world to me.

My brother had friends of all different races. I met all these people through him, so when I got to Jefferson, I hung out with people a few years older than me. I went with them to Speedway Meadows at Golden Gate Park and saw the Grateful Dead, Jefferson Airplane, etc. My brother's friends had suped-up muscle cars, (Corvettes, '57 Chevys, etc.) so we'd cruise through the Haight Ashbury neighborhood. We'd go to concerts at Fillmore West and Winterland. We also went to car races at the Fremont drag strip.

My best friend also got to go to the concerts and ride around with us. In high school his mother remarried so he wound up going to West-moor [majority White rival high school]. He seemed to be okay there. I met a few people he hung out with.

When Ron was still in eighth grade he was going to dances at Jefferson, dancing with older girls who were freshmen.

A wonderful world unfolded. We didn't have anything like that at Catholic school, and I was glad I'd learned to dance at the garage parties. It was a great experience getting to know all these people—I realized Jefferson was a real melting pot. I also had a lot of friends that were girls. It was nice to just hang out and get to know each other. In Daly City people seemed to get along pretty well. I never experienced people trying to denigrate me based on my ethnicity. From my observations, Blacks tended to hang out more with Blacks, whereas other races seemed to mix more with each other. There were plenty of times when we'd integrate. There weren't racial slurs or anything.

Ron's adolescence was full of "side hustles," part-time jobs, which led to new experiences and more part-time jobs.

When I was thirteen, a friend from Jeff who was three years older than me, helped me get a job at Fisherman's Wharf at Fabulous Confections. My friend worked inside making popcorn, caramel corn, peanut brittle, and taffy. I worked outside in a kiosk, making snow cones and cotton candy. I learned a lot. I met kids who lived in the nearby projects. I met Gypsies, topless waitresses, several of the famous Aliotos [a prominent San Francisco family who owned a landmark restaurant at Fisherman's Wharf and became politicians]. I met so many Italian Americans, networked and got other jobs. I loved being there and getting paid for it.

To get to and from the Wharf, until I got my first car at sixteen, I would walk from W. Cavour Street, to the "Top of the Hill," catch the 14 Mission bus to Seventh and Mission, walk down Seventh past the Greyhound depot and famous tattoo parlor owned by Lyle Tuttle, make my way to Market St., go down to Fifth and Market, and catch the Powell Street cable car in front of Woolworth's. The ride took me through Nob Hill, Chinatown, North Beach to Fisherman's Wharf. As much work as it was to get to the Wharf, I didn't mind it. In fact, I embraced it. I took in my surroundings and learned that there was a lot more to life than living in Daly City. On the way, I saw microcosms of various people and lifestyles. Anywhere from hardworking, small business owners and employees, to winos on Seventh Street, to Jehovah Witnesses on Market Street, beautiful women shopping on Powell Street, fancy hotels along the way, the different world of Chinatown, the Italian flair of North Beach, and Mecca of Tourism at Fisherman's Wharf. I learned far more about life riding that bus and cable car than I ever could have learned from books or in a classroom. Those experiences taught me to always be aware of what is going on around me and, just like a cable car, be prepared to pivot and do a 180-degree turn if the situation requires it, or just react; don't panic, ever, and you will survive.

Ron recalls occasional racial tensions at Jefferson High.

I think it was mostly about testosterone—guys smoking in the bathroom, someone says something, etc. After these flare-ups, which didn't last long, people would get over it and were friends again. The conflicts were usually between White and Black students. Being Hispanic, I wasn't the target. I did see a few White people get attacked. That was my first exposure to racial tension.

Ron had met a girl at their Catholic teen club some years earlier who became his high school girlfriend. Her father was from South America and only spoke Spanish, so she was 100% bilingual, and talking to her father challenged Ron to improve his fluency. To this day, although Ron is bilingual, he sometimes gets the tenses mixed up in Spanish.

My wife is from El Salvador and says my Spanish is fine. We have a time-share in Puerto Vallarta [Mexico] and when we go there, I'm fluent after a week and begin thinking in Spanish. I was definitely exposed to people being biased against those with a heavy accent, which annoyed me a lot. When I worked at Fisherman's Wharf I probably heard every kind of accent from around the world and I could understand everyone.

When Ron got to Jeff, he ran into several people he knew from the War Memorial Recreation Center.

I knew Ken and Pinky [Black brothers] from the Rec Center and I would talk to them all the time. I lived near Jeff and would take my dog, an Irish Setter, there to walk him. Pinky would be there by himself doing these explosive sprints that made him look like a gazelle; he was amazing to watch. He was relentless with his practice so he was often there on his own and we got to know each other. I remember other Black kids who were super-smart. I admired them. We'd acknowledge each other, but I didn't feel I had access to becoming part of their world. We'd have brief conversations.

Part of the reason Ron didn't feel he could become part of their world related to his education.

In first grade at OLPH, I was a straight A student, but I was also a daydreamer. My parents worked hard but didn't get involved in my education. The pace at Catholic school was much faster than at public schools. If I'd had help, I'm sure I would have done better, but for most of elementary school I was not a good student. I used to read a lot—comic books and storybooks. After we moved to W. Cavour Street, I'd stop in at the library to get books on my way to or from school. When I got to Jeff, I started getting A's again, so I realized I was smarter than I thought.

In freshman year I went out for wrestling, and really enjoyed it. One day, an acquaintance, who was a bit of a troublemaker, came in after practice and challenged me to climb the ropes in the gym, which we weren't supposed to do. The coach came in and kicked me off the team. He wouldn't let me play any sports at all anymore. I started hanging out with people going down the wrong path, so to speak. I didn't have sports anymore; my grades started going down. Then in my junior year I said, "I don't care what Coach said," and I signed up for the wrestling team again. He didn't even remember me, so I got back on the team. I shaved my head to a crewcut. I buckled down with my studies and started getting As and Bs again. The teachers couldn't believe how much I'd changed. I felt like, "This is who I am." I knew I wanted to go to college. If I didn't make this change, I wouldn't be able to move forward in a positive direction. I still had some catching up to do.

English grammar was always hard for me. I took Business English and Grammar from Miss Schmidt at the same time, and she took an interest in me. She helped me a lot. A lot of kids in those classes just wanted to pass time and get through class, but if you wanted to learn, she'd be there for you.

In my junior year I became the class president. Two things I'm very proud of were establishing a "crash pad" and a suicide hotline. There were a lot of drugs on campus during our time. As class president, I approached the principal and vice-principal and discussed the epidemic of barbiturates ["Reds"] we were experiencing. People were literally passing out all over campus, usually at lunchtime. It was no secret, and something had to be done. My idea was to take an empty modular building by the tennis courts and let students come in to "crash" and sleep it off, without the fear of being turned in to the police or the faculty. Believe it or not, they liked my idea, implemented it, and it was a success. It was supervised by staff or faculty who took the opportunity to talk to these students about the dangers of what they were doing, make it an educational process with some warning behind it. It lasted that one year, as Reds were no longer a big thing in '71.

The same year, unfortunately, there were a lot of drug-related suicides. I was truly concerned about people dying from drug overdoses and suicides. I got involved with some people and established a suicide hotline at a call center in Westlake. I obtained funding from Daly City for the hotline.

The real mentor I had at Jeff was Mr. Toibin, the photography teacher. I went to summer school at Jeff before I started there. I took photography and a math class. He saw potential in me, and we became friends. I took photography all through high school. After graduation, we went on a group trip to Europe. Mrs. Toibin [Abby] became a surrogate mom for me on that tour. There were about forty kids, six of us from Jeff, most from Southern California. We flew on a charter plane and went to eight countries in seven weeks. My mother gave me that trip as a graduation present.

Ron won a scholarship to study at San Francisco State University, the preferred training college for teachers. It was a melting pot similar to Jeff, but the issues of race seemed more obvious.

Angela Davis was there, Dr. Hayakawa was president, Reagan was governor. The Vietnam war was ongoing. All the stuff that happened in the summer of 2020 reminds me of my time at SF State. There was a lot going on with protests back then, but they weren't violent at all compared to now. My perspective was more liberal, but my moral values are more conservative—going to Catholic school helped to ground me and made me who I am.

While at SF State, I served as a teacher's aide to Mr. Toibin at Jeff and got credits. I was thinking about becoming a teacher. I wanted to major in photography, but they didn't have it as a major, so I got into fine arts so I could take photography classes. I minored in broadcasting. Mr. Toibin and I became even closer once I was his aide. I'd have long conversations with him at his house. Abby, his wife, influenced me by telling me she didn't want to see me grow old and be alone. I was thirty-one by then. I had an aversion to making a commitment. She wanted me to get married. It took me another year.

At age twenty Ron bought his first house while attending SF State. He rented rooms out to help pay the mortgage, taxes, and insurance. That was the beginning of his successful real estate investing career. He also worked as a painting contractor and hired other Latinos.

For about twelve years I had a lot of workers from Guatemala, Mexico, etc. I'd encourage them to speak in English. They were embarrassed, but I tried to encourage them because the Latino population was growing so much and it's important to learn English. I'd tell them, "Don't worry about your accent."

Ron has thought a lot about what Jefferson meant to him, as well as who we were collectively as students.

Jefferson had a profound and lasting effect on me. What made it so special was the diversity of the people. Despite potential conflicts based on race, our diversity united us. Teachers, administrators, students alike, we all knew we were considered the "underdog school" because we were not in an affluent, highly educated community and had more minorities than other schools in our district.

We wore the underdog label as a badge of honor. I believe we transcended Black and White. Our colors were blue and gold. Collectively we were the Jefferson Indians and were proud of it. We never thought of our school mascot as being racist or denigrating to Native Americans. Instead, we saw ourselves as warriors, honoring the proud tradition of Native American Indians. Just like them, we were a tribe that did not back down from our rivals. When it was time for a big game we had rallies in the gym inspiring us to support our athletes. It's called school spirit!

Spirit and tradition were at the heart of Jefferson. One tradition I remember being told as a freshman was, "You can never walk on the gold-colored J surrounded by blue mosaic tiles within a circle. You must walk around it." As far as I know, nobody dared to walk on it.

It was that tapestry of experiences at Jeff that prepared me for the next phase of my life and beyond. I graduated with confidence knowing my future looked bright. I knew that as long as I applied myself, remained disciplined, and worked hard, I could achieve whatever goals I set for myself. Jefferson will always be a big part of my life. Eleven years ago I sponsored our forty-year class reunion.

But it was also the early death of my father that taught me I had to survive at all costs, and I could never feel sorry for myself. Just get up in the morning, go to work, do what you have to do and try to get ahead in life, or you will be left behind. I attribute my "success in life" to God, family, and hard/smart work, in that order. Without those three elements I would not have come as far as I have.

Kathy

(White, class of '72)

* * *

I asked a couple of my Black friends, how does a White person talk to another White person about White privilege? Most of the responses were, don't bother, they won't get it. One guy said, just tell them it's the color. You're automatically privileged because of your color. You never have to give your kids "the talk."

* * *

Kathy is a proud San Francisco native, born at the original Mary's Help Hospital (which later moved to Daly City). She was the oldest of four children born to a single mother, with ten years between her and her youngest sister.

My siblings all have different fathers, but we always called each other just brothers/sisters. I don't know a thing about my father. My mom passed a few months ago and she refused to give up that information to the very end. The person she said was my father wasn't, because DNA testing points to somebody else. My siblings all knew who their fathers were, which was strange for me.

My mom raised us four on her own. She kept the men she dated pretty much behind the scenes; there were a few over the years, but she didn't bring them home so it was pretty much her and us. We were on welfare when I was growing up—the poor Irish kids who couldn't

afford Catholic school. Then Mom was a nurse's aide for twenty years;
finally, she worked as a bartender at Serra Bowl for fifteen years.

In today's world, Kathy's family might easily have ended up
homeless.

Every time our rent went up, we'd move, and eventually we had to
leave San Francisco because we couldn't afford it. We moved so much
that it became normal; you just pack up and move on to another house.
I went to five different elementary schools in San Francisco, and I went
to one of them twice—first in kindergarten, then in second or third
grade. As a kid in Daly City, I lived in four different houses. When I
moved back there as an adult, I stayed in one house for almost thirty
years.

Growing up, I didn't feel like I was poorer than anyone else be-
cause it felt like we were all in the same boat. We didn't know rich or
poor back then. We all played outside. Even at Jefferson High, it felt
the same.

Kathy reflects on her schools prior to Jefferson.

We were a melting pot back then. We had all different races and we
all got along. When I was in fourth and fifth grades we lived in the West-
ern Addition of San Francisco. I was the only White girl in a couple of
classes. We got along well for the most part. There were a couple of
Black girls who were jealous of me talking to their Black friends. At
most of the schools I went to, everyone was poor, so there was nothing
about status with clothes or shoes or anything.

In another elementary school, I was the only White girl. I noticed
we were different colors, but things weren't so divided back then.

For a while I kept in contact with some of my elementary school
friends from San Francisco, but after a couple of years we grew apart.
I had one friend I knew since I was seven, until she passed away a few
years ago.

Kathy's family ended up moving to Daly City in time for her to go
to junior high school.

After we moved to Daly City, we'd hang out in Marchbank Park.
One time my brother was going to start a fight with another kid who
was being watched by a girl, Linda. My brother said to Linda, "I'll
get my big sister to beat you up." Linda said, "Bring her on." When

I went down there I saw that Linda was a big girl and I'm a scrawny little thing, so I turned to my brother and said, "I'm gonna kick your butt"—for dragging me into that situation—and that's how Linda and I became friends.

I had a good two years at Colma Junior High. The dances were fun. We used to play soccer on the field. My homeroom teacher was Mr. Ramirez, I think. Elaine (see page 139) and I flunked home economics because we couldn't sew. I don't remember racial issues there. People sometimes picked on others for this or that, because they didn't like the way they look or something, but it wasn't about race.

However, much of what was going on in the world was very much about race, and Kathy describes her own mother as racist and sexist.

The night after Martin Luther King, Jr. was killed, my friend Toni [Black], her cousin Cindy, and I cut school, or maybe they sent everyone home early. We went down to the Haight in San Francisco. Black people were jumping off the buses and punching any White people they saw. They were breaking windows and throwing things. I stuck close to my "sisters" Toni and Cindy, and they helped me get home safely. I'll never forget that day.

My mother was very racist and sexist. She was mostly raised in a convent until she was sixteen, but her mom performed as an entertainer for servicemen—singing and dancing—and would take her out for a couple of weeks at a time to travel. I don't know where her attitudes came from. My sister and I would always give her a hard time: why did she serve our brothers their food before serving us? Why didn't the boys have to help with housework? We'd have to correct her often, especially when we had our own children. She'd use the n-word when something didn't go right. We'd tell her, "You shouldn't say that, Mom." Her perceptions changed after she got old. My sister's husband is Black, and my mom embraced him. She'd never say anything bad about one of our friends unless they did something wrong. But it was a pick-and-choose thing. If she didn't like someone, she'd use the n-word.

In high school, at Jefferson, Kathy continued to have friends and relationships with people of all races.

My friends were absolutely of all races, and that's continued until today. I also dated all different colors. It's the inside of the person that matters.

When we were freshmen and sophomores at Jeff, I remember hearing a few stories about not being able to go to certain bathrooms, but
not when we were juniors and seniors. I'd just go to whatever one was
available. Back then we used to go to "the Road" to celebrate. We were
all different colors down there. In my experience there weren't any racist teachers. We had great teachers—it was love, peace, happiness. I
think we all got along pretty well. We grew up at a great time.

At Jeff I benefited from ESEA [the Elementary and Secondary Education Act]. A substitute PE teacher invited me to go in the program,
which offered life experiences instead of academic study. I was the first
girl who got to join as a freshman and I was part of it for a few years.
Later it was called the Wilderness Program. We went up to Humboldt
County and helped build a dome; I learned about identifying types of
rocks and soil. We slept in a chicken coop we built on a farm. Someone
drove us to Marin County and we hitchhiked the rest of the way. We also
did a two-week trip to Hidden Villa [a ranch south of San Francisco
that had educational programs], staying in cabins there. We did a lot
of hikes; we took some psychedelics—the teachers found out after the
fact!—we just laughed a lot.

The ESEA program helped me gain more self-awareness. It helped
to ground people and made us city kids appreciate nature much more.

I took a lot of pre-med/science classes at Jeff and got good grades. I
liked the science teachers—Mr. Sinor, Mr. Tierney. I had always wanted to be a nurse. After high school, I started out at the College of San
Mateo, but some of the teachers rubbed me the wrong way, so I became
an emergency medical technician and then a paramedic instead.

The only thing I regret about high school is not going to the proms.
Now I make it a point to go to all the reunions.

Kathy shares her thoughts about why she understands White privilege, while many who also benefit from White privilege don't.

Growing up in ghettoish areas, I was so aware of it even back then.
We were poor, but Black people were poor and profiled. Nowadays they
are treated even worse. I have a Black brother-in-law, so I notice how
the cops pick on them. My sister and I would make a joke, saying if we
got pulled over we'd blame the Black guy. Her husband laughed with us
about it, but it isn't funny.

I got into a debate with some of my White friends—Trumpsters—
I don't really want to bring politics into it, but they don't get the message about White privilege at all. Oh man, did I get my butt brow-
beaten on that! They'd say, "I worked so hard for what I have." But

they don't get that they're privileged because of their color. They just don't get it.

Some of these people went to Jeff with me, and some of them are very racist. I asked a couple of my Black friends, how does a White person talk to another White person about White privilege? Most of the responses were, don't bother, they won't get it. One guy said, just tell them it's the color. You're automatically privileged because of your color. You never have to give your kids "the talk." [What their kids should or should not do if they have an interaction with the police or other authority figures.]

My daughter married a Michigander and moved there. It's a beautiful area, but it's very White and racist—a great place to visit, but I wouldn't want to live there. It's weird how a lot of affluent people are more Republican and look down upon people who don't have what they have. I see that a lot in the Midwest and back East. We're lucky to live in California.

Today Kathy lives north of San Francisco in Petaluma, which is predominantly White.

I live on a little ranchette and all around us are all kinds of farm animals—cows, goats, chickens. I love living out in nature, out of the Daly City fog. Yesterday I was at Linda's house in San Bruno. I took the slow way going down through my old neighborhood, driving through the streets, the Top of the Hill, Daly City, and going down Hillside. It looks so poor and run-down. There are all these apartment buildings on the hill and next to the War Memorial Center, where we used to go to dances. The War Memorial is still there, but I don't know what they do with it now.

Kathy's final reflections:

You've got to move away sometimes to really appreciate what you have. I moved to Syracuse, New York, for a year in 1991. I hated it. The people were friendly to me, but they would never invite an outsider into their home, and they treated people of color like dirt. It was horrible. That really opened my eyes to discrimination in other parts of the country, which I hadn't known about when I was growing up.

George

(Filipino, class of '74)

* * *

It's sad that kids stoop to name-calling, and they know nothing about you. You could have been the one that helped their mom carry groceries or did a favor for one of their friends.

* * *

George and three of his four siblings were born in the Philippines. Their father was in the U.S. Navy.

My whole family came to the U.S. when I was two-and-a-half years old. When we first moved to Daly City, we lived with another Filipino family for about a year. Mom and Dad found a house two blocks away. Most of the relatives who are in the U.S. today were able to come because Mom and Dad petitioned for them to come.

Dad was a carpenter for the Veterans Administration and Mom was a seamstress. I remember Dad dropping Mom off at work in Chinatown every morning. One time I went with her and sat on a pile of material on the floor while she worked.

George regrets that he lost the ability to speak Tagalog, his native language, due to growing up in the U.S.

Our parents wanted us to learn English so badly that they wouldn't speak Tagalog in front of us kids, and I lost the skill of speaking it. It's too bad because I think it's beneficial to be bilingual, but you don't think about it at that age. I think all languages are beautiful. My oldest sister can still speak Tagalog, and my next oldest sister understands it. My younger sister also speaks it because she was exposed to more family gatherings where everyone was speaking it.

George's integration at school began early.

I was bussed from Hunters Point [in SF] to Fairmount Elementary School. I guess because of the location, there weren't a lot of Filipinos there, but there were quite a few Mexicans, Blacks, and Whites. I really never noticed any color as a majority. At that age all you want to do is play.

In Daly City I started third grade at Woodrow Wilson, then was bussed to Fernando Rivera [FR] in the Westlake District for fourth through sixth grades. At FR it was mostly White, but everybody got along. There weren't any racial tensions, so I didn't notice anyone being different from each other. I was fortunate to have friends that didn't see me any other way. No one made you feel out of place.

From what I remember, there weren't any problems until probably in middle school, where there were disagreements, kids who were bullies, and feeling like you had to protect someone from being bullied—stepping up and speaking out. I couldn't really say who was doing the bullying in terms of White, Black, or Brown; it was just kids being kids.

The first time George noticed racial differences in a significant way was in junior high school.

When I got to Colma in 1968, there was a divide between the Black students and everyone else. The biggest impression was Black students hanging out together and pushing others away. It was the first time I noticed racial differences. At the time, there was the Black Panther movement, and I think that had a lot to do with what was going on at school. It put everyone who wasn't Black on defense, even other minorities like us, so many people weren't as comfortable around Black people. I still had a handful of Black friends from my neighborhood, and they reassured us that the protests were nothing to do with us personally.

There would be an occasional fight that teachers would break up. It was mostly a lot of shouting, and more pushing and shoving than actual fist-fighting.

My parents never really said anything about race. I'm sure they watched the news, but I can't remember a time where my mom or dad said, "Watch out for Mexicans, or for Blacks or Chinese." I think if we had come home with a problem involving another race or nationality, they probably would have told us to stay away from them, but nothing like that happened to me.

George shares about his friendships and attractions to others.

By the time I got to Jeff, the racial divide that I saw at Colma had kind of leveled off. It may have been that Vietnam took people's minds off the racial stuff. Some people still had a chip on their shoulder, but it wasn't like "them against the world." Going to Jeff was like starting over. A lot of Latinos hung out together, a lot of Blacks, too. The Filipinos who hung out together were—the term was FOB, "fresh off the boat"—from the Philippines. I think they hung out together because they spoke the same language. I didn't speak it, and they knew it, but it was all right.

As a freshman I hung out with my older brother Vic's friends, which helped pave my way. They all called me "Little Vic" when I got there, so that was how I got to know a lot of people that I didn't go to Colma with. Everybody's sisters and brothers had at one point gone there and got along—you knew people and met them because of siblings.

My first friend of my own at Jeff was White. When I first saw him, I was curious about a birthmark on his neck. He was not embarrassed, and just told me about the birthmark, and we've been good friends ever since. I also became close friends quickly with a guy from Brisbane, who was also White.

The girls I liked were Filipino, Chinese, African American, Mexican. From an early age, if I was attracted to someone, if they turned out to be not how I perceived them—not a nice person—I'd lose interest, and no longer wanted to be with them. I never stuck with a person because of looks, no matter how beautiful. If they showed their ugly side, that was it.

George was friendly, but he had no ambitions to stand out.

I was in the glee club. We had an annual spring festival concert. I remember doing a solo of a Frank Sinatra song called "My Way," and everyone loved it. I wrestled for four years and played basketball. Those were the only two sports I played.

When we had a rally, I'd sit with my friends or my class, not with just one group [by race]. There were certain cliques who always stuck together. You'd see them in a group at every event.

At one time, Mr. Toibin [photography teacher] wanted me to head a dance committee, but I kept brushing it off, saying I didn't want that responsibility. Finally I said I'd do it this one time. He put me in charge of the fundraising for our class. We picked the night for the dance. It was a dud! Not many people showed up; it was a waste of time, so it affected my confidence.

Like many young people, George was called various names at different times while growing up.

Name-calling was something I experienced all the time at an early age, usually just outside of school, when I was twelve, probably in fifth or sixth grade. I remember some kids used to call me "Ching Chong Chinaman" or "Chink." I guess it was because Filipinos weren't a well-known nationality, so we were all lumped in with other Asians. At Jeff, people got more creative with their name-calling because they knew you were Filipino or Japanese. They shied away from Chinese insults because they knew it didn't fit. In high school I was called FOB because now I was thrown in with the guys from the Philippines. Blacks who didn't know me called me that. It's sad that kids stoop to name-calling when they know nothing about you. You could have been the one that helped their mom carry groceries or did a favor for one of their friends.

I have no memory of my siblings sharing anything about racial problems at home but, thinking back, it must have happened to them as well, and they never said anything about it. I think because of who we grew up with, we were more conscientious about not offending other nationalities.

After graduation, I went to the College of San Mateo [CSM] for a semester. A lot of my friends who came from similar backgrounds went there. College life was different from high school—everyone's doing their own thing. People are busier. I didn't really see a lot of racism.

I worked in San Francisco during college, juggling the two. It was too much, so that's why I only was at CSM for one semester. I worked downtown for an insurance company. My supervisors were Chinese. I had two Black coworkers. One guy was kind of a knucklehead, the other was a musician. We were friends as coworkers. We got along fine.

Just listening to them talk, you could tell they'd been through some stuff with other people, not just Blacks. I understood their situation because I'd seen it growing up: profiling, people in authority talking down to them, acting superior. I've heard snide remarks when I was with other people of color, not so much if I was with White people. Occasionally you come across it, you see it on the news, you hear about it from other friends, and you know exactly what they're talking about. I would always say that not everybody is the same, so you can't hold that against everybody, which was hard for them to hear and believe. As long as I was cool with them, they were cool with me.

George's final thoughts:

Honestly, I believe Jefferson was a very, very special school. I had friends at other schools in the district—Westmoor was predominantly White, Serramonte predominantly Black. My friends would tell me that everyone was always on guard. At Jeff you never felt like you had to be on guard. Everyone from every race got along and knew each other.

Teacher: Nancy (Davey) Jermaine

(White; taught physical education 1963–1975)

* * *

In my opinion, it's not the color but the socioeconomic background.

* * *

Nancy was born in Kansas in 1936 and grew up on a dairy farm in the tiny town of Bonner Springs until she was nine. She went to a two-room schoolhouse which had grades one through eight.

While my schools were all White, the town was essentially segregated, with one part all-Black and the other all-White. Each side of town was self-contained. I never saw Black people at the grocery store; I assumed they had their own.

The movie theater was a shared space, but Black people always had to sit upstairs. They entered from a different door around the back. The attitude [of White people] was that you didn't want to touch them. They also had to sit in the back of the bus.

My dad used to hire farm workers to work on our dairy farm off and on. One time he hired a Black man. I talked with the man and he was very nice and polite. All the other hands ate lunch inside with us, but the Black man ate on the back porch. I asked my mother why. She said, "Oh, they have their own way of eating."

There was one mixed-race family in our town. A White woman married a Black man and they had children. They had to ask the school board for permission to send the kids to a White school. None of those children were in my class, but I know they were looked down upon. At that time, not many Black people went to high school. There were no Black high schools near us, so again, any Black children who wanted to continue their education had to attend a White school. They didn't join any clubs or anything. They must have figured they wouldn't be welcome.

From an early age I realized that racism wasn't right and questioned it.

174

I asked my mother about it, but she just accepted it. I remember the downtown area of our town where there was a paved sidewalk that dropped off at the edge to where it was all dirt. If a Black person was walking past us, they would have to go into the street, onto the dirt part, while passing. I always thought that was strange. I was raised to respect my elders, so why did an older Black person have to step into the dirt to get out of my way?

When Nancy's family left Kansas, they went to Los Angeles for two years, then to California's Central Valley when she was twelve.

Los Angeles wasn't much different from Kansas; almost everybody in my school was White. In the Central Valley it was a little more mixed. There were four Mexican kids in my class, four Japanese, and one Filipino. That was where I first heard about Japanese Americans being sent to concentration camps during World War II. This seemed wrong to me too. I'd never known any Japanese people, but we were taught to hate them during the war. As I got to know them, I realized they were just like everybody else.

I attended Manteca High School. There was one Black girl at my school. She was very friendly. The Black families were always very well-groomed and they dressed better than White people.

As farmers, Nancy's parents didn't have a lot of money, so they couldn't help her with college. During her senior year of high school Nancy took a survey to find out what career might be good for her.

I always liked education and sports of all kinds. I was also interested in becoming a children's book illustrator, but someone told me it was really hard to get into the art field, especially illustration. I knew there would always be teaching opportunities and wanted a secure job, so I pursued teaching. I thought I would teach history and physical education.

In 1954, Nancy enrolled at San Francisco State. While there, she worked at Joseph Magnin's, a higher-end department store in downtown San Francisco. SF State was originally a small teachers' college located at the corner of Market and Octavia Street near downtown. By 1954 the campus had moved to 19th Avenue and Holloway Street.

It took an hour on three different buses to get to school and an hour to get downtown. I told myself that it would be worth it in the long run.
During college I lived in eight different places. First, I lived with my sister, then out on 33rd Avenue near the ocean, then with a widow

who had a room in her house. After that there were girls in the same program as me who had an apartment—I was the sixth girl to live with them. In the summer they'd go home, so I found a rooming house near downtown on Nob Hill. It cost $7 a week and had a bathroom down the hall. There were about ten girls living there. We had a good time. There was always something to do on weekends. We went dancing on Friday nights. At the department store I was a cashier on different floors. The salespeople had to come down every morning and get their change bag from me. I wore my tennis shoes and could beat the trolley car as I ran down Powell Street at 7 a.m. to go to work. At that time of day, there were few people around. I'd bring my good shoes for work.

Nancy was supposed to do student teaching to get hands-on classroom experience. However, she ended up skipping it because there was a teacher shortage.

That's how I ended up teaching at Downey Junior High School in Richmond, CA, where no one wanted to teach. I lasted one year. It was so upsetting and frustrating. I would have quit teaching if I'd stayed there.

Downey was originally an all-White upper-middle-class middle school, and they were integrating. The Black and White students didn't get along at all. There was such a difference because the Black kids came from a very poor part of town. The kids just didn't have much in common, being from such different backgrounds. In my opinion, it's not the color but the socioeconomic background that makes it harder for people to understand each other.

It wasn't until my first year at Downey Junior High that I encountered such poor Blacks—all the Black people in Kansas were probably poor, but we were so segregated that I didn't have much experience with them. At Downey, their attitude was very negative. It seemed that many weren't motivated to improve themselves because their lives were so hard. It was sad to see students with such negative attitudes at such a young age. They kind of took over the school.

We had to walk through the cafeteria to get to the gym. All year long I noticed a Black girl staring at me when we walked through. I didn't have her as a student so couldn't figure out why she stared at me. One day she started calling me terrible names. I told her to knock it off or I would report her. She continued, so I reported her to the principal. In a couple of days, I heard back that they'd had that problem with her before—she hated anyone who had blonde hair and blue eyes.

By the time Nancy graduated in 1958 she was so tired of school that she decided to do something else before going into teaching. She taught dancing for a while. She went to Hawaii on vacation. In 1960 she went to Reno and dealt craps and blackjack for a year.

When I was in Reno I met the man of my dreams, so I moved back to the Bay Area to be near him. He went to San Jose State and drove up every weekend to see me. We got married but within three years he had an affair with his secretary, so we divorced. It broke my heart, so I decided to go to Japan to teach for a year. Everyone was so respectful there. I had nothing but positive experiences.

After Nancy's adventures abroad, she decided it was time to settle down and start teaching. She applied to Jefferson High School, not knowing anything about it.

In 1963 I started teaching at Jeff. I got the job because someone I'd gone to college with worked there and vouched for me. She said I'd be able to get along with others, which the principal really valued. These were the hippie days, and it was very liberal. It was a good opportunity. You get tired of teaching the same things after a while, so I liked that I could come up with ideas for other things to teach, like yoga, and posture and grooming. I joined the teachers' union. I remember going to a meeting where a teacher brought a big poster board—a collage of different protests.

While Nancy enjoyed teaching at Jeff, she had some concerns about it when she started.

It was the 1960s and we were very close to liberal San Francisco. There wasn't a lot of teaching going on. There was a rift between the older teachers and the more radical younger ones coming in. The newer ones said, "Oh, we just talk all the time." Many of the newer teachers wanted to be their students' buddies, not to have a teaching or counseling role.

I always observed that students of different races got along fine. Being in PE, we were somewhat isolated down in the gym, which may be why I didn't observe everything. Sports brought people together. I never heard anything from other PE teachers that was racist.

Jeff never had a very good football team. There were these husky Samoan kids and the coaches wanted them to go out for football, but

*they were very peaceful so they weren't interested. Several Samoan stu-
dents asked me if I would sponsor a pep rally. It was wonderful. They
sang in beautiful harmony. They did fire dancing as they passed under
a limbo bar. It was both fun and scary—they were dancing with real
fire, which they hadn't used in rehearsal, so I didn't know! But there
was one problem. They put rags which they lit on the end of their ba-
tons. When the rags burned all the way down, the ashes dropped on
the basketball floor, which upset the coaches. I had to go get the fire
extinguisher.*

*In my gymnastics classes the students always wanted to do better
than other schools because they knew other schools thought they were
better than those at Jeff. They particularly wanted to beat Westmoor,
the "rich kid" school.*

Nancy was very aware of the diversity at Jeff.

*I was aware that Jeff was different but didn't give it a lot of thought
because everyone got along. I noticed that in the cheering squad there
was a girl from every nationality—Monita [mixed race Japanese and
Latina], Dorothy [Black], a Chicana girl, and a White girl. I thought
how wonderful it was and was impressed how they got along so well.
People seemed to really mix as friends, but at a prom I attended I only
saw one mixed-race couple. I think the kids got along so well because
they were integrated from such a young age.*

There were other things that stood out for Nancy while at Jeff.

*In my early days there we took a survey where we were asked how
many Asians, Blacks, etc. were in our classes. On my softball team there
were four Black girls who all said they were Indian. I thought it was a
shame they didn't want to admit they were Black. The survey didn't offer the possibility of identifying as more than one race. This was before
the days of Black Power, which might have influenced their answers.*

*There was a fashion show once, so we went to a boutique in West-
lake Shopping Center to get the clothes for it. The salesclerk commented on how beautiful the Black girls' skin was. I was so used to seeing
them at school I hadn't really thought about it before.*

*Another thing I remember was when a lovely Chicana former stu-
dent got a scholarship to Stanford. She came back to visit and I congratulated her. She told me that a teacher from Jeff told her the only
reason she got it was because she was Mexican. I felt badly as I knew
she had worked very hard.*

Outside of work Nancy experienced something that really bothered her.

In 1975, when I was planning to move to San Carlos with my husband, a realtor showed us all around. I realized I hadn't seen any Black people and commented on this. The realtor responded, "Oh, we steer them to Redwood City." Even five years later, there was a pizza parlor that had an old-time framed photo that said something like "Welcome to San Carlos, no Blacks allowed." It was offensive and it was taken down not long afterwards.

On one of her vacations Nancy went back to Kansas on a visit.

I remember driving around and realizing that this is 1980 and I still don't see any Black people. Later, I questioned my sister about it. She commented that there were now some Italians around, which I thought was strange—Italians are White Europeans, after all! Also, on that trip I was disappointed to realize my nephews seemed to be just as racist as their parents. It was shocking. If someone had brown eyes, people said, "Do you think they're part Black?"

Nancy's final thoughts:

I would have continued teaching at Jeff but for a lack of support from the principal. There were incidents with other students—not mine—coming into the gym and disrupting my classes. I had no problem managing my own students but I had no way to discipline those who were not mine, and the principal wouldn't take any action. Teaching was impossible in those circumstances, so I left.

I never heard any bad things about Jefferson. Even after I retired, a teacher I knew who taught at another school in the district never said anything bad about Jeff.

Teacher: Bob Brandi

(White; taught 1968–2002, physical education and math)

* * *

Jeff wasn't a "kumbaya" place, but everyone got along well enough to make things work.

* * *

Bob grew up in the Sunset district of San Francisco, the child of an immigrant family. They weren't exactly poor, but his father never graduated from high school—despite getting a baseball scholarship—because earning money was more important than studying. Bob's Italian grandfather, on his father's side, collected garbage in San Francisco with a horse and cart until 1907; households paid five cents to have their garbage picked up. Being non-English-speaking made it hard to find a good job, and he was pleased to get a permanent one as a janitor at City Hall. When he'd made enough money, he sent home for his wife. Bob's paternal grandmother duly came over from Italy but never learned English. On his mother's side, his Slovenian grandmother was a seamstress.

The street where I lived as a kid had all White people of various nationalities, some Jewish, and mostly European descent. For kindergarten to eighth grade I attended Holy Name School, which was all White. At St. Ignatius High School (SI) we had a couple of Black kids, several Asians, and a few other nationalities. After graduation in 1960, I attended San Francisco State with about 20,000 students from all backgrounds. I played football one year and remember the team as being very mixed racially/ethnically. I  *also played baseball for four years, but the team was mostly White. All of my friends were White at the time because that was who I knew.*

From sixth grade on, I knew I wanted to be a teacher and a coach. That's why I went to SF State—at the time, if you wanted to be a teacher, that's where you went. The tuition was only $30 a semester!

Bob did his student teaching at Mills High School in Millbrae, where everyone

180

was well-off and White. He remembers that the students' cars in the parking lot were nicer than the teachers' cars.

After graduation, Bob was hired at Ben Franklin Junior High School in San Francisco, whose student population was about 97% Black.

The school was just up the street from the People's Temple head-quarters. [The People's Temple, run by the Reverend Jim Jones, was a racially integrated Christian church which became a controversial cult. In 1978, in Guyana, Jones incited his followers to mass suicide; 900 people died.] I was at Ben Franklin from fall '65 to '68. There were riots in the Bayview-Hunter's Point District and the Fillmore District where the school was located. There were also minor spillovers of the riots at the school during that time, possibly related to the assassination of Martin Luther King, Jr.

My student teaching at Mills gave me zero preparation for teaching at Ben Franklin. I taught physical education, as did one other new teacher. The head of our department worked with us, emphasizing certain things that were important, such as making sure everything was under control before you tried to teach anything. In a couple of classes I had fifty kids, so I had to make sure they were paying attention. The kids were really pretty good. After a few weeks I was comfortable there and I enjoyed it.

When class was over the kids had to shower. Over time they got comfortable with each other undressed. Everyone's calling each other the n-word. These are Black kids, so I asked them, "If I call someone that, I'd get in trouble, but why are you doing it?" One said, "Oh, Mr. Brandi, you don't understand, this guy over here, he's a [n-word]." It was their way of calling someone uneducated or ignorant, but it wasn't as derogatory as it is when a White person says it. The kids weren't bashful using that word in front of me, and it was something that raised my awareness about it.

During my three years at Ben Franklin I worked on my master's degree at night. I didn't want to be at a junior high school for the rest of my life; I wanted to teach high school and coach. In those days San Francisco had some outstanding high school coaches, so I knew it would be hard to move up. I'd heard about a job at Jefferson High through Coach Johnson, who was also in the master's degree program with me. Don McCann, Coach Gary Leahy, and other Jeff coaches had gone to SI ahead of me and I'd see them once in a while. They encouraged me to interview at Jeff.

My wife and I had been invited to a party with some coaches, including Coach McGrath, who was the head of the PE department at

Jeff. I went to the party, thinking they invited me to get an idea of who I was. McGrath asked me a few things. I didn't realize I was being interviewed on the spot. Then I got a call to go and see the principal, Mr. Cereghino. I went in and he said, "Hi, Coach McGrath speaks highly of you. You've got the job."

During Bob's first summer of college, he had worked for Daly City Parks and Recreation as a playground director. One site he worked at was "Little Jeff," a local elementary school that was a "feeder" school to Jefferson High.

A lot of the kids I knew from my summers as a playground director at park and rec were now in high school. My first day at Jefferson, one of the kids I knew from then said to me, "Hey, Bob, how you doing?" I said, "Hey, Gary. I'm okay, but it's Mr. Brandi." He said, "Yeah, okay, Bob." That was my introduction to Jeff. The kids were great.

Bob remembers hearing that the year before he started at Jeff there were some racial problems between Blacks and Whites that got resolved in fights on the football field.

When I got there in '68, there weren't any problems. With any group of kids, everyone knew who the tough kids were—the kids knew better than the faculty what was what socially. You just kind of stayed away from the tough ones and kept your mouth shut. My first year, I was the freshman football coach. Everything was brand new to me. I was twenty-six years old. I had my eyes wide open—I have some wonderful memories.

Jefferson was a different kind of place. When I first arrived, there were some strange teachers there, not in a racist way...extremely liberal, not worried about class control. Kids told me about what was going on in classes. With coaching, you have to get the kids' attention so they can focus on what they need to do, the opposite of what was happening in some of the classes.

There was a teacher from another part of the country who may have grown up with racism. He was a little rough around the edges, said things without thinking, but he really liked the kids there. Maybe I was oblivious and didn't see racism. I'd really have to look hard to find something.

I remember one time when I was coaching football with another teacher. The Black kids always called each other the n-word. It was just what they did, part of their growing up. I'd say, "Come on, guys, knock it off." The other teacher would get really upset and stop the practice, saying, "No one's going to respect you if you keep doing that." He made it a teaching point.

I don't remember any of the Black kids at Jeff my whole time there doing race-related stuff. There was a Black student union in my first years there. Maybe some kids would tell each other, "He's not a problem; she's not a problem." They'd let each other know which teachers were okay and which were unpopular. As a teacher you didn't see all the other teachers, so you didn't necessarily know what was going on, but the kids got real comfortable telling things to us coaches. They would tell stories about a teacher who was so laid-back that kids would be smoking dope in the back of the class.

After teaching PE for a while, Bob got into a disagreement with the principal, who moved him to the math department.

I think he wanted me to go to another school. A lot of the teachers weren't very happy with him. I had said something to him that he didn't like. I was teaching general math, mostly working with remedial kids. I was teaching things like, "Sally has four yards of cloth and is going to make a dress," etc. First of all, there's nobody named Sally at Jeff, and—dressmaking? It seemed totally irrelevant to the students' lives. I realized the kids weren't interested because they couldn't relate to what I was teaching.

One day I was having a difficult time trying to explain how to find averages; partially it was me, partially the kids weren't interested. I thought about it and decided to try something different, so I said, "Yesterday I went to a 49ers game and a receiver caught ten passes for ninety yards. What was his average?" Half the class raised their hands immediately; they had no problem working out the answer.

Eventually I created a class called Sports Math, initially called Statistics of Sports. Every day I'd get thirty-five copies of the San Francisco Chronicle. The kids didn't need a textbook, so no one had the excuse that they'd forgotten their book. We'd do all the applications with percentages, averages, decimals, fractions. They'd find quarterback completion percentages, average carry per completion, etc. We also did a lot with different types of graphs and I taught them about probability. I liked being in the math department. As the years went on, I went full-time in math, and really, really enjoyed it.

As well as teaching PE and math, Bob coached football and baseball at Jefferson. During his first five years he taught mostly freshman football, then lightweight basketball, and refereed basketball for a few years. Bob continued to referee basketball for four decades.

To be a referee I believed you had to be knowledgeable and you had to hustle, so I was and I did. I came back two more times to football— two years of varsity, then soph/frosh [sophomore and freshman], for about fifteen years total. I coached soph/frosh baseball until the varsity coach, Tom Martinez, left to go to the College of San Mateo. I coached the varsity team from '76 to '86, and then was hired by City College of San Francisco (CCSF) to be the pitching coach and worked from '87 to '92 while still teaching at Jeff. The head coach at CCSF left and I was offered the job, but it wasn't a teaching job. I would have had to leave Jeff, which would also have meant I'd take a big pay cut, since I wouldn't be teaching anymore. You can't teach five high school classes and coach a major sport at college.

I ended up with the best job of my life, coaching baseball in Italy. In '93–'94, I took a sabbatical, went to Italy, and coached baseball. I thoroughly loved it. Because of that, I decided that the next time I was eligible for a sabbatical, I would bo back to Italy. My next sabbbatical was 1999–2000, so I returned to Italy to coach. After officially retiring in 2002, I continued coaching in Italy until 2010. I made all kinds of friends. The team was based in the town of Rovigo, an hour southwest of Venice by train. I got my Italian citizenship—my dad's family is from the Genoa area and my mom's family was from Slovenia, just east of Italy. I got to see my Slovenian cousins several times because I could easily drive there from Italy. I probably would never have met them otherwise. Baseball helped me to be able to do that.

Bob reflects on race/ethnicity and coaching.

I don't remember initially having any kind of diversity training related to working with Jeff's student body. Later, when Daly City had become heavily populated by Filipinos [Daly City has the biggest population of Filipinos outside the Philippines], they had a representative from the community come to talk with the staff about working with Filipinos.

Almost all the coaches were White. We did have one Black coach for a while. The thing about coaching is you're trying to put the best players out there. You teach them the skills, but you want to win the game. It never, ever occurred to me to play one guy ahead of another because of skin color. It absolutely never entered my mind. All the guys I coached with felt the same way. Maybe there was one coach who might have used the n-word once in a while. Even he would use the best players, the ones who deserved to play. As a coach, you wanted the best players in the position that was going to help the team to win.

In the early eighties, we played a game against Washington High at Golden Gate Park [in San Francisco]. My aunt brought my nephew to the game. My mom, dad, and aunt were all first-generation Americans. Back in their day they got picked on here and there. That generation wasn't embarrassed about saying something [about race]. When the game was over, I went up to my aunt, who said, "You don't have any White guys on the team." I replied, "I've got White guys. What are you talking about?" I looked at the bench where the team was waiting for me, and I realized she was right—I had no idea! I realized it didn't make a difference who was on the team in terms of what they looked like. One year I had a girl who played with the boys on the soph/frosh team. What mattered was whether or not someone could play the sport.

When coaching or with the kids in my classes, I don't remember intervening in any racial incidents—if there was a problem in class, it was because someone was being a jerk. Maybe he had said something to someone. But I don't remember anything involving race.

I had a chance to go to Terra Nova [another district high school] in the late seventies/early eighties. They were always loaded with great baseball players and some made the big leagues. They had a community lead-up program, a really good, well-structured youth baseball program, which gave the kids a huge advantage. I was recruited to go there, but I remembered some of my experiences with people there, almost all of them White. I didn't want to go. People of color, Black, and Latino kids like those at Jeff, would just come right up and tell me the way it was. They were more direct, which was fine with me. As I got older, I was never comfortable around all White people; I was more comfortable with mixed groups. Italy was funny because almost everyone was Italian, but the non-Italian residents were usually from Senegal and other African countries.

Bob felt that the school district didn't care about Jefferson High.

They cared more about other schools that made them look good. Jeff's test scores were low, so that dragged the district down a little. I admired the teachers who stayed because they liked the kids. You kind of felt like you were doing something for somebody. Other teachers who transferred from other schools and spent their last years at Jeff felt they were really doing something. We never expected to get anything other than, maybe, a "thank you." We never thought twice about it. After fifteen years of retirement, I helped out coaching a Little League team in Belmont, down the peninsula from Daly City. At the end of the year parents gave me Starbuck's gift cards and gift certificates for dinner. I got more presents in one year at Belmont than in all my years at Jeff. But that's not why you're in it. You like coaching, you like the kids—you get close to them in ways you couldn't in the classroom.

You grow up with prejudices just from your neighborhood, the things people around you say and do. As you get older you realize some of these things are wrong, so you lose these prejudices. Today we use "racist." A racist is someone who has his beliefs but knows better. A prejudiced person might not know better or is someone who is still learning and evolving.

Jeff wasn't a kumbaya place, but everyone got along well enough to make things work. There were rules. If a student missed practice, they didn't play in the next game or didn't get to start. Everyone was subject to those rules. You were consistent. Everybody saw it so they knew you were being fair. As a teacher, I was responsible for teaching not just the sport, but also life lessons.

Margine

(Japanese American, class of '72)

* * *

It seemed like Jeff encapsulated a special Daly City culture, with both Filipino and Black culture very prominent.... Because of those dominant people of color, I felt like the White kids and everybody else, like Japanese, we just kind of blended in. We took our cues—our fashion, our slang—from the cool kids, the kids of color.

* * *

Margine, the oldest of three girls, was born in San Francisco to Japanese American parents. Her family lived in the city's Japantown until moving to Daly City when she was about three years old.

Margine's mother was born and raised in Cupertino, California. During high school, her mother was sent to live in Japan for a few years, like many children of Japanese immigrants at the time.

My mom was on the last ship coming back to the United States from Japan after Pearl Harbor was bombed. Shortly after arriving, she and her family were forced to go to an internment camp. She talked a lot about "camp" and being uprooted from her home.

She was eighteen years old and suddenly her family had to pack up everything, leave their home and their community. They were directed to go to the Tanforan racetrack [the "assembly center"], where they stayed in horse stalls. After a while they were put on a train to Wyo-

*ming. They had to keep the shades down because the government didn't
want anybody who saw the train to know who was on board.*

*They were not given much food in the camp and the quality was
poor. My mother said the water was also bad and it caused boils on her
skin. Health care was not very good. Her mother, my grandmother, died
of breast cancer in the camp.*

*I didn't get the sense that there were guards everywhere, but they
were definitely around on the periphery. Toward the end of the war
people were allowed to work outside the camp. My mom ended up doing
live-in housework for a family in Wyoming. She said they treated her
very well. I don't know if she experienced any overt racism in the camp,
but clearly it was a prison.*

Margine's father was born and raised in Salt Lake City, Utah.

*My grandfather left Japan to work in the sugarcane fields in Ha-
waii, which were recruiting Japanese and Chinese laborers. In Hawaii,
he was recruited again to work on the railroad near Auburn, CA, and
then to work at a copper mine in Salt Lake City. After arriving there, he
sent for my grandmother from Japan.*

*My father didn't end up in the camps because they only interned
folks from the west coast—California, Oregon, and Washington.*

*People who were in the camps had a bond based on that experi-
ence. My dad and his family felt like outsiders because they had not
gone through it. His sister said once that it might have been easier if
they had been in a camp because anti-Japanese racism was so strong
[in other places]. Wherever they went, there were people who said very
racist things. But there were also White families who weren't like that,
so they had a support system. There was a very small but tightly knit
Japanese community in Salt Lake, mostly doing physical labor. They
had a Buddhist church.*

*After the war, my mother's family returned to the Cupertino/Sunny-
vale area of California. My dad's sister had married a guy from Japantown in San Francisco. When my dad went to visit his sister, he met my
mom.*

*My family ended up in the eastern part of Daly City because my
dad tried to buy a house in [more affluent] Westlake but they wouldn't
sell to people of color. He told the story about going into the real estate
office with my mom and us kids and they wouldn't wait on him. They
waited on everyone else, but they completely ignored him; they never
acknowledged him at all. He never forgot that.*

The war, anti-Japanese prejudice, and the internment camps cast a very long shadow over Japanese Americans. Margine's parents tried hard to make their daughters into Americans who would fit in, beginning with their names.

My sisters and I all had Anglo first and middle names. My parents spoke Japanese to my grandparents but always spoke English to us. My mom wouldn't teach us Japanese. She really didn't want us to "be Japanese." She didn't want us to stand out. If we asked, she would teach us little things, like the alphabet, but she didn't want us to know enough to make us culturally Japanese. Our family friends went to Japanese school, but we never did.

Although we had a strong sense of community, we never felt part of the close-knit J-town network because we lived in Daly City. Japantown is such a small area. We did go there for shopping, church, and social events, and we knew all the families, but we didn't socialize with them. I always felt more mainstream American, but I was taught that we were not White, and because of it we had been persecuted and could still be treated badly. Mom repeatedly told my sisters and me, "I don't want you to experience the same problems that I did. The government will always know where to find you because you look different and are not White." Her telling us this made me feel a little victimized—okay, we stick out. At the same time, we were expected to do well in school and not cause any trouble. I don't know if part of that had to do with us being all girls.

My mom sometimes talked about the holocaust, so I was acutely aware that there were parallels between the Jewish experience and ours. Whenever we met other Japanese Americans, the first discussion was "What camp were you at?" It told a lot about your story, just knowing that.

The neighborhood in Daly City where Margine's family lived was very mixed.

Our block where I grew up had three Japanese families, a Black family, some Italians, and a few Mexican families. School always had every color; that was just normal. I was bussed to George Washington Elementary School near the Excelsior District, where it was very mixed. Nobody took any issue with it. Every time we went to a new school, there were more Black kids, a lot of Filipinos, Mexicans. I don't ever remember being in a class where it wasn't multiracial. My mom made friends with a Black woman who was fostering kids—White kids, Black kids, etc. My mother never referred to anyone by their color: it was never "a Black family," it was just "a family."

When I was in second grade, a Filipino kid called me Tojo [Japan's prime minister during the war]. I didn't know what it meant, but I must have told my mom when I got home because she got very upset. She went to meet with the teachers, and nobody ever called me names again. She didn't harp on it with me. This was the only racist thing I remember from growing up. However, I started taking judo when I was at Colma [junior high] and I knew that the judo teacher favored my sister and me because we were Japanese. This made me feel like there was more pressure on us than on the others in the class.

I was a Girl Scout, with mostly White girls in the troop. There was definitely an "American apple pie" subtext, but I was doing what everyone else was doing in mainstream America—you go to camp, you take swimming lessons. The reason I talk about these two things is because most of the kids doing them were White, yet I felt absolutely accepted.

We talked about race and identity at home, but not at school with our peers. With all my friends, all my life, color has been secondary. Friendships are based more on common interests. I enjoy learning about my White friends' backgrounds and share common experiences with my Asian friends: your grandparents weren't born here but your parents may have been. It's not so much experience as culture, like with my Filipino friends, there were food commonalities. Going to school together for most of our lives, we all went through the same things.

Going on to Jefferson High School, Margine plunged into student life. She was a class officer, she played bells and percussion in the band, and she was in various clubs, like model U.N. and CSF (California Scholarship Federation). Outside school, she continued taking judo classes two nights a week.

At Jeff, my closest friends were Filipino, Italian, and Greek. There were no cliques based on race/ethnicity. The most popular kids were all colors. I always felt comfortable and I don't remember any racist incidents in high school. We acknowledged everyone's race but didn't trip on it.

It seemed like Jeff encapsulated a special Daly City culture, with both Filipino and Black culture very prominent. I remember that "Flip" was a good word [for Filipino]. It's hard to articulate, but there was this part of Daly City that was a hodgepodge, a potpourri of all these subcultures. Because of those dominant people of color, I felt like the White kids and everybody else, like Japanese, we just kind of blended in. We took our cues—our fashion, our slang—from the cool kids, the kids of color.

My parents were very open-minded, but there were different expectations when it came to dating or marriage. One time my sister Lori had a date with a Black guy who came to the house to pick her up. We knew my dad wasn't thrilled, but he never said anything. Another time I was going on a date with a Latino guy who had dark skin and sort of kinky hair. My grandmother saw him waiting for me in the living room and she thought he was Black. She didn't say anything about it either, which is typically Japanese—we were not a very verbal family—but we knew she wasn't happy. Then my mom explained that he was Mexican, and my grandmother was fine with it.

What stood out to me in high school was that Westmoor [the big high school rival] was viewed as "White." It seemed to be better-funded and the students thought they were superior to us. I was really aware that there was an imbalance between the two schools—we had older buildings, there wasn't much money, we had a lot of people of color. I think I knew intuitively there was an economic difference. It always seemed like kids from Westmoor had more money. I was becoming more socially aware. It was the sixties. There was the anti-war movement, Black Power, etc. I remember going to Glide Church [a Methodist Community church serving people of all races/ethnicities in the heart of the Tenderloin, a poor and very "colorful" area of San Francisco]. I identified with those movements.

During the summer Margine was a counselor-in-training at a diabetic youth camp.

That camp was a big learning experience. Most of the campers and a lot of the other counselors came from Pacific Heights, a very wealthy area of San Francisco, and went to private or Catholic schools. I'd never been exposed to so many people who had so much money. All the kids at the camp were White, as the camp didn't offer scholarships for low-income kids at that time. I think the only people of color were those of us from Jeff. It was the first time I realized that there are some really rich people out there. Throughout my career I would meet people who remembered that camp.

After graduation, Margine was one of a few Jeff classmates who enrolled at the majority white, wealthier University of California at Davis.

The Jeff vs. Westmoor dynamic taught me about the feeling of not having money or influence. Going from Daly City to Davis, I became more aware of class differences. I became closer to other students of color because we seemed to be from the same economic background.

In college I learned that people of color and lower economic classes are not equally represented in the power structure. I was a sociology major and was taking all these classes in ethnic studies. We had classes in the temporary buildings, not in the venerable ivy-clad halls reserved for more important subjects. Sociology really opened up the world for me about institutional racism, or even studying the institution of racism. The oppression was so obvious, and the women's movement was like an awakening: when you look at present-day power structures, the gender differences stand out.

Asian American studies was expanding. There was a Board of Regents meeting at Davis and I remember picketing them, I think around the Bakke case [a reverse-discrimination case]. There was such a social movement going on when we were in college and high school...the sexual revolution, bra burning.

After graduating from Davis, I gravitated toward working/volunteering on women's issues and I staffed a women's academic equity project. Later I became a senior legislative aide to California Speaker and San Francisco mayor, Willie Brown, where my primary responsibility was for the Asian/Pacific communities. My commitment was always to underrepresented groups.

Margine's final reflections:

My home life was relatively conventional for that time. Our values were study and hard work, assimilating as much as possible, and "being a good girl." At school I learned about drugs, sex, stealing, fighting, and how to stay out of trouble; how to navigate among the "stoners," juvenile delinquents, and tough kids. I learned I could smoke pot and still get good grades.

I had a real sense of community in high school. It was small and I felt like I knew everyone really well. What began as a strong school identity as in Jeff vs. Westmoor morphed into an "us vs. them" mentality as I got older: i.e., those on the lower end of the economic scale needed to challenge the "old guard," the power structure, the establishment. In the sixties and seventies, we began to articulate what the problems were, and now there's a platform for trying to solve some of them:

racial injustice, sexism, harassment at work. You couldn't sue people for the kinds of things you can today. Back then the attitude was, "suck it up, it already happened, don't cause a scene." Now there's more recognition that people and institutions need to change their behavior. You have to include everybody.

Gary G.

(White, class of '73)

* * *

I think some of the Italian kids got racist attitudes from their parents. I could have gone that way, too, if it wasn't for my mom being so open about everything. They would never have a Black friend, or if they did, they'd never have a Black friend over to their house. The only diversity in their lives was at school.

* * *

Gary was born in Honolulu, Hawaii, where his father was stationed in the Marines. His family was a European melting pot with roots in California on both sides.

My father's family was from a small town on the border between France and Germany which was fought over a lot. I like to claim we're French but we're probably more German. His family was in San Francisco in 1918 when the Spanish flu pandemic hit. They moved to Santa Rosa, and later they moved again to Daly City, which was where my dad grew up. He graduated from Jefferson High in 1937.

My mom's father came from what is now Ukraine to Kansas after getting kicked out for being a Mennonite. He made his way to the Central Valley of California, where there was a Mennonite community, to work in the oil fields. Mom's mother was of English descent—her grandfather was born in the United Kingdom and immigrated to Los

194

Angeles. He became a dentist. My grandmother taught school in the Bakersfield area, where she met my grandfather. My Mom was born in Bakersfield.

After my dad was injured (shot in both legs during WWII), he was rehabbed at Oak Knoll Hospital in Oakland. He wasn't fit for active duty, so they stationed him in SF, where my mom was stationed as a Wave—she became his secretary. There was a little office hanky-panky going on!

When Gary was two years old, his father was transferred to Camp Pendleton in Southern California, where the family of four relocated. In 1960, his dad left the military and moved the family back to his home-town, Daly City, where Gary started school.

We lived off Hillside Boulevard. Across the street from our house was a new elementary school, kindergarten to fourth grade, which had just been built. Since the school only went through fourth grade, I was bussed to George Washington Elementary School in Southern Hills for fifth and sixth grades.

Our neighborhood was mostly White, with a few Filipino families who lived around the corner. There were a few Black kids and a few Filipinos at my first school. George Washington Elementary school was much more racially diverse—a lot more Blacks, Hispanics, and Filipinos. I absolutely loved George Washington because it was a whole new world for me, coming from a White area to a very mixed place. I loved the kids there. I think it was the first time I opened my eyes about race.

Gary reflects on his family's attitudes about race.

Dad was a hardened Marine. [Racism] was more a thing of their era. I think at first they weren't sure about me going to George Washington, but when they saw what a great experience it was, they embraced it. My dad would occasionally use the n-word, and as I got older it made me cringe. I'd say, "Come on, dad, knock it off!" I think with the WWII guys, using the n-word flowed too naturally.

When the Watts riot happened (1965), my dad said something like, "They deserve this. Look at them doing that. It's the wrong thing to do." I'd tell him, "Dad, they're poor people. They're disadvantaged." Their situation was very different from ours.

My mom really appreciated the schools we went to. She wanted us to meet and experience a lot of different people. I think she was the one who, once we went to these schools, absolutely thought it

*was good for us. She was very religious and I think she didn't want
to judge anyone.*

*My sister Diane, who's three years older, was very involved in the
Girl Scouts. She had a very diverse group of friends and was popular
at Jeff. Her best friend was Japanese American.*

During elementary and junior high school Gary's best friend was
of Puerto Rican descent.

*He and I were in band together; we played saxophone, and I also
played clarinet. We'd go to each other's houses to practice. Sometimes
he'd come over for dinner. I loved his mom's food better than my mom's.
I love black beans and rice to this day. My mom was open to having him
over. I don't remember any uncomfortableness with my father around
him. I think my dad was slowly evolving. If someone was a friend of
ours, he'd be okay with it.*

*My earliest memories of racism were when I was at Colma, and
Dr. King was shot. A lot of the White kids were really crass, speaking
ill of Dr. King, and a lot of the Black kids did not appreciate it—being
told that Dr. King deserved it because he was a radical, etc. I thought
he was like Gandhi, so peaceful, and I didn't understand White people
criticizing him. At school they were worried about minor riots happening, so they let us go home earlier. Things were kind of simmering.*

*Music divided us. The surfer kids were White, and they listened to
rock and roll—the Beach Boys, the Rolling Stones. Black kids were soul
and listened to Motown. I loved the Black kids in fifth and sixth grade.
They were so cool, and fun. We'd hang out after school, play records,
and they'd teach me to dance—which was quite a feat for a White kid
like me! They turned me on to Motown. I tried to bridge both sides.*

*In eighth grade, we already knew that my Puerto Rican friend was
going to Serramonte High and I was going to Jeff, so I drifted more
toward the kids I'd be going to Jeff with. In high school, we had joint
school concerts so were in touch some, but by our junior year I wasn't
communicating much with him. When I was at his school for a game,
he'd come by and it was like old times, but he wasn't part of my daily
circle anymore.*

Like many kids who went to Colma, Gary didn't find Jefferson
High a big transition.

*I remember my first year at Jeff, there were some Black guys who
wanted to take our lunch money. It ticked all of us off. That was kind*

of minor stuff, which was probably more because we were freshmen, dorky little kids.

I was in the band and played sports, and we always had kids from all different ethnic backgrounds. Again, I loved it. I thought it was super! I don't remember any other incidents regarding race. I just thought we had a great time. I met some really nice Black people. They weren't just great Black people; they were great people. I enjoyed myself in high school, even though I was too shy to ask anyone out.

I think some of the Italian kids got racist attitudes from their parents. I could have gone that way, too, if it wasn't for my mom being so open about everything. They would never have a Black friend, or if they did, they'd never have a Black friend over to their house. The only diversity in their lives was at school. They weren't out-and-out racist; they were on the same teams as me in baseball and basketball, and we all got along, but outside of the team they wouldn't have any interactions with non-Whites. They used the n-word every once in a while. I think sometimes people say that stuff without even thinking about it. It's so dismissive and stupid.

After graduation from Jeff, Gary went to college and became an air traffic controller.

I went to the College of San Mateo, where I took aeronautics for two years. Then I transferred to San Jose State. In both places it was mostly White. I don't think many minorities got into that program—it was probably perceived to be a "White guy" thing. Part of picking a career is awareness of what's available, and I don't think many minority kids knew about aeronautics. Someone growing up poor and Black in Oakland probably wouldn't even have thought of going into it, and our guidance counselors wouldn't have encouraged it. The only Black people I knew in the field were those who had been in the air force or the navy.

I was an air traffic controller for thirty years and retired while I was still young. It was a great career. After retirement, I took a year off to do nothing. I was bored stiff, so I went to work for the San Francisco Giants, doing security up in the booth. Once again, it was one of the most diverse places and so fabulous, meeting all these great people that I probably wouldn't have known otherwise. Many of us are close friends today—several Blacks, several Hispanics. A mixed bag. It was so much fun. We'd get together when the Giants were on the road.

Gary's final reflections:

Jeff was a great place. I had an absolutely fabulous four years and it was great preparation for the big world out there. You have to wonder about kids who go to an all-White school and are thrown into a situation of mixed races one day—how do they react? If you don't have the exposure, how do you deal with it? Even having the exposure, sometimes people can be racist. My time at George Washington, Colma, and Jeff taught me that there are good people of every race, and bad people of every race.

Richard

(Chinese American, class of 1970)

* * *

The fact that it was naturally integrated at Jefferson High made it special. There was no bussing to get us integrated. I thought that was really great.

* * *

Richard was born in 1952 in San Francisco, a fourth-generation American whose great-great-grandparents immigrated from China in the late 1800s. He spent his first seven years in an apartment on Russian Hill [a San Francisco neighborhood]. His extended family, including his uncles and their families, all lived together in the same building.

A highlight of Richard's childhood was their frequent trips to the nearby Swenson's ice cream store. Ice cream cones cost six cents. He and his older cousins would sit in front of Swenson's and sell newspapers.

Richard was the third of six children; the eldest was three years older, and the youngest eight years younger than he. Despite the extended family, Richard learned very little Chinese, and hardly speaks any today.

My mother would switch over to Chinese when she didn't want the kids to know what she was saying. After I graduated from Cal [University of California at Berkeley], I took a Cantonese class at City College of San Francisco. However, my mom made fun of my intonations, so I stopped.

199

The first school Richard attended was Sarah B. Cooper Elementary School in San Francisco.

It was different for me because there were maybe only about five percent Asians; the majority was Caucasian. From that experience I got used to the fact that there weren't going to be as many Asians at my schools.

Sarah B. Cooper Elementary was renamed later and is now known as Yick Wo Elementary, and it's predominantly Chinese. Richard's wife's family owns an apartment house across the street from the school.

In 1959 Richard's family and his uncles bought brand new houses in the same block in Daly City, not far from the San Francisco city limit. Another relative lived two blocks away, and a cousin lived three blocks away. Richard was enrolled at General Pershing Elementary School, not far from home.

I met Riley [White (Jewish)] in grammar school and Bob [White] in middle school. Riley and I got closer in third or fourth grade and are still friends to this day. Unfortunately, Bob passed away in his early fifties.

For most of elementary school I didn't realize that there was some racism against me. In fifth grade there was a Black kid who was making his eyes slanty. At some point we got into a fight and we had to go to the principal's office.

In sixth grade, there was a White guy named Sam who went with me to a Giants baseball game. When we were waiting for a ride home, we got jumped by some Black teenagers. We weren't hurt badly, but we did go to the police station.

Richard's mother had her own way of being "color-blind."

One time we were watching a Giants game on television. There was a White centerfielder, Ken Henderson, and a Black right fielder, Bobby Bonds. She kept getting them mixed up. I pointed that out to her. She said, "Who cares? One's White, one's Black. They're not Chinese." While she didn't seem to care much about race, she didn't like Japanese people, most likely because of the war. [WWII, when Japan invaded China]

My parents both worked at the post office, so they were exposed to Black people all the time. I think their casual acceptance carried over to me. I wasn't fearful or mistrusting of Black people.

The first girl Richard asked out was Filipina.

I also dated a few White girls. The first girl I kissed was Cauca-sian. Eventually I went on a trip to Taiwan where there were a lot of Chinese Americans, and that's where I met my first wife. Unfortunately, that marriage didn't last long. While I was still attracted to other races, most of the women I dated were Chinese American, as is my current wife. We've been married thirty years.

While Richard and his two older siblings went to Jefferson High School, his younger sisters went to Serramonte, which opened at the beginning of his junior year at Jeff.

Richard recalls his years at Jeff as being a happy time.

I really enjoyed my friends. I had several close friends who were Black, including Iris, Sarah, and Deana. I also had a close friend who was Latina, Helen. My old friends from elementary school, Bob and Riley, walked to school with me, about a mile away. We went to each other's houses all through high school. But I didn't bring people home often because there were six kids at our house. I remember fun parties at Iris's, Rebecca's [Filipina], or Sarah's. Their parents would be there and there was alcohol. But I don't remember anyone getting wild.

While I was at Jeff, I consciously thought about how racially di-verse we were—Caucasians of different nationalities, Blacks, Asians. I don't remember racial divisions or fights. Before I went there, it was said to have some racial issues, but it didn't happen when we were there. Maybe at first I was a little concerned, but once I was there, it wasn't a big deal.

One incident does stand out in Richard's memory.

I ran for commissioner of elections against Ken who was a Poly-nesian/Irish friend. We had to campaign in front of the student body. I remember Ken saying, "And if you vote for my opponent, you will be an unfortunate cookie [a reference to Chinese fortune cookies]." I felt that his comment was inappropriate and nowadays would be classified as racist—but, since I won, I guess I got the last laugh.

After graduating from Jeff, Richard went to the University of Cali-fornia at Berkeley [Cal], a public university, while most of his closest friends went to private colleges in Southern California.

My friend Bob went to San Jose State, which wasn't too far from Berkeley. A few times we visited our friends in Claremont. I wasn't nearly as happy at Cal as I was at Jeff. I didn't have that many friends, but one of the people I met there became a good friend. He was also of Chinese descent.

Richard worked for twenty-nine years for the San Francisco Department of Public Health's [SFDPH] environmental health division.

Since it was a public agency, having diversity was so important because staff had to go all over San Francisco dealing with the public. We intentionally tried to enforce diversity in our hiring. Since I was a manager, I had to deal with any complaints—sexual harassment, people not working when they should have been, etc., but there was never anything racial. It's surprising that I can't think of any racial issues after working with that department for so many years.

Richard's final reflections:

The fact that it was naturally integrated at Jeff made it special. There was no bussing to get us integrated. I thought that was really great. I don't know of many places like that. Now it's changed a lot; I think Jeff is almost all Filipino today. Back then we had Polynesians, Italians, Jewish, Irish Catholics, Chinese, Japanese, Blacks, Filipinos, etc. We were joking one time, saying that the only race not represented there was Eskimos!

Michele

(White, class of '72, younger sibling of Marc)

* * *

I feel really sad that in later years many people in Brisbane felt Jeff was too rough for their kids, so they sent them to other schools. A few do still go to Jeff, but I feel like Brisbane kids need to go to Jeff to get integrated into the real world, more than ever.

* * *

Michele was born in San Francisco and has lived most of her life in Brisbane, CA. In 1930, Michele's paternal grandmother, originally from Missouri, bought several lots in Brisbane for $100 each—$10 down, $10 a month. Her father's family were "Okies" who migrated to California as described in Steinbeck's, *The Grapes of Wrath*. Prior to leaving the dust bowl, the family was literally starving, so they loaded everything they could on top of their Model A Ford, packed the family of five inside, and headed west.

Michele's mother, who was half Italian, also grew up in Brisbane.

Michele remembers wondering about her ethnicity when she was little.

I asked, "What am I?" and memorized what I was told: Scottish, English, Irish, Dutch, French, Danish, German, and one-quarter Italian. My dad's family shows up in the 1690 census in Virginia, then again in the 1790 census in Tennessee. I worked at the Brisbane library,

so I got to look at the census books. I knew it was my family because they had first names that got passed down through the family lineage.

The 1790 census said our ancestors "were poor and only listed two slaves." I was shocked that my ancestors would even have slaves. Can you imagine that in 1790, having "only two slaves" in Virginia was considered poor? These relatives migrated west and eventually to the Oklahoma Territory, where my grandfather was born.

After my father's mother died when I was forty-seven, I found out that I was also Choctaw and Cherokee, which my grandmother had kept a secret. I had suspected this because one of my sisters had really straight black hair. People used to think my dad was Spanish, but he had bright blue eyes, which apparently wasn't that unusual with the Choctaw.

Brisbane was a very White town when Michele was growing up—but not completely.

There were some people of Italian descent, some of Spanish/Mexican descent, and very few Asians. There was one Samoan family with whom I am still good friends. I don't remember being conscious of the fact that it was mostly White. It just "was what it was."

Another of Michele's earliest best friends lived on the same street and was half-Japanese and half-White.

I remember her mother trying to teach her little brother how to use chopsticks, but he was left-handed so it was very hard. I got a good dose of Japanese culture at that time. Sadly, she moved away about the time we started kindergarten.

Michele reflects on her earliest memories related to race.

I remember my dad used the n-word at the dinner table one time. Mom freaked out and told him she didn't want him to ever use that word in front of us again. My mom, being half Italian, had experienced a lot of prejudice growing up in the thirties and forties so she was very sensitive—she was called a dago and a wop, even by her half-siblings, who weren't Italian. As a teenager during the war [World War II] she played saxophone in an all-women's jazz band at the USO club. She had a much broader view of both Black people and prejudice. We were strictly taught to always accept people for who they were and not judge people by their race, color, or economic status.

Both of Michele's parents were teachers, which broadened their family's horizons.

My father taught at Berkeley High School in the sixties and it was very mixed ethnically. I remember him using the expression "blackboard jungle" [a 1950s movie describing a violent, unruly inner-city school] and telling us that he had to use the fire hose to break up fights. He didn't want to get in the middle of a fight and get stabbed, but he didn't want to tolerate fights in class either.

Dad had two exchange students from Mexico who invited us to visit, and we had friends from Hungary who had lived in Mexico and encouraged us to go. So, in the summer of '64, when I was ten, we bought a travel trailer and drove to Mexico. We were gone for two months, going all the way to Acapulco and back. The whole trip, including gas, food, and purchases, came to $864 for our family of six. [Equivalent to $7,795.63 in today's money.]

On that trip we saw starving people—children with extended bellies living in extreme poverty. You don't ever forget that. In many places the roads weren't even paved. We had brought piles of used clothes and canned food because we were told that we'd be able to give everything away, and we did.

I remember standing on top of the Pyramid of the Sun near Mexico City. The only others there were a dozen Catholic school girls. We girls danced to the Beatles' music on the top of the pyramid! That trip changed my life—the fact that my parents had the courage to take us out of the country and go to Mexico by car with a trailer. Nobody did that in those days, especially no one from Brisbane. This gave me the desire to travel and see how other people lived, and it made me unafraid to do that. It made me want to learn the difference between cathedrals and pyramids.

Both of Michele's parents supported the civil rights movement, especially her mom, so Michele knew a lot about it prior to going to Jeff. Her mother was adamant that no one use derogatory racial words in front of the kids. Michele recalls a funny incident when her grandmother was in her nineties.

She lived in a nice neighborhood in Santa Clara. A lot of Vietnamese families started moving in, including right next door. One day she was complaining about all the Vietnamese families moving in, so I said exaggeratedly, "Oh my god, it's just like when those dang Okies came here and wrecked California." Her eyes suddenly got big. She was hor-

rified to realize what she was doing. The next thing I knew, she was babysitting the kids next door and bringing them homemade pies and cakes.

My dad served on the first Brisbane city council for thirteen years. He was a driving force for Brisbane becoming a city, and I was singled out because of his political views—he had enemies, including some of our neighbors. It was ugly. Decades later, some of these guys called me and apologized for how they treated me.

Racism still shocks and horrifies me when I see it today. I even see it sometimes with people we grew up with. I live on the same street where I grew up, but I didn't see racism as much back then because I was focused on other things and, frankly, there were very few kids that weren't White. Now I am so much more aware.

Michele was excited about going to high school and especially to Jeff, even though it had a reputation for being a tough school. Her parents had gone there; her older twin sisters had gone there; and her older brother Marc was still at Jeff, a senior when Michele was a freshman.

When Marc was a junior, he took me to Jeff with him one day, and I met some of his friends. I already knew the Brisbane guys and some of his soccer buddies, but not his other friends. This was near the end of the 1968 school year. When they played soccer that summer in Brisbane, I was often their goalie. Marc was a very peaceful, highly respected, loving person with friends across the whole racial spectrum— Black, Brown, Yellow, White.

While Michele was excited to go to Jefferson, she had a rocky start.

I never had gone to school with so many people. It was exciting, finding my locker, attending football games, etc. About three weeks in— fall of '68—I was sitting on the field where all the daisies grew, having lunch with new and old friends. There was already some strain developing at Jeff when the race riots were happening all over the country. A group of eight Black girls came up to our circle of eight. I didn't think anything about it. One of them asked, "What grade are you in?" I answered, "Freshman, what of it?" I said this because I was proud to be a freshman at Jeff. Then she responded, "Are you sassing me?" She came right up and hit me in the head.

The next thing I knew, all eight of them were attacking me. I was trying to protect my face, my eyes especially because I had contact lenses. Not a single one of my friends stood up for me. Not one of them!

I finally was able to get to my feet and hit back. My brother's friend Lavelle, a big man on campus who was Black, came over, grabbed one of them, and slapped her, yelling, "What are you bitches doing? This is my bro's little sister. If you touch her again, you're dead." I was bleeding and had a black eye. I was absolutely stunned. I had never been in a fight, let alone hit back at anyone, except my brother. Lavelle asked how I was. I said I was okay. Another friend took me to the bathroom to help me clean up.

She asked if I was going to report it. I said, "No! If I report it, it would cause a race riot. And my mom would probably try to take me out of school. This didn't happen!" My brother found out about it, but I swore him to secrecy. I told my mom that I ran into a locker. That incident ended my friendship with one person who had been one of my best friends, but didn't lift a finger to help me.

One of the girls who attacked me later apologized. Over the next few years I became friends with a few of those girls. It was a rough start, but it made me sensitive to race relations and what was going on. I developed a sort of super-awareness of what was around me. If you were smart, you paid attention when walking down the hallway.

One reason I was targeted was because I was blond and sitting with some Brisbane kids, even though there were a few Daly City kids too. Lavelle's "blessing" changed my time there. It made me untouchable. It put a protective halo around me so I could go anywhere on campus and not feel threatened.

Later there was a younger girl who was getting hassled; she couldn't go into bathrooms, etc. For one week I escorted her around, and after that she was golden—untouchable, like me. Lavelle's legacy protection gave me a big gift that I shared whenever I could, especially to build bridges. I refused to let that horrible experience on the field affect my life, but it made me super aware and super sensitive to others. It also made me appreciate what the Black kids were up against, and why the BSCO [Black Student Cultural Organization] made a point to integrate.

Michele believes the kids at Jeff tried hard to integrate and make it work.

For kids from Daly City, maybe they didn't have to think about it much since they'd been integrated in grade school. For me, I had to work at not falling into just hanging out with Brisbane kids.

Jeff was great, but it was rough; I get it. It changed a lot in the four years I was there. I remember when we couldn't have night games any-

more because of the race riot we had with our mostly White rival school Westmoor, my freshman year. Westmoor broke our quarterback's leg at half-time. He was a White guy from Brisbane, a local legend. We were winning 17–0 but the game ended in a tie. The schools said it was a race riot that led to the broken leg and the post-game strife, but it wasn't. It was because we were winning. I remember it so clearly because it was one of the few football games I was able to go to, because I had a part-time job after school. Even though that game was in the afternoon, night games were suspended because we were "dangerous." We couldn't even have our homecoming game at night.

Jefferson gave me a dose of what life was going to be like. It opened that whole world of diversity to me, of what people brought to the table. It made me unafraid of going out in the world and being around people who didn't look or sound like me.

Yes, there were the stoners, the rah rahs, but there were also the brainiacs, the musicians, the philosophers, and the Wilderness School. When I graduated, Jeff had the top ten, or more, SAT scores in the district. We weren't a bunch of dummies. It's just that Jeff was so poor— they took away our physics class because of low enrollment, and we had to fight to keep it. We could barely get the pre-university classes we needed. In my freshman English class we learned to meditate instead of reading Shakespeare; my mom called the school about it. We students had to take control and demand that we were offered the education we needed to get into a university. That was balanced out by all the positive things and the great teachers we had—truly dedicated and brilliant educators. It was a rich experience all the way around. It was a much richer experience even than my college years.

After graduating, Michele went to San Francisco State to study biology.

I went to San Francisco State University because that was what we could afford. I was immediately thrown into classes with people of all ages and from all walks of life, not just eighteen-year-old freshmen, and from more economically diverse backgrounds. I had to buckle down and study the material. I tested out of so many classes that I was able to take higher-level classes such as Greek literature and geology. There were some people who didn't appreciate having an overly bright freshman, who got really good grades, in their graduate classes.

After university, I was more involved in my life than my career. I danced in an international folk-dance company. I did a lot of traveling and had a lot of friends from all over the place—more Asians. Even today, while there are a lot more people of color in Brisbane, there still aren't a lot of Black people.

Michele's final reflections:

I felt woven into the fabric of life at Jefferson. When I look through my old yearbooks today, I think, "Wow, you were part of this." Each interaction had a good influence on my life. I feel like our time at Jeff was so incredibly important for helping me to be open-minded and develop a good skill set for dealing with real life. It wasn't all rosy, but it was very real. It gave me a good foundation for moving forward in my life. Jeff was a really amazing experience, the depth of it and its cultural diversity; it was so different from growing up in Brisbane. I feel really sad that in later years many people in Brisbane felt Jeff was too rough for their kids, so they sent them to other schools. A few do still go to Jeff, but I feel like Brisbane kids now need to go to Jeff to get integrated into the real world, more than ever.

The most important thing about my experience at Jefferson High was it gave me the courage to know I could handle myself anywhere in the world– as a cocky college freshman taking graduate-level courses, or when I went to Thailand in 1978, years before it became a popular destination. Because of that I've traveled all over the world, near and far, met and talked with so many people, and have not been intimidated or prevented from living my best life. The very fact that we're talking right now...that probably wouldn't have happened if we had gone to some other high school with some other people.

The love I feel now for what we had is real. I feel it when we have our annual picnics. It's been amazing to go back and see people we haven't seen in so long. To connect with people again is so special.

Marc

(White, class of '69, older sibling of Michele)

* * *

Even though I didn't learn a lot about math at Jeff, I learned a lot about people and really enjoyed the diversity of the environment. That was a whole education in itself—being able to hear other people's points of view and understand the things that impact them.

* * *

Marc was born in San Francisco and grew up in Brisbane, California, where he still lives today. He attended the same elementary school that his mother did, but was bussed over the hill to Jefferson High, like most teens from Brisbane.

Both of my parents also went to Jefferson. Mom came to Brisbane in '36 when they opened Brisbane Elementary School. Dad came when he was in high school. His family left Texas when he was twelve and lived in Visalia for a few years. My mom had a part-time job collecting tickets at the theater, and that's how she met Dad. He'd ride by on his bike, which he had all fixed up. He was a year or two ahead of her at Jeff. They got together again after the war and got married.

Although Marc's family was White, they were conscious of not being as White as other Americans.

210

I was always told not to tell anyone I was Sicilian because it meant I was part African. The Moors [from North Africa] ruled Sicily; it was part of the Mediterranean culture. Italians think of us Sicilians as being Black. I didn't find out until I was a teen that Mom spoke Italian, which was her grandmother's only language. She was called a "dirty little wop" [racial slur for a person of Italian heritage] and other things when she was growing up.

I never knew I was part Native American until I was about forty, either—my father's great-great-grandmother was half Indian, either Choctaw or Cherokee.

Apart from this, Marc's parents didn't talk to him much about race/ethnicity. Although Brisbane was a mostly White, blue-collar town, Marc, nevertheless, made friends with a diverse group.

I can't recall any people of African or Asian descent, but when I was around seven, a Mexican family moved in across the street. I quickly became best friends with one of the boys, but after several days my mom told me I couldn't play with him. She was afraid I might catch a disease! I didn't expect that from her. I had to let the kid know we couldn't be friends anymore, which was really difficult. Within a few years I made friends with two more boys of Mexican descent, but my mom never said anything about either of them. I guess their families lived in nicer houses. I don't know if it was the poverty part that she objected to.

My best friend growing up in Brisbane was Samoan. As a kid I'd go over to his house, where only adults could sit at the table; kids sat on the floor. A few years later I went over and his grandmother let me sit at the table. My friend said, "She must really like you!" I knew her until she died. She had the whole history of the Samoan tribe tattooed on her body—her whole body covered with tattoos that expressed the history of the people. It was a sacred ritual that would happen upon the chief's passing. Her son was supposed to become chief, but he was away in the military, so that's why she ended up getting the tattoos. He never returned to Samoa. After his military service, the family moved to Brisbane. They were good friends with my parents and would have dinners together.

All in all, I thought of my parents as pretty open. Mom was a jazz musician. She played with a lot of African American friends.

Another one of my best friends in school was Japanese, and his father taught me about the internment camps [where Japanese Americans were sent during World War II]. We were missing a very important part

*of history by not being taught about this in history class. I never knew
about them.*

Marc was not particularly aware that Jefferson High had a reputation until he got there.

*Everyone from Lipton Junior High, like me, went to Jefferson High,
but I didn't know much about it. Jeff was an eye-opener. I felt there was
racial tension, but I thought our class was pretty good with mixing it up
and being open. Although there were scuffles, it didn't seem like there
were any more than when I was in elementary school. I had friends of
all ethnicities.*

*As a freshman I was only 5'6" and 103 pounds. I didn't grow until
my junior year. I had hassles with people of all different backgrounds
at one point or another, one or two a year, so I always felt like I had
to be on point—ready for something. One time between classes this
Filipino guy steps out of the bathroom, dressed to the nines. He's got
this cane, bangs it on the floor and says, "Give me all your money." I
kind of laughed and started walking away really fast because I knew he
wouldn't chase me.*

*A friend of mine [Black] came into the gym while we were chang-
ing and cuffed me on the ear. It kind of hurt. We were waiting to go
upstairs, and as soon as the bell rang, I popped him on the head. Everyone freaked. When I got to the top of the stairs there was an African
American kid trying to get at me. My [Black] buddy grabbed me in a
full-nelson and told me not to do anything as it would really start something, so I let it go and walked away.*

*Jeff had a Black marching team. It was very military, and they used
broomsticks as rifles. I could feel the anger of the era—people saying, "We've had enough," and I couldn't blame them. I had African
American and Asian friends. A Filipina friend invited me to her party. I
was the only White person there, but I didn't feel uncomfortable, except
when someone spoke Tagalog and I felt a little left out.*

*One of my good friends was African American. One time he took
me into the inner sanctum—a half-size room between the chemistry
room and another classroom where Black students hung out. It was full
of Black Panther posters, etc. One other Black guy there was not happy
that my friend brought me there, so we left after a few minutes, long
enough to let him know we weren't leaving just because he wanted us
to. In three years at Jeff I'd never known that room existed.*

*I met most of my friends through sports. My Japanese buddy and I
wrestled together and were in the same weight class. In my junior year*

I started playing soccer. A couple of guys took me under their wing and taught me defense and offense. Most of the team was from Mexico, Honduras, or El Salvador. We had some Europeans, one English guy. My Japanese friend and I hung out together. We'd go to parties and race our cars. I never heard anything from him about experiencing racism.

Once, in my junior year, I was in PE with one of the (Black) guys who was considered to be the toughest in the school. We were picking teams for volleyball. He looked at me and said, "You're on the other side," and shoved me. I came back and knocked him, and he fell on his butt. That night at the bus stop, no one would stand near me—word travels fast. Other kids were worried that a car might pull up and some guys might jump out. A few days later I saw this guy in PE. He came up and said, "We gotta talk. Why'd you tell the coach on me?" I said, "What's there to tell? I didn't tell the coach." After that, we were cool. About a year later I went out the back door and there were about five or six African American guys staring at me. I wasn't going to go back in, but I did feel intimidated. All of a sudden, I heard from the back of the group, "My man," the group parted, and that guy came forward. I think he saved my butt that day. There was always that tension.

We had a good group of teachers at Jeff. Some were pretty liberal. It seemed for the most part that everyone was treated fairly and I thought it was a pretty good education at that point. Once I got to the University of San Francisco (USF), I realized my education had been lacking. At Jeff, I cut half of my math classes because we'd be on the same page for days at a time. It left a hole in my math skills.

Marc found USF to be much different from Jeff.

USF was predominantly Caucasian, not the mix that I had experienced in high school. I missed the diversity. I didn't even know it was a Catholic school until I got my acceptance papers. They asked me to fill out a few pages about my religious background. When I got my acceptance, they'd checked me off as "other." It was "Catholic" or "other." They didn't make me take religion classes, but I had to take philosophy instead. I had to work a little harder at USF to make up on the math, but I was able to catch up. I had a hard time with calculus because I didn't have the trigonometry background. I just hadn't gotten that far my senior year.

I started out wanting to be a mechanical engineer, but I had to take computer classes. In the process I got interested in artificial intelligence and started studying psychology and got a degree in that. I worked at Letterman Hospital for a year and a half with kids who'd lost their fathers in Vietnam, but they closed the program.

I lived in San Francisco for about six years and moved back to Brisbane when my wife and I were expecting our first child.

Today, Brisbane is more mixed than it was during Marc's childhood.

It's about fifty percent European descent, fifty percent from other countries. It's a lot more fixed up, more up to code—some of the old houses were boxcars with no foundations. There are many more white-collar families. There used to be three or four stables: now there's only one, with just three or four horses. There used to be cattle, too; they're gone now, replaced by an industrial park. But there's still kind of the same feel, semi-rural. People come here to step out of the mainstream a little, get to know their neighbors.

This year the Brisbane Lions Club couldn't do their annual crab feed because of Covid-19. It draws about 200 people and raises several thousand dollars for the kids' college fund. We did a drive-through at-cost thing, just to have it as a placeholder. It ended up being the most money we ever raised! We have a community that's really giving. I appreciate that about Brisbane—people care.

It's a Brisbane tradition to put stars up on our houses during the holidays. It used to be the chamber of commerce that made them. Today the Lions Club makes them. They're made of wood, which rots and shrinks, so we need new ones periodically, and they're different sizes depending on where they're put. Making them has always been a collaborative effort.

Marc's final reflections:

Even though I didn't learn a lot about math at Jeff, I learned a lot about people and really enjoyed the diversity of the environment. That was a whole education in itself—being able to hear other people's points of view and understand the things that impact them. I found it illuminating, especially during the Black Panther movement and the protests.

Jerry

(Japanese American, class of '72)

* * *

Parents teach their kids in subtle ways, especially about race.... The parents of a lot of the kids at Jefferson kind of had it figured out, and they passed it along to their kids.

* * *

Jerry's parents were both west coast Nisei—Japanese Americans born in the U.S. to immigrant families. Jerry was born in Chicago, the second of two children, and moved to San Francisco at age four, then to Daly City a year later.

Both of Jerry's parents went back to Japan in early adulthood. Jerry's father went back with his brother after high school to work, whereas Jerry's mother's parents decided to move back to Japan when she was sixteen, "to teach the girls more Japanese ways." His mother remained furious about this until the day she died.

My mom was independent, an avid reader who planned to go to college. Being uprooted put all her dreams on hold. She, her parents, and her sister moved to Tokyo—they were there for the duration of the war [WW2]. She saw all the American planes flying over, bombing Tokyo. She said that the bombs rarely hit residential areas, but someone she knew was killed.

215

It was a traumatic time, although possibly less so than if her family had remained in the United States.

My mother's family went back to Japan almost ten years before the war, so they were part of a community by then. I assume they already knew other families because her parents came from there. It doesn't sound as if Japan discriminated against Japanese Americans. They didn't stand out, whereas in the U.S., people could see immediately that they were "different."

After the war, Jerry's mother got permission to return to the U.S. with her father; her mother and sister remained in Japan. The American government wouldn't allow them to return to the west coast but sent them to the midwest with other Japanese Americans who had spent the war either in relocation camps or abroad. That was how Jerry's mother ended up in Chicago—starting over with nothing.

His father's experiences in the war were even more dramatic.

Dad came back from Japan to California in the late 1930s. In 1940 he enlisted in the U.S. Army. When war with Japan broke out in '41, he was honorably discharged into the army reserves, but he was sent to live in an internment camp anyway. His brother, my uncle, had already been drafted before the war started and was stationed at Fort Sam Houston in Texas, Since he was already there, and was not working in any way with weapons, he was not perceived as a threat (like west coast Japanese Americans were), and was allowed to serve in the Army in Texas for the duration of the war. Kicking out Japanese Americans was a west coast thing.

My father was shipped to the Topaz camp in Utah. Camps had desert-like conditions—freezing in winter and baking hot in summer. Families were only separated by canvas walls, and the rooms were divided by clotheslines hung with blankets. Dad never, ever talked about this part of his life. It's the same with most of the third-generation Japanese American kids I've talked to—no one in their families talked about this. I didn't even know about the relocation camps until high school, and I learned about them from my mom, not my dad. There are a few Japanese Americans who were more open than my family.

A lot of Japanese Americans on the west coast worked on farms, and many farmers were sympathetic to them because they were neighbors and friends. But because of the hysteria after Pearl Harbor, very few other people questioned the injustice toward Japanese Americans.

Most Japanese Americans had to either leave their possessions or sell them when they went to the camps. My father gathered all his things and gave them to the Buddhist temple in Berkeley for safekeeping. He and his uncle were able to pick up their belongings again after the war.

Years later, Jerry acquired additional information from a Japanese American friend whose father was also in the Topaz camp.

My friend typed in my dad's name and found the Topaz Times—the Japanese American monthly newspaper. It turns out that my father was the first from Topaz to be re-inducted into the military when the war department decided they were desperate for more men! He went directly into the 442nd, the all-Japanese American regiment. They were sent to fight in Italy, where they were in quite a few of the main battles. They saved a Texas regiment and became the most highly decorated regiment in American history. Many of them were killed because, since they were of Japanese descent, they got all the most dangerous jobs. They were the sacrificial lambs.

When Jerry's father came back from the battlefields of Europe, he also went to Chicago, either because he wasn't allowed to go back to the west coast or because it was too unwelcoming. Some Japanese Americans banded together and bought an apartment complex on the south side of Chicago. Jerry's family lived in that complex until 1958. Slowly, the displaced families started moving back to the west coast.

Jerry's family first moved to the Western Addition [a neighborhood] of San Francisco. In 1959 they bought a house on Los Banos Avenue in Daly City from an Italian family that was moving to the more upscale, all-White area of Westlake. Jerry remembers Los Banos Avenue as more of a melting pot, with families of Irish and Italian descent, and some who were Asian, Hispanic, and Filipino.

However, the "melting pot" didn't melt thoroughly enough to smooth his mother's path to employment.

Around the time I started school, my mom applied for a secretarial job at Bank of America in Daly City. She was very well qualified—she could do shorthand and type, and, of course, she was fluent in English. During her interview, my dad and I waited outside in our Ford station wagon. When she came out my dad asked, "How'd you do?" She replied somberly, "I guess they didn't want me. I could do shorthand, type faster than anyone else, etc. Maybe because I was Japanese I didn't get it." That was my first memory of others not liking us because we were Japanese. When it comes to race it kind of gets you, it really sticks on certain things. It's so subtle sometimes, you don't even realize it happened.

Jerry's first school was Woodrow Wilson Elementary School, which he attended from kindergarten to third grade. It used to go up to sixth grade, but the population grew too fast for the school. Jerry and his classmates were bussed to White, middle- and upper-middle-class Westlake Elementary from fourth to sixth grade.

All of us who got bussed there were minorities. I was an introvert, so it felt very different, a little bit awkward. There were few Asians, so our skin color and facial features stood out. It made me feel a little insecure. I don't remember hearing any racial slurs, but it may be that I didn't notice them. I don't know what the other Asians at the school experienced. The people at Westlake were okay. There was a little bit of snootiness, but I can't remember having problems.

Junior high school was a much more intense experience.

Colma Junior High was intimidating because it brought in so many people from everywhere. I saw the power of the Black cultural movement coming out, which was so different from everything about Japanese culture. That was when I started to really understand that I came from a different culture. My parents were only one generation removed from Japan, and they were very reserved—they were never emotional, they never told me they loved me. So when I went to Colma it was a little scary. Everything and everyone was bigger and louder, even the music at school dances, and I was shy and insecure.

One time I got into a fight with this Black kid. I think he was a year younger than me. We had accidentally bumped each other on the bench at lunch; he grabbed my potato chip bag. Then he "called me down," which meant we were going to fight. We went outside and started fighting. I guess I did okay as I was punching him on the ground. The teachers came towards us, so I got up and went off to another part of the yard. The next day some other Black kids came up to me and asked if I was the one who beat him up. It made me wonder if there was a thing about Asians.

According to Jerry, in high school he fit the mold of the studious Asian person and often ended up being the teacher's pet. He became involved with an all-Japanese church group in San Francisco. That was also when he got more into Japanese culture.

My church group reinforced my being Japanese American and gave me more confidence about being Japanese. My parents had their Japanese friends, but most of them weren't in Daly City.

In high school you start to figure things out. I understood more about Black Pride, more about distinctions of races and nationalities. I actually embraced it; I thought everybody at Jefferson High was pretty cool. There were certain people who I think didn't like Asians, or Japanese specifically. Occasionally I got funny looks from some people. How do you distinguish a jerk who wants to be a bully versus someone whose family looked down on certain races?

Some people clashed, and sometimes it was because of race. I was kind of in between. I got along with a lot of Blacks, Filipinos, etc., but also got along with a lot of Whites. Maybe my experience wasn't as harsh as a lot of other people's. Japanese Americans were more accepted by African Americans because we had both suffered from discrimination and hardship. I felt sort of between the White and Black cultures.

In high school I hung around mostly with people in the band. Every lunch time it was me, along with two White and two Latino friends. We'd jump into my station wagon, and drive either to A&W in Westlake or McDonald's in SSF [South San Francisco]. I got to know my friend Robert's mother pretty well. She had a Mexican restaurant in the upper Mission and was very much into her Mexican culture.

I don't remember any specific racial incidents at Jeff. Maybe I didn't see it; maybe I wasn't around when there were fights. I know it was a lot different from other high schools. I have a Japanese friend who went to Balboa High School (in San Francisco). He told me, "It was ugly. Blacks and Whites were always clashing, always going up against each other. I couldn't wait to get out of there."

One personal incident stands out for Jerry.

We were in U.S. history class with a teacher who played favorites—I was one of them. If another guy talked, she would kick him out, especially one big Hispanic guy. One time she was talking about the internment of the Japanese during the war. She referred to "the Japs." My buddy Robert [Latino] was seated a few rows away. He looked at me and I looked at him. I shrugged. Suddenly Robert cleared his throat loudly and said, "That's kind of a derogatory word." The teacher immediately apologized. I'm sure that was the normal way of saying things where she was raised. My mom told me that some people think that way because they were raised that way. If they had no experiences with other ethnicities, they wouldn't know some things would be offensive.

Jerry remembers distinctly the Brisbane students who were bussed over the hill to Jeff.

I didn't hang around with the Brisbane crowd much. They didn't have any assimilation like most of us did at Colma. Lack of exposure can lead to fear and stereotypes, and that made it more challenging when they got to Jeff.

Jerry has a lot of very positive memories of his time at Jeff and its diversity.

I thought of it as a fun thing. I'd go into the cafeteria and see different groups of people hanging out. We were lucky. Maybe we all got along because economically we were all the same. We were a working-class school. Later, when my kids had events at their high school, half the stands were full of parents. At Jeff, our parents worked all day. My parents never went to any of my high school sports. That was a big eye-opener for me when my kids went to school. I do remember Ken's [Black] father used to show up at high school games to support his sons, who were huge basketball stars.

There was never any tension or anything when I went to any of my friends' houses, and most of them weren't Japanese. A few times I was over at Ken's house. I noticed his mom, but it seemed to her like I was just another kid over at her house. I went to Sue's [White] house and would talk with her mom for a while. You could tell right away whether it was awkward or okay. Visiting told us a lot about how our friends grew up. Ken and Pinky [Black brothers] were real leaders. They had the ability to show the rest of us that we could get along, mix, and be friends with each other.

I was extremely insecure about girls, but otherwise I loved it at Jeff.

In Jerry's adult life he has experienced racism.

My wife [at the time] and I decided to move to Petaluma before our kids were born. We got a realtor who referred us to a broker to get a loan to buy the house. At the broker's office I put my hand out to shake his. Men always look right at each other's eyes. Instead of looking at me, he looked at my [Caucasian] wife. We started talking, what we do for work, etc., and he never once made eye contact with me. We left and

I said, "We're not getting the loan." My wife didn't understand why. I told her that the broker didn't like me and, sure enough, we didn't get the loan. Fortunately, there was no problem in getting a loan with another broker.

I used to drive to work with another plumber who is Black. We'd talk about racism. My friend said, "Yeah, you can tell, you can just feel it. You can feel it when you see the person, their body language, how they talk to you. Is it phony, is it genuine?" The older you get, the more sensitive you are about it.

Jerry's final thoughts:

Because of where I was raised, I was lucky enough to know many cultures—my friends, their parents, their food, lifestyles, etc. We're still all the same, despite these differences.

I think a lot of the minorities who were at Jeff were from families who had been in Daly City for a while. They were comfortable in what they were doing and who they were. They didn't have that rage and anger that some people felt [at other schools] who didn't have a lot more diversity, which led to racism.

Parents teach their kids in subtle ways, especially about race and racism. Sometimes they'll blurt something out. These nuances I understood through the Japanese tradition. You can sense the mood of your parents through what they did, how they acted. The parents of a lot of the kids at Jefferson kind of had it figured out, and they passed it along to their kids.

Sue

(White, class of '72)

* * *

One time, a group of us got a ride to the airport to sell candy. When my dad arrived in his pick-up truck to take me home, he realized that my African American classmate also needed a ride. When my friend got into the truck, my dad stiffened up. He didn't say anything, but his discomfort was so apparent, it was the longest ride from SFO I can remember.

* * *

Sue was born in San Francisco, the third of five children and the oldest girl in an Italian American family that moved to Daly City when she was eighteen months old. Her mother was a second-generation American whose parents were both living in SF during the earthquake of 1906. Her grandfather hauled produce from the SF vegetable market to San Jose every Sunday through Thursday and spent his days off fishing on the delta. Sue's father's parents came from Sicily and his mother died when he was two; his father remarried two years later. In 1950 he died and Sue's father, still in his twenties, took over the family business. Sue believes that his stepmother inherited her husband's money but contributed nothing to the business, making it very hard on her stepson (Sue's father).

Dad's stepmom lived with us for several years due to her failing health. She and my dad always spoke to each other in a Sicilian dialect.

222

Because they were loud and I didn't understand what they were saying,
I assumed they were arguing most of the time.

Sue's childhood was marked by the death of her ten-year-old brother, Charlie, in an accident at home, when Sue was eight. Her elder brother was four years older and her younger brother four years younger.
Their sister, nine years younger than Sue, was born the year after Charlie's death. Sue reflects on that time.

My older brothers would be outside playing and I wasn't allowed
to join them. I have vivid memories of being in the garage, laying on my
stomach on the cold cement floor, peering through the door vent wish-
ing I could play outside. I often felt I didn't have the same privileges as
my brothers because I was a girl.

After my brother's death, I felt I had a duty to be successful, by
getting good grades, to give my parents something positive to hang
on to. Unfortunately, it seemed the only things that caught my mom's
attention were the things I didn't get right. One example is that my
parents expected me to take my younger brother to mass every Sun-
day, from the time I was eight years old. I would sit in the front row
in order to see the altar but felt obligated to control the behavior of
my fidgety five-year-old brother. On one occasion we were fighting
and pinching each other, and the priest disciplined us from the pul-
pit. My mom was terribly embarrassed and criticized me for sitting
in the front row.

After my brother's death, my parents' relationship with my father's
stepmom deteriorated and business challenges mounted. I can only
imagine how difficult it was for my parents to meet the needs of three
children while grieving the loss of their son and dealing with a very dif-
ficult woman in their home.

Like most families in Daly City, Sue's family was working-class,
with their own struggles.

Until my baby sister started kindergarten, my mom was a stay-at-
home mom, but she took small jobs such as babysitting, ironing and typ-
ing to supplement our family's income. When I was a freshman in high
school, she went to work on nights and weekends at a local department
store. I assumed many of the "mom" roles and spent several summer
vacations doing housework, watching my younger siblings, and prepar-
ing meals. It was during this time that my dad left self-employment and
became an entry-level civil servant.

I remember how difficult it was for my dad to accept a job cleaning jail cells and have his wife working outside the home to contribute to our upkeep. He told us that he would take cigarette butts off the floor to smoke during his break because he couldn't afford to buy his own. After much encouragement from me, he reluctantly agreed to apply for food stamps, but was denied based on the amount of his paycheck, which was particularly painful. But he continued taking civil service exams until he qualified for a more "respectable" position with the Public Works Department, where he worked until his death, at age sixty, in 1984.

Sue has few memories from her childhood regarding race.

We lived in an all-White neighborhood. There were lots of Italians, Irish, Germans. Definitely no Black or Asian families, and maybe one Hispanic family. I remember there was a house for sale on our block and overhearing my parents talking with our neighbors in a way that sounded as though they didn't want Black people to move in. I didn't understand, but clearly it was a big deal to them.

I'm ashamed to admit there was a time I was one of the "mean girls" in grade school. In an effort to fit in with the popular girls, I actively participated in bullying a classmate because she had red hair and freckles. In retrospect, I also now realize overt racism was present at Colma Elementary School. Everyone seemed to ridicule a tall [Black] girl with an unusual name.

Sue continues, sharing about the challenges in her family life.

After my brother Charlie died, things at home became increasingly difficult. When my dad came home from work, I would watch him drink several shots while cleaning up in the garage. By the time he came to the dinner table he was usually drunk. In addition, my eldest brother started cutting school and using drugs in his early teens, not long after Charlie died. He often came to dinner stoned. He developed a serious problem; he spent many years in juvenile and adult institutions for drug-related offenses.

Life with a family member who's addicted to drugs or alcohol is unpredictable. I never invited friends to our house because I never knew what to expect at home. I was always on "high alert" at dinner because of my father and my brother. I would behave badly, knowing I would be told to leave the table and go to my room. That's how I avoided potentially unpleasant situations. To this day, I find it challenging to relax and enjoy myself at a dinner table.

As an adolescent from a troubled family, Sue really struggled with her self-esteem.

At Colma, in junior high, I thought the new kids on campus seemed to be smarter and better than me. I didn't feel worthy enough to seek them out as friends until my sophomore year at Jeff. As my confidence grew, I pushed myself to follow my instincts and gravitate toward the "smarter" kids who inspired me to broaden my horizons. I sought people out (and still do to this day) who were more involved in a variety of activities, who valued education, who made better choices than my family, and who were less naïve than me. Surrounding myself with people who seemed more confident and were doing good things helped me to build my confidence. People who seek out challenges encourage me to challenge myself more.

Before I started at Jeff, I felt reluctant about going there because of my perception that the "rough kids" went to Jeff. There was an incident in junior high when my favorite wool scarf was taken by a group of older girls with darker skin, possibly Hispanic. They were very intimidating, and I was frightened about confronting them, but the scarf was a present from my godmother and I wanted it back. I suspect that incident contributed to my concerns about attending Jeff.

When I got to Jeff and was at a rally, I recognized that the tall Black girl with the unusual name who had been picked on at Colma was a cheerleader, standing proudly with a huge warm smile. I was very happy for her. She was in such a different place from when I first saw her. Seeing how well she was doing in the "right environment" probably helped me to feel that Jeff was a safe place for everyone.

I gravitated toward friends who accepted me for being myself and were respectful of one another. There was a shared sense of pride in being from the same school, sort of like, "This is our family." We were unified by our school colors and school spirit. This is how I saw my world at that point. In addition to my Caucasian friends, I had close friends who were Japanese American, Filipina, and Black.

One time, a group of us got a ride to the airport to sell candy. When my dad arrived in his pick-up truck to take me home, he realized that my African American classmate also needed a ride. When my friend got into the truck, my dad stiffened up. He didn't say anything, but his discomfort was so apparent. It was the longest ride from SFO I can remember. I had not expected his reaction to be so strong.

Because my world was very small, I felt insignificant around others who I perceived as being better. This was part of the reason why I gravitated toward people who seemed smarter than me. Other kids from school would get together after school or on the weekends, but I was babysitting my little sister and taking care of the house while my mother worked. I had a definite sense that all my friends came from better families than I did.

Early in my sophomore year, I remember thinking, "I have to get out of here [home]." Realizing that I was elibigle to apply for a work permit at age fifteen-and-a-half, I jumped on the opportunity, and the very next day was offered a postion at Jefferson Adult School. I worked there for the next three years, every Monday through Thursday between six and ten p.m.

Cecilia, the Latina receptionist I worked for, started driving me home after work because I didn't want my dad picking me up. We'd sit chatting in her little Volkswagen bug in front of the house, so we got to know each other well. Mr. Redmond, the adult school principal, would come into the office several times a week, and I'd hear him and Cecilia talk about politics and other things, normal adult conversations that I'd never been exposed to in my family. Mr. Tierney, one of Jeff's daytime teachers, was also around during night school and I got to know him better. I was earning money and learning new skills while observing healthy banter and stimulating conversation among adult educators. That got me through to graduation.

After graduating from Jeff, Sue attended San Jose State University (SJSU)—about an hour away from home, because, more than anything, it provided an opportunity for her to escape.

SJSU was huge, but I felt comfortable there. It felt similar to Jeff because it was ethnically and racially diverse. The resident advisor in my co-ed dorm was a young Black man who was supportive and willing to provide "big-brotherly" advice to this naïve young freshman.

I had done well academically at Jeff—most subjects came easily to me, and I could sweet-talk my way into turning papers in late because I had a part-time job—but college was a different story. I was totally unprepared for the academic work, but at least I was finally out of the house. I buckled down and got through.

After college, I lived in San Francisco until getting married in 1980, when I moved to Oakland and started my thirty-year career with Alameda County. I worked in a variety of racially diverse environments. I didn't think about race until, as a manager, I was accused of treating an employee unfairly based on race. It was a deeply troubling experience, but I was grateful for the support I received from our executive

*officer and HR director, both Black, based on my reputation and writ-
ten documentation.*

Sue's final reflections:

*The quality of my time at Jeff improved significantly after getting
the clerical job with the adult school. It provided a lifeline by rescuing
me from the nightly chaos at home and giving me exposure to positive
adult role models: Cecilia, the principal, the teachers. I truly believe
their influence had a direct impact on my self-confidence, which inspired me to engage in extracurricular activities (cheerleading, etc.),
apply to college, and surround myself with a diverse and talented circle
of friends.*

Jaime

(Latino, class of '71)

* * *

I saw a former math teacher from Jeff who asked me what I was doing. I told her I was a guidance counselor at James Logan High School and she said, "I would never have thought that of you." She was proud of me and congratulated me.

* * *

Jaime was born in San Francisco and is of Puerto Rican descent on both sides (his mother was born in Puerto Rico, his father in the U.S.). The family lived on Potrero Hill, San Francisco, until he was thirteen, then in the Hunters Point Projects for a year, before moving to Daly City—"out in the country." They bought a house near Colma Junior High School, down the street from Jaime's cousin.

It was different coming from SF, where my schools had predominantly Black students and people of color. Whites were the minority, a few first-generation Russians, and Italians. A lot of my friends were mixed, Blacks and Latinos. Colma was a little Whiter. I was shy and kept to myself. I felt comfortable that no one caused me any problems because my cousins were there looking out for me. My first real friend was also Latino.

From kindergarten to seventh grade, when Jaime was still in San Francisco, he remembers some people, even family members, talking about "those Black guys."

It was the late sixties during the civil rights movement. There was lots of stuff on the news, lots going on in San Francisco. Even some Latinos, like us, said that Black people were doing "bad stuff," but I had Black friends and I knew they weren't doing anything bad. When other people would say things about Black people, I'd point out that they were talking about my friends.

What I heard in the neighborhood came mostly from first-generation adults. There are plenty of Black Puerto Ricans, but to my family, they didn't count as Black—they were Puerto Ricans, not the same as African Americans.

Having a light complexion and blue eyes, Jaime could "pass", and he blended in with Whites—but he was 100% Latino and proud of it.

Grandma lived next door and she didn't speak English. We listened to salsa music, Puerto Rican music. My mother would talk about how she grew up very Latina on her maternal side, with a lot of cultural pride; women should take care of their men and we should all marry Latinos, etc. On my paternal side, my grandfather was the president of Club Puertorriqueño de San Francisco.

It was mostly my father's side of the family that was racist toward Blacks. I was never taught that Black people were bad, just to be careful around them. All my friends had my back. Black friends knew I was Latino because they'd hear me speaking Spanish at home. Even though I'm light-complected, I'm actually twenty-two percent Black, which I found out from DNA testing a few years ago.

Jaime was aware of racism around him but never felt it directly affected him in school.

All the way back in kindergarten I had a crush on a White girl. Most of my crushes over the years were on White girls. To me, race didn't matter; if you're a good person, I like you.

At Jeff I had a lot of friends from the soccer team, mostly Latinos and Filipinos, even though I didn't play soccer. I also played football and wrestled and had many friends from there. Some of my friends spoke Spanish. My Filipino friends and I were similar in thought—I felt we could be cousins in terms of our cultures, due to the Spanish influence in the Philippines. We'd go to each other's houses and our mothers would feed everybody. I didn't hang out with the White guys on the football team because some of them had attitude. Some of them used the word "chachas" (a racial insult) about the soccer team, saying they were going to take over the football field. They'd say this freely around me because I was light-complected, so they didn't realize I was Latino. Chinto, Willie, Jessie (all Latino), and I were accepted because we were on the football team. The comments didn't bother me because they weren't directed toward me, but they were directed toward my friends.

As a sophomore I remember two juniors going around together, a Black girl and a White guy. They were making out in a car, holding hands, etc., but no one said anything. It was normal. We had a lot of progressive teachers, but there were also individuals who had their thing [racism]. I think it was more about stereotypes than overt racism. I definitely don't remember any teacher saying anything specific.

Jaime joined the Wilderness Program at Jefferson and ended up becoming a counselor in a summer program.

During the summers I was a counselor-in-training (CIT) at Bearskin Meadows, a camp for children and youth with diabetes. Jeff sent the largest number of CITs—about eight of us—because of our Wilderness Program (WP), which was a national pilot program for outdoor education. The reason I was in the WP was because it was alternative education and I had been identified—wrongly—as an at-risk kid, though I had no idea about this at the time. The kids in the group were Black and Brown, urban kids who were targeted by the Early Secondary Education Act (ESEA) under President Johnson.

I didn't know I had been in a special at-risk program until I was working in a high school years later. I'd been hired as a counselor, and I was meeting with other counselors. Someone mentioned the ESEA program, and that was me—I'd been in it. I shouldn't have been there. I wasn't at risk. My parents both worked; we definitely weren't poor. I played sports. I didn't get into trouble. But my family name is Huertas, so.... I think this was about stereotyping or even tracking. Institutional racism.

"Tracking" wasn't entirely benign; it meant that Jaime was steered away from academic classes. In order to continue his education after high school, he had to start at junior college. So it was that Jaime went to Skyline College, where he made the wrestling team—and felt judged by his color for the first time.

I met a White girl, Tammi, and used to visit her at home, proudly wearing my letterman jacket. We went out a few times. I even took her to a Puerto Rican dance. One day me and a buddy, Tony, were in her neighborhood. We walked up to Tammi's door with our leather jackets on. Her father answered the door and saw Tony's darker skin and black hair, and he told us that Tammi wasn't home. I didn't hear from her for three days, so I drove over to see her. It turned out that after Tony and I were there, her father asked her what I was doing with a Brown guy. He told her, "Don't bring him around here anymore. Those people live differently than we do. If he comes back, I'll call the police." It wasn't enough that I was a college kid and a lettered athlete. I was a Latino who hung out with a Brown guy. That was the first time I was judged by race/ethnicity, not by who I was, and it made me angry. For twenty years afterward, I only dated Brown women and I refused to date White women.

Skyline was mixed, including a few Latinos, but there were a lot more Whites than at Jeff. I learned about the MEChA club (Movimiento Estudiantil Chicano de Aztlan), founded in 1967 at the University of California, Santa Barbara and still going strong. It was a very political group, and the first Latino club that I ever joined. We did Cinco de Mayo activities (thirty of us in the club).

I had an injury so I couldn't wrestle for a year. The coach from San Francisco State wanted me to transfer there, but I didn't want to because it was too close to home. The head coach for Cal State–Hayward wrestling was married to Mrs. Meekins [a former Black teacher at Jeff]. He told me that if I ever wanted to wrestle on a college team, reach out to him, so I did. I ended up transferring to Hayward, living with a cousin in Milpitas. A whole new life started. I competed and got my two degrees, including a Master of Education.

At Cal State, most of the other students were White, but there were a few Latinos from Bakersfield. A lot of my friends were La Raza [a pan-Latino movement]. We were in ethnic studies and hung out together.

I felt real passion about my race and the inequities that existed. I had to integrate this into all areas of my life. I was competing in wrestling and I was a kinesiology major. Other jocks would say it wasn't cool to bring politics into the sports arena, that we should leave all that out of it.

At La Raza I introduced myself as Jim and they responded, "Hi, Jaime!" which is the Spanish for Jim or Jimmy. All through college I was called Jaime and eventually I adopted it. But my family and everybody I grew up with still calls me Jim or Jimmy.

In 1975 the Cal State student paper interviewed me about racism and I said, "Yeah, it still exists." I got hassled for that. Even though Latinos were accepted in the athletics building where most of the athletes were White, they didn't want trouble in the other parts of the school.

Jaime's life took a totally unexpected turn that brought him a completely new lifelong passion.

One of my friends, who was Chicano, joined a Mexican dance company in Oakland with his girlfriend at Chabot College. They had a gig at Paramount Theatre in Oakland in '76 and he gave me a free ticket. The theater was beautiful—Art Deco [from the 1930s]. I'd seen dance on the street and at outdoor festivals, but I wasn't impressed until I saw it on stage with lights, costumes, live music, and the ambience of a theatre.

That show made a huge impression on me. While I didn't grow up with Mexican music, when I saw it on the stage, I thought it was beautiful! A few days later I met the director, an old-school Mexicano. I had a big afro and a goatee. The director said, "Who's this hippie cholo coming in?" But I told him I wanted to join, and he welcomed me. I'm a natural dancer. A wrestling coach from San Francisco State once told me that wrestlers make the best dancers because we have great balance. I guess he was right.

From 1976 all the way to summer, 2020, I was involved in the group. We performed many times at the Ethnic Dance Festival at the Palace of Fine Arts in SF, with high-profile people in attendance. I danced with them for almost fifty years—folklorico (traditional) and Aztec dance. In 1990 I founded my own dance troupe at James Logan High School which is still going strong. I also performed with Luiz Valdez Teatro Campesino (founded sixty years ago). When Dolores Huerta and Cesar Chavez were trying to organize farm workers, they went to the fields and presented skits to show people the benefits of being in a union. This evolved into Teatro Campesino. Valdez also produced "La Bamba" and "Zoot Suit."

Dance has been my passion. We've toured Mexico and the U.S. In fact, I've been to Mexico more times than to Puerto Rico! This year I was supposed to go to the International Dance Festival in Beijing, but it was cancelled because of Covid-19. We're supposed to dance at Carnegie Hall in 2023.

Some years after graduating from Jeff, Jaime went to a Hall of Fame banquet for athletes.

I saw a former math teacher from Jeff who asked me what I was do-ing. I told her I was a guidance counselor at James Logan High School and she said, "I would never have thought that of you." She was proud of me and congratulated me. I wasn't sure how to take it and was think-ing about it when I left. I think she thought that this Latino kid in a gen-eral math class wouldn't be doing something that required college. A similar thing happened six years later when I ran into a former counsel-or from Jeff. She also said, "I never thought you'd be doing something like that." They thought because I was Latino and not in the academic classes, I wouldn't go to college. I wasn't brilliant in high school, just a quiet, shy jock, so it was easy for teachers and counselors to assume I would go into some field that didn't require a degree.

Jaime's final reflections:

Jefferson was incredible. It was multicultural, and I made a lot of great friends.

Teresa

(White, class of '72, Speedway High School, Speedway, Indiana)

* * *

That was a culture shock [moving to the Midwest]. I remember my first day at Speedway High. I walked into my class and I was almost immediately aware that there were no people of color.

* * *

Teresa was born in San Francisco and lived in Daly City, very close to Jefferson High School. She went to Woodrow Wilson from kindergarten through fourth grade, and to Colma for the rest of elementary and junior high school.

Our section of Woodrow Street, one block from Jeff, was all Caucasian for many years. That's who you hung out with, the people on the block. Margie [Latina] lived one street down and we became friends. My group of friends didn't seem to have any problems with race. I had another friend who was Japanese American.

My mom was very active in the PTA and held every position in it. At Woodrow Wilson, the PTA had international night. My older sister and I would sing Italian songs and wear Italian dresses. I remember long tables with traditional foods from a variety of countries. I was drawn to Filipino food.

Teresa says she never gave much thought to race or ethnicity in her early years.

234

I don't think there was ever much talk about nationality in my household other than being Italian. Dad was busy working, building engines for race cars. He wasn't a very involved father. Mom had five kids in the house, cooking, cleaning, etc.

When I was still at Woodrow Wilson, my older sister was at Colma, and my brothers Mark and Charles were at Jeff. My brother Charles got jumped by a couple of Black guys outside the War Memorial. I don't know why, maybe he said something smart. Mark also got jumped for money in the boys' bathroom at Jeff by a couple of Black guys. As a result, my dad put them in a martial arts program. At Colma, my sister had had a couple of fights in the hallway with girls of color, not just Black. My dad's solution was to put a brick in her purse.

Family life was stressful.

When I was eleven, my oldest brother Charles, who was eighteen, got his girlfriend pregnant, and they lived with us, so there was a lot of stress at home. While Dad was back in Indy (Indianapolis), building race car engines, my mom was holding down the fort. He used to go back just for the month of May, but when I was in seventh grade Dad joined the race team in Indy. It was my father's engine in the car Al Unser was driving when he won his first Indy 500. Dad "won" another Indy 500 and lots of other races, giving him recognition in the racing industry. He became the "engine man," and when my mother got sick, he wasn't around.

I have a hard time remembering that period. There's nothing else significant other than our music instructor, who I didn't think was very good, until I got into seventh grade. That stuck in my mind because we changed classes every hour. I was a hall monitor.

Tragedy struck at the end of Teresa's time at Colma.

When I was in eighth grade, in '68, my mom died. If she'd had better medical care and made a lifestyle change—her eating habits, stress level, etc.—she could probably have lived a long life. From my young perspective, my dad was not an advocate for her. My mom's best friend wanted to help out, but my father didn't want her around.

I think I kind of checked out of life for quite some time.

During this time of mourning, Teresa moved on to high school at Jefferson.

After I lost my mom, I kind of walked around in a fog. When I got to Jeff, I do remember sitting in the office and two Black girls came up to me and asked if I was related to my older sister. They said, "She's a bitch, but we've been watching you, and you're okay." It didn't dawn on me that it was racially motivated. It's likely it was because my sister was very popular, which also meant that some people didn't like her.

I was popular enough. It doesn't hurt to have older brothers and sisters, and that probably helped me get chosen to be a cheerleader, but that can be a burden, too—the whole coming-of-age thing, coming out from behind the shadow of the older ones.

I had crushes on a Filipino classmate and other guys of color. I never gave it much thought that one person was Latino or Filipino, until my dad pointed it out. He had friends of other races, but they didn't come home with him. The racing industry was predominantly Caucasian.

I remember two specific times when my father said something like, "Don't you know any White boys or Italian boys?" I said, "No, because Italian boys are spoiled." That was how it was in my family. It always seemed like the women did everything around the house and the men didn't do anything. All my crushes were on guys who weren't White, but none were reciprocated. While I noticed a person's looks, it was about whether I liked the person, not about race. I was attracted to other races, and sometimes White guys. But not Italian guys.

I've never liked the n-word, and I don't think my mother ever used it or labeled people, but my father was another story. One time I went to Indiana with my step-mom, the summer before we moved there. During that trip, I learned about the White River, which ran behind the shop where my father worked. My dad said, "That's the river where all the [n-words] fish." I always wondered where that came from: what happened to make him label people like that? When Dad was growing up during World War II and Japanese Americans were being put in camps, his mother was upset because she had a lot of friends of Japanese descent. How did my father get to a point where he would single out a culture or group of people?

Losing her mother at such a young age was extremely difficult for Teresa. To make matters worse, her father remarried the woman who had been his first wife—only four months after Teresa's mother's death.

My stepmother arrived with a chip on her shoulder. She hated my mom. I think she felt Mom was responsible for her divorce. Everyone felt she was harder on me than on the other kids because I looked so much like my mom. She was very cruel to me.

In the middle of Teresa's sophomore year at Jeff, the family suddenly moved halfway across the country to a small town, Speedway, on the outskirts of Indianapolis, population around 14,500. They moved to be closer to Teresa's father's work.

Nobody consulted me; that wasn't how things were done in my family. You did what you were told without questioning. Maybe my father and stepmom didn't trust my older siblings enough to leave me and my younger sister with them. I don't know if they even considered asking if we could stay with family friends.

The move was really traumatic—socially, it was heartbreaking. I had just started to feel more grounded again. I had a lot of friends at Jeff, and I knew every inch of the campus because I'd lived so close to it all my life. I felt so secure when I got to Jeff, after being at Colma. I felt like I belonged.

I loved being a cheerleader, and I lost that. I was not allowed to perform at one final assembly since I was about to move away, so an alternate performed in my uniform. I resented this long into my adult life. It could have been my farewell performance.

Moving to the Midwest was a culture shock. The region was about three years behind the West in all things—dances, etc. I remember my first day at Speedway High. We lived just on the outskirts, so my parents had to pay for me to go to school there.

For my first day I wore this cute purple mini-dress and teased my black hair. I walked into class and was almost immediately aware that there were no people of color. It was a strange experience to see so many White faces in one place. Likewise, they were under the impression that everybody from California had blonde hair and blue eyes.

If Speedway High had been designed to make Teresa unhappy, it could not have been any more effective. So much about it was a stark contrast to Jefferson.

The principal and my stepmom took all my extracurricular activities away. My stepmom may have thought it was best for me to focus on academics, but it felt more like punishment. Instead of PE, they put me in study hall. I never got to swim in the beautiful swimming pool with the big high dive.

You didn't go home for lunch; we had assigned seats in the cafeteria. There were very strict clothing rules. You weren't allowed to wear pants unless it was a pants suit. You walked the halls quietly in an orderly manner. Every teacher stood outside their door. Girlfriends and boyfriends weren't allowed to hold hands.

I hated it. My whole life had been turned upside down. I remember writing a paper about the "welcome wagon." I wrote about how phony everyone was, venting my feelings. I never got the paper back! I also wondered why no one talked with me. I was so unhappy. "Friends" turned over every semester, and I never felt close to anyone. Band was my outlet, the only thing my stepmom let me keep.

The band room was the only way I'd get out of going to study hall every day. I had to start at third chair, third clarinet and challenged my way up to third chair, first clarinet. At Jeff, I was sitting first chair, second clarinet, which was pretty good for a sophomore. The first three of us would go to state contests and do well at them.

There were no families of color at Speedway until my junior year, when a Black family moved in and their son started at school, a freshman or sophomore. It created a social stir. Everyone wanted to be his friend. After the phony welcome wagon I felt sorry for him, as I didn't know if everyone was being phony with him or not. I don't know where he lived.

People could be real snobs. They had sororities and social clubs in school. The only reason I was invited was because of my father's connection to racing. I knew that the Sigma Taus were upper-class elitists. From my perspective, they did next to nothing other than being a social club. The Phi Omega Gamma at least did charity work every year, which I liked. We would go to orphanages, bring cookies, clothing, and hang out with the kids. I wanted to be associated with a service club. I had a pretty good time, not that I'm close with anyone from there now.

I always felt like the outsider looking in. When we stepped on the plane to fly back to Indy from visiting in CA, I fantasized about not getting on the flight. Academically, Speedway was better, but I didn't want to be there. For my algebra class at Jeff, the teacher would always let me out of class to practice clarinet. I didn't know anything, but still got a B+ in the class. I struggled academically at Speedway. I'm not sure if it was because I resented being there or I was just not smart.

At an assembly near graduation, they had a couple of popular people from the class open up a sort of yearbook. The entire thing was a look back at their lives from kindergarten through graduation. They read out all these fun memories, and I realized I had nothing to show for my time there. I actually had more than two years in band, but it wasn't in the book. I tried to get the yearbook changed to show my time in band. I sat in the audience, unsure if I was going to pass my government class and graduate.

My life was absolutely sad. My stepmom hated me. I got caught with some weed, and after that the only extracurricular activities I had were the sorority and band activities; everything else was associated with racing. My stepmom picked us [Teresa and her younger sister] up from school, took us to the race shop [where Teresa's father worked], and we'd occasionally clean race cars, watch old race films, do homework, or just hang out. I would have done anything to run back to Daly City and get my life back.

Speedway was so much like a box. I don't remember anything related to racism. Everything was very protected and scripted. On the other side of town, there was a racially mixed school with a killer band that had gone to Europe to perform. I don't remember any kind of tension at football or basketball games.

At Jeff, it seemed to me that there were more rivalry tensions than racial tensions. When they built Serramonte [high school], kids were ripped from Jeff to go to Serramonte. It seemed to me that Jeff's rivalry was more with Westmoor.

Having survived Speedway, Teresa belatedly got her wish to move back West -- to Torrance in Southern California, too late for her ruined adolescence.

As quickly as my parents decided to pull us out of Daly City and move to Indy, the racing team decided just as quickly to move to Torrance. It was all White, but I was thrilled because it was closer to what I still considered home. I went to junior college because my stepmother didn't think I was bright enough for a four-year college. I would have liked to study dance and be a PE teacher, but I was sent to do a secretarial course. Life was still all about my father and racing. One day he came home for lunch and said he was retiring. We almost moved to Texas, but returned to northern California instead, to the house on Woodrow Street.

In the early eighties I worked in Silicon Valley, which was a melting pot that only wanted the brightest employees. Sexism really existed there and, as a woman who wasn't an engineer and didn't have a degree, my prospects were limited, although it seemed that some women could advance by sleeping with the right people. There were several African Americans, East Asians, Latinos, etc.

In the nineties I was visiting a friend in Idaho. We were driving around and she commented, "This is Aryan country." I was shocked that people like that really existed. I shouldn't have been surprised, after Indiana.

For a while Teresa and her husband, Randal, lived with a Black couple. Teresa had worked with Rich and needed a place to live after coming back from a cross-country motorcycle trip for which they had put all their things into storage.

I needed to have income before we could get a place of our own. Rich and his partner also needed to share. Rich and I had a really close relationship, and Randal and Rich hit it off—Rich rode a motorcycle, too. We all lived together. It was a great relationship. Randal and Rich painted their motorcycles together. When Rich's family visited, Randal and I had to hide because they would be upset. It was the same when my family visited. It didn't matter to us, but we knew it wouldn't be okay with our families. When our landlord found out we were all living together, she made us all leave. My guess is it was because of race. We stayed friends, though.

Rich wanted to introduce us to Black biker culture in Oakland. He coached Randal on how to behave when we walked into one of their events. It was always after hours, the building windows were all boarded up, there was a lot of graffiti. Rich told Randal, "When you walk in, you have to grab your balls, you never uncover your drink," etc. I'm thinking, "Do we really want to do this?" Randal's attitude was that we'd experience it and survive. We hadn't spent much time around bikers except to go on a few picnics when we were on our big road trip. I was always concerned any time we got around the "one-percenters," the ones who ride to live. They're usually the gang type, like Hell's Angels. I was attracted to the movie and TV version of the mystique surrounding it. As a young, impressionable girl, it was very appealing—the tattoos, the toughness—not knowing much about the lifestyle.

We rode over to Oakland and walked into this club. Randal did as he was told and plopped me down at this one table. Absolutely no one else there was White. Everyone was nice—rather charming, in fact. It was anything but scary. I had the best time...dancing, etc.!

Once I had a conversation with a friend about White privilege. I know I have it. My friend grew up in Daly City with an alcoholic father. She felt that because her mother had a difficult time providing for her and her siblings, they were often discriminated against because they were poor. I asked her, "When was the last time you worried about your son getting shot at or pulled over because he's White?"

Teresa's final reflections:

I loved my time at Jeff and I mourned the loss of my life there. I felt like I was just coming into my own. My older sister was gone. It was my turn to make my own mark at the school. In my memory, there were no bad times. Other than not being able to attract the attention of the guys I had crushes on, it was perfect. I felt a strong connection to Jeff. I still feel that loss now.

I don't know if I'm better off now because I left. Nearly ninety-nine percent of students at Speedway went on to four-year universities, but I wasn't one of them. I've often wondered what I would have done differently if I'd had all four years at Jeff.

Growing up and going to school in Daly City prepared me to interact with a variety of worlds, so I was more accepting. Speedway seemed so closed in, so limited. In Daly City, we walked off campus, we protested against the Vietnam War. I felt more empowered and more alive. There was so much more to do than just the social club, the yearbook and sports.

As an adult, I always hoped and wanted to believe that America had come farther than we have as a society. There is so much more diverse representation in the media—different races, mixed races, genders, people with disabilities, etc. I hoped that the U.S. was more open and accepting, and I'm appalled and embarrassed that there are so many Caucasians who behave the way they have in recent years.

John

(White/Japanese American, class of '73)

* * *

Jeff was racially inclusive. I felt that was the norm and that was important to me.

* * *

John's family background is mixed: his mother was Japanese, and his father's side was English, Irish, Scottish, German, and Seminole Indian. They came to North America from England twenty years after the Pilgrims, on the ship with the original settlers, Smiths, Joneses, and Worleys. At first they settled in the Carolinas, then moved south and west—to Florida, Alabama, Texas, and finally to California.

John was born in San Francisco in the Tenderloin district and lived there until he was four. After his sister Joy was born, the family moved to the Geneva Avenue area of the city, and, eventually, to Daly City.

I remember walking into the new house and seeing a piano for the first time. I got excited because I thought I'd be able to play it. But when we moved in, the piano was gone.

Music was very important to John from childhood and eventually became his career. Early in his professional days, he played in the pit

242

orchestra for a rehearsal of "Hello Dolly" in San Jose, CA. The main actress was Jo Anne Worley from *Laugh-in* [a TV comedy show during the sixties and seventies]. John mentioned her to his father, who said, "Make sure you say hi. She's one of our third cousins." During a break he introduced himself and told her they were related. She said, "Really? Tell me some of your background." She had researched some of her ancestry and it matched John's family story.

John's father was a merchant seaman who sailed to Japan, where he met John's mother, Hana.

My father was looking for a wife, someone who could be a good family person, raise kids, etc. He met my mother in a restaurant in Yokahama where she was working. My dad was there on a date with another woman. Despite the language barrier (Dad didn't speak Japanese and my mother spoke very little English), they must have shared a vibe, because he went back later to meet her. They kept in touch somehow and, soon, she would meet him in different ports around Japan when his ship came back. Eventually, they got married in Japan and came to San Francisco in 1950.

Years later, when my mother passed away, my sister, Joy, and brother, Richard, took some of her ashes to the Kyoto prefecture in Japan to put in her family cemetery. Two years later, I got an opportunity to play some gigs in Kyoto, Osaka, and Tokyo. I went to my mom's hometown, Yosano, and played music for her and my family who were laid to rest there. In that graveyard were fifteen generations of our family. It was very moving to play music for her, along with all those generations of my ancestors.

I walked through her neighborhood, saw the school she attended, and visited the house where she was born and grew up. I met my cousins and my eighty-year-old aunt. Through them I got a glimpse of what it was like to grow up Japanese. My mother used to tell me stories about Japan. One was about a bay and a land bridge in Amanohashidate that surfaced after an earthquake. You see pictures of people/tourists there with their backs turned to the bay, bent over and looking between their legs. When you do that, the mountains look like a giant winged dragon. It was so gratifying to see the story come to life, as well as meet my Asian family.

My mother learned English from my father. When she came to San Francisco, she made friends with some Japanese people here. The first two years of my life I spoke only Japanese. I can still recognize and understand a little, especially the way they put together their sentences and their inflections.

John's mother made him very aware of his ancestry.

From the time I was very small I knew I was Japanese from being with my mom and hearing the language. She read Japanese books to me and told me stories and fairy tales. When I was around five, my dad's father and brothers moved to San Francisco. They would come over the house and play poker all night. They'd smoke cigarettes, drink, and the whole house would stink. I never really identified with my Caucasian side, especially listening to the way they talked about people of color.

I remember when I was playing with a couple of White friends and we were noticed by a gang of older Caucasian boys, eight to ten years old. They saw me and started calling us names—I was the only Asian boy there. We ran, but they chased us and backed us up the stairs in front of my house. They were standing there with homemade spears, calling us names, and threatening to kick our butts. One of my friends had a rock in his pocket. He threw it and it hit the head of the leader, cutting his forehead. He bled badly so they left to take care of his wound. Thank goodness we never saw them again.

After that incident, I became aware of being singled out and called Chink, Jap, etc.

John began his long musical career at Jefferson Elementary School.

I first took trumpet lessons from Mr. Snyder in fifth grade. It wasn't easy, and it made me cough at first—an excuse not to practice—but I sure enjoyed it. Before moving back to Daly City I played drums in fourth grade band in Rohnert Park, where we lived for a little over a year. I used to set up my dad's MJB coffee cans with the plastic lids and beat on them with my mother's chopsticks. One day I saw a picture of Louis Armstrong [famous Black trumpet player] on the back of a book called Treasury for Young Readers that my parents ordered for us kids. I read the story about Louis Armstrong, and it blew me away. His message was that he could go anywhere in the world and communicate with people even though they didn't speak each other's language. Music is a universal language that is understood by listening and feeling it in your heart and soul. I still have that book to this day in my teaching studio and I show it to all my students. I tell them the story in the book is the reason I became a musician.

At Jefferson Elementary ["Little Jeff"] I had my first African American teacher, Mrs. Gilton, in sixth grade. I remember her taking our class to see the opera Rigoletto. Little Jeff was very mixed. I didn't feel a lot of racial pressure there. In fifth grade I had my first girlfriend for the whole year. One of her parents was from Bolivia, another mixed-race family like mine.

John doesn't remember much about junior high school. What he does remember is related to music.

When I got to Colma Junior High, I was the worst trumpet player in the band. I was so bad, the band director decided to put me on baritone horn. It was a big stinky-ass instrument, but I put up with it for a whole year. It really bummed me out because I liked the trumpet so much better. In eighth grade the teacher asked if I wanted to play baritone again and I said, "Either I play trumpet, or I'll quit." She replied, "If you want to play trumpet, you're going to have to practice." That was the beginning of taking control of my trumpet playing and fulfilling the dream of being able to communicate through music.

At Jefferson High, John started hanging out with musicians.

Mr. Larson, our band director, told us that the San Francisco Fireman's Honor Band was holding auditions at Mission High School in San Francisco. The honor band included kids from SF and all the way down the peninsula to San Mateo. Mr. Larson said everyone should audition because playing in that band was a great honor and you might get free music lessons. I auditioned and got in—first chair second trumpet. I not only received free trumpet lessons, but I wound up playing with some very talented young musicians.

In my freshman year at Jeff I made friends with a junior who also played trumpet, Johnny Serrano, Jr. He was a fine player who got a lot of attention, which he deserved. We all stood in his shadow. In our school jazz band, he could improvise better than everyone, play the drums, and knew more about jazz than anyone I'd ever met. He had learned everything from his dad, John, Sr., who was a professional musician in San Francisco, and his trumpet teacher, Johnny Coppola.

I started taking lessons from Johnny Coppola when I was fourteen. He taught in his apartment, across the street from University of San Francisco, and was called the "grandfather" of the Bay Area's trumpet players, teachers, and students. Back then, my parents couldn't afford to pay for my lessons. We rented my trumpet by the month and to pay for my lessons, I got a job at a music store downtown as an apprentice brass repairman, but eventually I got laid off. I told Mr. Coppola I had lost my job and would have to stop taking lessons. He said, "You just keep coming. When you finish your lesson, you can take out my garbage, sweep my porch, and go home and practice. And, if you do what I tell you, I'll make you a professional musician by the time you're sixteen." I took this to heart, worked hard, and played my first gig at fifteen.

Johnny Serrano had been gigging for a while and was in a soul/ rock band called Far East Coalition [FEC]. He took me under his wing and helped me to get into FEC. My very first gig was at the Kabuki Theater in Japantown, SF. The walls and curtains were covered in red velvet. It was very classy, but my first thought was, "I've never seen so many beautiful Asian girls in my life." At age fifteen, that was the start of my professional career, and my first solo in front of a live audience— the opening trumpet solo of Tower of Power's big hit, "You're Still a Young Man."

One episode at Jeff that really changed me as a person came from Bruce Williamson, my freshman English teacher. The first day of his class, we were sitting in rows and the first thing he said was, "You've been learning how to read and write for the past eight years. I'm going to teach you how to communicate." We put all the chairs in a circle so we could see each other and he had us talk about our experiences, about our racial backgrounds, gender, etc. I'll never forget it. Instead of looking at people and thinking of the various stereotypes, I saw them each as a person. I remember him saying to someone, "John over there, he's Asian. What do you think about that? What are the stereotypes?" The person would say them, and then he'd ask, "Does John act like that?" "No." "See, you can't really put those stereotypes on people because everyone is an individual. The sooner you put those aside and see who they are, the sooner you will become friends. The same with stereotypes about women and men. When you learn to look past stereotypes and see who they are inside, you learn how to communicate." There was a girl I became friends with after that class (a White girl of German origin) and because of what I learned in that class, we're still friends to this day.

John remembers some uncomfortable experiences he had at Jeff.

One day I was in the cafeteria and had to go upstairs for something. At the top of the stairs, there were two big, tall African American girls standing in my way, and they wouldn't let me pass. I could feel the hostility coming from them. One of them finally said, "Are you Anna Worley's brother?" I said, "Yeah." She turned to the other girl and said, "Oh, he's cool." They stepped aside and let me pass. It was scary, but afterwards it was funnier than hell that one of my sister's friendships could save my ass.

I left high school a semester early to pursue my dream of becoming a musician. I had plenty of credits, so it wasn't a problem to leave high school behind.

John attended the College of San Mateo, where he met his mentor, the director of the college jazz band, Fred Berry.

Fred Berry is an African American trumpet player who played many of the top gigs in town for the last five decades. Now 82 years young, and still sharp as a tack, it was the start of a friendship that continues to this day. Fred taught me many valuable lessons about life and music, on and off the bandstand, and through him, I met and got to play with many incredible and well-known musicians.

In 1977 I got a job at Marriott's Great America in the "Broadway" show pit orchestra. I met so many talented young musicians there. One of them was a kid named Louis Fasman. I heard him play the first day and was amazed by his technique and range. I walked up to him and said, "Man, you sound great! What's your name?" That was the start of another lifelong friendship, forty-five years so far. Louis convinced me to go to DeAnza College and play in their jazz band with him, and study trumpet with Dr. Herb Patnoe.

While I was going to DeAnza, I was contacted by a local trumpeter/ educator and asked if I was interested in taking over his trumpet teaching studio. I said, "Absolutely!" That led to teaching forty students five days a week, along with working in a music store two days, gigging five nights a week in SF, and going to school. I was so busy, I finally burned out and needed a change. The next school year, Louis and I went to Cal State Los Angeles, which had one of the best collegiate big bands in the country. I worked in the school pub as a bartender, played in the CSULA Jazz Ensemble, LA Jazz Workshop Big Band, and played whatever gig that fell my way. By the end of that school year, I ran out of money and was looking for a chance to go on the road. That summer I went on the road with the Circus Vargas band and toured the U.S. I also went to sea with various cruise ships and played shows in Las Vegas, Belize, LA, etc.

For a few years I continued to travel on and off, playing music and making new friends. But I always knew I wanted to come back to the Bay Area. Not only was it home, but I also knew I could always teach trumpet and make a living from music because of all the different genres of music I had the opportunity to perform in.

I have been fortunate enough to back up and/or to share the stage with Pete and Sheila Escovedo, Ella Fitzgerald, Dizzy Gillespie, Mel Tormé, Lila Downs, James Brown, The Temptations, Four Tops, Malo, Wayne Wallace, Lester Chambers, Dave Pell, Wayne Shorter, Jon Jang, Glen Campbell, Kenny Rankin, Linda Ronstadt, and many others in the music business.

John's final reflections about Jeff and his life as a musician:

Jeff was racially inclusive and that was important to me. After taking Mr. Williamson's freshman English class, I felt confident that I could communicate with most people. I thought it was a great school to go to because most of the teachers were very open-minded and progressive.

One of the best things about playing music is that you can go anywhere in the world and share your feelings and thoughts. You might not be able to speak someone's language, but you can pick up your instrument and play something they can relate to. Music has the potential to touch hearts in ways that words cannot. That's what I got from reading that Louis Armstrong article in 1963. I'm very fortunate to have this gift bestowed on me, and I don't take it for granted.

I called my old teacher, John Coppola, just before he passed in 2015 and said, "Johnny, we're in a book together called 'Trumpet Greats' that recognizes 2,400 trumpeters of note since the 1600s." I wanted to share with him that it really meant a lot to me to be included with him and all these great trumpet players. I have the "Treasury for Young Readers" in my library next to "Trumpet Greats," side by side, like the beginning and the continuation of my life's dream.

Carol B.

(Arab American, White; class of '72)

* * *

Growing up, I identified as White, but felt like that didn't quite fit me, even though it was what people saw when they looked at me. As I got older, when filling out forms asking for race/ethnicity, I started checking "other," as I didn't want my Middle Eastern heritage to get lost in the White box.

* * *

I am third-generation Lebanese (Arab) American on my father's side, and White on my mother's side. A few days after I was born, in San Francisco, I was whisked off to Daly City, California, where I lived for the next eighteen years .

My father was born in Oakland to Lebanese immigrant parents and grew up in San Francisco. Arabic was his first language and he didn't learn English until he started school. As the eldest, he had to drop out of high school to support his family after his father was seriously injured in a motorcycle accident. My dad eventually got his GED, but he always felt limited by his education. His biggest dream was that his three daughters would go to college. We did, although he didn't live to see any of us graduate.

My mother grew up 106 miles from Tulsa, Oklahoma. She was only a few months old when a White mob in Tulsa instigated a massacre of Black residents, killing hundreds and burning down their homes and thriving businesses. I am not sure if she knew about the massacre; we

never talked about it; but her father was the editor of their local newspaper and he would almost certainly have been fully aware of it. I do know that when my mother was about six years old, she was walking with her nine-year-old brother and saw a Black man for the first time. She pointed at the man, and said, "Look!" Her brother scolded her, telling her that she should never point at people or think differently about others because of how they look or the color of their skin.

Both my parents were Navy veterans. They met in 1947 at a dance, and they kept dancing together until my father's premature death twenty-six years later.

As newlyweds, they rented an apartment in San Francisco until my eldest sister was a year old. My father had already bought a house with the help of the GI Bill, but his family was living in it. My mother gave her new in-laws $1,000 from the sale of her father's house to put a down-payment on a house of their own. I've always lamented that I could have grown up in a nice area of SF instead of cold, foggy Daly City, but my mother insisted that the SF house was too small for a growing family. As it was, I shared a bedroom with my two older sisters until they left home ahead of me.

My mother's relationship with her in-laws was challenging. She wasn't Arab and never learned to cook Lebanese food (although she loved it). Her mother-in-law and sister-in-law would drop in at any time while she was juggling the demands of family life. My mother felt judged if the house wasn't in perfect order, and it's possible that her in-laws may have blamed her for not having a son to pass on the family name. She got along better with my father's brother, and after my father died, my mom eventually got closer with my aunt.

My father's salary as a mailman was enough to meet our needs, and my mother was a stay-at-home mom who led Brownie troops and taught piano. Gifts were practical, never big or expensive—pajamas, a game, a doll. I wore my sisters' hand-me-downs until I learned to make my own clothes in home economics class. I never felt I was missing out on anything, because no one had any more than anyone else. Each summer we took road trips to national parks and other famous places. On a few of our trips we crossed into Mexico and Canada.

Playing outside one day, when I was about seven years old, I heard my elderly Italian neighbor use the n-word. I was shocked, but I kind of felt sorry for him; I thought he just didn't know any better. I didn't really understand what the n-word meant, but I knew never to use it. My parents taught us to be kind and respectful to *everyone*.

Our immediate neighborhood didn't have any Black or Hispanic people. We had lots of Italians, some German, some (White) Jewish. A close friend who lived nearby was half White, half Chamorro (father from Guam). All three schools my sisters and I attended were within walking distance, and all three were racially mixed. My world, my "normal," was a true mix of people, even though our elementary school, "Little Jeff," wasn't very big.

My sixth-grade teacher, Ms. Gilton, was a very nice Black woman who took our class to the San Francisco Opera to see *The Barber of Seville*. When the show began, I just about fell out of my seat. Although I grew up in a musical home, I'd never heard opera, and it was shocking. A part of me wanted to laugh. But I looked over at Ms. Gilton and decided to behave myself. She looked so proud of us.

At Colma Junior High I was thrilled that there were hundreds of potential friends to choose from. I met three people who would become some of my closest friends in high school: one from the Philippines, one Japanese American, and another Italian American. I played violin in the "string ensemble." Recently I discovered a photo in which I'm standing between three Black girls, all with our violins tucked under our right arms. While I immediately remembered the names of two of the girls by my side, I realized it had never registered that our string ensemble was quite mixed in its racial makeup.

On one summer vacation, around 1966, my family drove cross-country to Pensacola, Florida. I distinctly remember a physical sense of racial division while driving through long stretches of the South. I'm not sure why I was so sensitive to it, but I definitely felt that something was wrong. The poverty I saw seemed worse among Black people.

When I started as a freshman at Jefferson High School, my eldest sister Jean had recently graduated, and my middle sister Peggy was a junior. I knew several kids from Colma, but Jeff was a much bigger school. I must have seemed more confident than many freshmen because I was friendly to everybody—our parents taught us to say hello to strangers if they made eye contact in the street, very different from today. Shy people liked me because I didn't wait for them to speak to me first. Being so open towards everybody helped me become more popular. Peggy's friends were very welcoming to me, which also helped pave my way. People who knew my sisters sometimes mentioned that I had the "Badran smile" (our smile actually resembled our mother's, not our father's).

I made a very wide circle of friends from all my activities: class officer (freshman vice-president and treasurer), sports, dance, orchestra, special ed assistant, counselor-in-training at a summer camp for diabetic youth, participation in clubs. Later I even went camping with the Wilderness School although I wasn't a member.

In sophomore year I was in the homecoming court. Our homecoming queen that year was a gorgeous, radiant Latina; one of the other "princesses" in the court was Filipina. In the group picture, I'm the only girl standing sort of bow-legged while everyone else is prim and proper. In another picture we're all sitting down and everyone else has her legs demurely tucked under her, while my legs are stretched out in front of me with my ankles crossed. This was in spite of my taking a PE class called

Posture and Grooming! I was (to use a politically incorrect term) a tomboy. To this day, I hate wearing dresses.

Everyone expected me, as a member of the homecoming court, to go to the dance with the "soph/frosh" team captain (Latino) because we were in the same class. However, I invited Jim (Black), whom I'd had a crush on at Colma, but he was at Serramonte High School. I probably made waves by choosing to take someone who wasn't from our school, even though the team captain I didn't go to the dance with had absolutely no trouble finding another date. I don't remember any reaction to the fact that Jim was Black, including from my parents, who thought he was very nice. It didn't make any difference to my social status at school, either. I was elected to be a pep girl in my senior year .

Through most of high school I belonged to the Model U.N. and Model Senate clubs. Every year we went to UC Berkeley for the scholastic U.N. conference. We were always paired with smaller and lesser-known countries, like The Gambia, so we had no power. This was an early introduction to geopolitics, but by senior year I had to reduce my involvement because being a pep girl took up so much time.

In Sophomore year Jeff staged a performance of "Like Hair," based on the huge Broadway show, with a multi-cultural cast. I did props along with one of my good friends. We would sneak off to smoke a joint (provided by her older brother), then return backstage and laugh through the performance. I think of this every time I hear the song "Aquarius," and of how representative it was of the era.

I had known my classmate Ken (Black) at Colma, and at Jeff we became closer friends as sophomores in a French class where almost everybody else was a freshman. On Friday nights during senior year, Ken and a few others who had access to cars would drive into "The Circle," just inside the school entrance, and pick us up en masse. We would pile into the cars (no seat-belt laws to limit the number) and head off to go ice skating, on a hayride, etc. It didn't matter who was dating or not dating; the drivers gave everyone a ride—Black, Latino, Filipino, other Asian, and White. It was a safe way to have fun. There was no alcohol involved. We were pretty tame in terms of taking risks. (Some people may have smoked weed before or after; I couldn't say.) After games we'd do the same, pile into cars and go to A&W or Toto's Pizza to get a bite to eat. At the end of the evening the drivers dropped us off at our homes.

While at Jeff, I didn't feel as different about my half-Arab heritage as I had in elementary school ("Lebanese? What's *that*?"). Like me, my oldest sister Jean was very open about her Arab heritage. Of the women in our family, she looked "the most Arab," though her skin was lighter than mine. People often assumed she was Jewish. She was very sensitive about anything anti-Arab and grew up to be highly political, like me; our sister Peggy was more focused on LGBTQ rights (as an adult she came out as a lesbian) and her career in social work. Jean and I learned to pronounce our name, Badran, correctly and we used that pronunciation as adults. Peggy stuck to the old mispronunciation we'd grown up with.

I never met any Arabs apart from our relatives, but high school was so mixed it didn't matter. People got along and chose their friends based on personality. My most serious boyfriend was during my senior year. He was half-Latino, half-Filipino, and played the conga drums. We had a lot of fun together. His family was very accepting of me, and mine of him.

Outside of Jeff, it was a different world. I remember hearing rumors that other schools in our district—which were mostly White—were afraid to play sports at Jeff because we had a reputation for being rough. For us, this was almost a joke, although we were a mostly blue-collar school and we knew there was some snobbery as well as the race angle. Even our cheerleading squad looked like a mini-United Nations.

After graduation, along with two of my best friends (Filipina and Japanese American), I enrolled at the University of California at Davis. I had not anticipated just how White it would be—it was shocking. But there I was, fulfilling my father's dream for his daughters. At Davis I began to understand more about social class, which I'd never thought about much before. Prior to college, I considered myself middle-class. Now I realized my family was actually lower-middle-class or working-class.

One weekend during my first semester, a friend from the suburbs of Sacramento came home with me. As we neared my house, she blurted out, "You live downtown!" It seemed like a silly thing to say. Downtown was San Francisco, with high-rise office buildings, big department stores, banks, etc. I lived half a block from Mission Street, a major street with businesses on it. The next semester I went home with this friend and realized that to someone from the suburbs, a business area was equated with downtown.

In college I started thinking more about my Lebanese/Arab background. Growing up, I identified as White, but felt like that didn't quite fit me, even though it was what people saw when they looked at me, with my light skin and Caucasian features. I don't know if other people didn't focus on it because not many people understood what "Lebanese" and "Arab" were, although the telltale pause whenever I revealed my heritage (as I often did) made it clear that I was "different." However, exactly what kind of White I was, or how much, didn't seem to matter to anyone during my school years, and it was pretty much the same at Davis. I was White enough to have full White privilege.

As I got older, when filling out forms asking for race/ethnicity, I looked for other boxes to check that included Middle Eastern or Arab. I started checking "other," as I didn't want my Middle Eastern heritage to get lost in the White box. I've struggled at times when sharing about feeling different. My non-White and (White) Jewish friends never question me, but some White friends and acquaintances don't seem to understand. I don't want special treatment. However, since many Americans don't know anyone of

Arab descent or have negative stereotypes of Arabs, I feel it's important for them to know we're just like everyone else. All the people I knew of Arab descent were very kind and loving. It's painful to hear others speak badly about Arabs .

When I was teaching in high schools and community college, I would often ask my classes to guess the origin of my last name. No one ever got it right! After I told them, it still felt as if most of them still saw me as only being White.

While researching some local history for this book, I spoke to someone who turned out to be a graduate of mostly White, affluent Westmoor. Even after all these years, I immediately felt that he had a sense of superiority.

In reflecting on my time at Jeff, I realize it was an exceptional experience, especially considering just how mixed we were. I've talked with friends whose schools had White and Black students during that same time period, but no one hung out together. Even with our friends from Colma who had to go to Serramonte High, they told me how segregated things were there, which was strange for them. Our Jefferson community was truly special. Although I didn't get the best academic education, I got something more valuable: a wonderful social/cultural education.

Epilogue

A deeper appreciation and some common themes

Writing and assembling this book has been a remarkable experience. I thought I "knew" many of the people I interviewed, since we'd grown up together and many of us were very close during that time. However, in quite a few cases, I have gained a different perspective on what other people's families and home lives were like. I have a new appreciation of all the classmates and teachers who contributed to this book.

Recording people's stories was also painful at times. Racism is mean, and it cuts deep. One nasty remark that singles out a child, makes fun of them, or puts them down, can wound them for life—shattering their innocence for something over which they have no control, their race or ethnic group. I learned that some of my classmates had racist experiences outside of school that I had no idea about. It was nice to hear some of them say that Jeff was a safe space for them.

As I worked on their stories, I noticed some common themes. Several people, including a former teacher, Bob, mentioned that they felt the school district didn't care about Jeff as much as it did about other schools. Because resources for public schools were based on local property taxes, Jeff definitely had less money than all the other schools in the district. Yet, it didn't seem like it mattered that we felt somewhat neglected. Knowing that we were the underdogs made us try harder with some things and fostered a school spirit that many of my classmates mentioned in their stories. This surely helped us all to get along.

Another theme surfaced that some of our teachers seemed to be more concerned with their popularity than with their effectiveness. I agree with those classmates who commented that the overall quality of education was not as good as it could have been. However, from interviewing six of our teachers, it became clear that many of them cared deeply about us and looked for creative ways to be more effective in reaching us.

Unfortunately, we did not always get good advice from our guidance counselors. One former classmate told me that she and two friends met with our class's counselor early in our freshman year. He told them point-blank that Jeff had a high drop-out rate and that one of the three

255

of them would not graduate. What a horrible thing to tell students! My friend left his office thinking she would be the one who would not graduate. (She went on to college to get a master's degree!) Another friend dreamed of going to a historically Black college but never got the guidance she needed to pursue her dream.

While doing this project I discovered that we had a lot of diversity within our diversity. Because of our proximity to Mexico, I had assumed that most, if not all, of Jeff's Latinx students were of Mexican descent. Among those I interviewed, there was a greater diversity: one was Nicaraguan, another Puerto Rican, another half Ecuadoran, and a brother and sister who were half Mexican and half Salvadoran. Of the Asian-Pacific Islanders at Jeff, while it seems the majority were Filipino, with some of Chinese, and some of Japanese descent, we had also had Samoans and Koreans, as well as classmates of Southeast Asian/Indian descent.

Three things that made Jeff work

As I worked on the interviews, I came up with three possible reasons why things at Jeff worked as well as they did. First, most of us came from working-class backgrounds, with some people a little poorer, and others closer to middle class. No one really had much more than anyone else, so we were all on a more or less equal economic footing. Children of our generation expected to do better than their parents financially, so we believed there was social mobility in our futures. I have no idea whether or not it turned out that way, but it seems that with most, if not all, of the people I interviewed, they did do better professionally than those who raised them.

The second reason is that most of us experienced integration from a young age (with the exception of those from Brisbane). By the time we got to Jeff, diversity was our normal, as our teacher Jeannine pointed out. While White was the overall majority race, we were rarely in any class that had only a few non-White people. So, if someone had a negative experience with someone of another race or ethnicity, they continued to be in class, daily, with other people of that same group. Anyone with an open mind would come to see that they couldn't judge an entire group by the behavior of one or two people. As several classmates noted in their stories, there were no racial or ethnic "gangs" at Jeff during our time there.

A third significant thing is that we had safe spaces for socializing together, away from school. Several people mentioned spending time at Marchbank Park and the War Memorial Community Center. Those places were well-integrated and everyone was welcome. Many young people today, especially in poorer urban areas, do not have safe spaces where they can hang out together when school isn't in session.

Then and now

None of my former classmates or teachers made any claim that things at Jeff were perfect. When I was a freshman, in 1968, there were some racial tensions and understandable anger and frustration after the assassinations of Martin Luther King, Jr., and Malcolm X, but that gradually calmed down. As people went to classes together, and interacted in sports, in band, and similar activites, they got to know one another as individuals, even when they may not have seemed to have much in common.

Several classmates from the majority-White town of Brisbane were challenged by their early experiences at Jefferson: having money taken, their watch stolen, or getting into a fight for their "attitude." They learned to look beyond that to realize that one or a few people of a particular race/ethnicity doing something to harm one does not mean that everyone of that race/ethnicity behaves in the same way.

Given the racial/ethnic makeup of Jefferson High, compared with the rest of the country in those days, and how we mostly interacted easily with one another, we were far ahead of our time.

Today my stomach turns when I see social media posts by a few White former classmates that demostrate hatred and racism. I wonder what had happened in their lives for them to have gotten to such a different place. What we learn at home can have a strong impact on how we turn out. Some classmates may have internalized racist messages from their families. If they did, some of them may have struggled at Jeff as they watched Black, Brown, and Asian Pacific Islander classmates achieve positions of power and prestige beyond them, and/or excel in academics over them. Possibly, they played sports, or an instrument, and were outdone by non-White classmates. Perhaps one of them even had a situation similar to our classmate who was beaten up at school, or they didn't feel safe while at Jeff.

So, while they got along—more or less—and maybe even had one or two non-White "friends," those friendships never went beyond the school gates and were really just acquaintances. In their adult lives, if they never looked beyond our reality at Jeff, they wouldn't understand just how different things were (and continue to be) for non-White people throughout our country. I remember seeing the movie *Mississippi Burning* in the 1990s and being absolutely shocked to learn that it was based on true events that took place in the south during the sixties. How could that be? We were living in the same country, but something like that would never have happened in the San Francisco Bay Area. Or would it?

Conclusion

I conceived of this book because I am deeply concerned about the future of our country. We are moving away from being a large White majority toward a racial mix closer to what we had at Jefferson High when I was a student, but we are in trouble.

Each of us is so much more complex than the color of our skin, our physical features, our religious beliefs, or other identifying character-istics like our gender identity or sexual orientation. People may look similar, but have very divergent views—on politics, the climate, etc. When we lump together everyone of a particular feature, we do a dis-service to all of us.

No one chooses where they will be born or their race/ethnicity. While your parents certainly influence these factors, you yourself have no say over them. We can't change these things, yet why do some people hate others based on something none of us has any control over? Why is it so difficult for them to imagine themselves in someone else's shoes: set apart and identified only by the color of their skin, regularly remind-ed as they go about their lives that they are different in a way they can do absolutely nothing about? How can humans be so unfeeling?

We all have more in common than not. Most people want the same things: a loving family, good friends, a decent job that pays the bills, food on the table, a clean home in a safe neighborhood, occasional va-cations. Yet we remain so divided about things we cannot do anything about, while other things that we can impact, such as climate change, are in serious need of our attention.

Americans are in love with "freedom." Yet what is freedom for a person who fears for their life each time they walk out their front door? For Breonna Taylor, for whom not even being at home in bed protected her from wrongful death. What is freedom for those who fear they will never see a loved one again because they were in the wrong place at the wrong time, even while doing nothing wrong? Why should one person enjoy more freedom than another, simply based on the color of their skin?

Heather McGhee in *The Sum of Us* writes, "The more you interact with people who are different from you, the more commonalities you see and the less they seem like 'the other.'"

At Jefferson High, we had exactly that. Proximity made us more comfortable. It was impossible to observe and interact with so many dif-ferent people without eventually dropping our guard. We had a chance to see different sides of people: someone who appeared intimidating outside the classroom might have tried as hard as or harder than the next person in class; or maybe they were funny, which you don't usually see when a person is trying to act tough. In spite of different physical features, we really weren't that different from each other. The school culture was that we were all okay, and most of us avoided stereotyping.

These stories open a window into the lives of a wide variety of people who came together at a particular place and time and got along somehow. My hope is that you will find common threads between your life and the lives of others who may seem very different from you. Or, if you cannot identify common threads, I hope you will at least see that we are all human and that inalienable rights apply to all of us, equally.

I invite you to think and do more about some of the themes that have been explored in this book, especially if you have not done so before. Get engaged in anti-racism, anti-poverty, equity-promoting activities. Start by reflecting, exploring, recognizing, reading, informing, involving, educating, and acting!

C.B.

Acknowledgments

Had I known how complicated it would be to write a book that includes the stories of forty different people, I don't know that I would have embarked on this journey. However, I did, and I am glad I did. I could not have done it without the help and support of many people.

First, I want to thank each person—teachers and classmates alike —who shared their personal story with me, believed in what I was trying to accomplish, and trusted me to tell their story in a way that their voices would be heard.

A big thank you to the following people who provided support throughout: Jennifer Tasto, the first person I pitched my idea to, who immediately "got it," even when I wasn't quite sure what "it" was and was steadfast in her support. Susan Stewart, my "COVID buddy," who had to listen to me weekly (on Zoom) as I told her about the ups and downs of trying to locate people, convince them to be interviewed, etc. Chinto Fonseca, who has been the "glue" of our class, who helped me connect with people, and more. Russell Toy, who helped with editing, among other things. To former teacher extraordinaire, Al Sinor, who, while he didn't think his personal story would be interesting enough to be interviewed, (not true!) connected me with several former teachers.

I am incredibly grateful to the following who encouraged me with their support and/or read various parts of the book while it was in progress: Tito A., Szari Bourque, Patricia Erwin, Ellen Frank, Lynn Hazen, Nina Hemenway, Yolanda Hippensteele, Judy Logan, Ali Morse, Alex Pagonis, Terrie Raphael, and Karen Sokal-Gutierrez.

A very special thank you to a few who went above and beyond in some capacity: My dear friend Barbara Sussman who read every word of the book and provided first edits. Nancy Stone (and Edda), Marsha Morrow, and Melissa Reiter for their much-needed and appreciated support.

Thank you to Tessie Bayangos and Lillian Martinez (Serramonte High, class of '72) for their willingness to be considered for this book project, even though they did not attend Jeff.

I am immensely grateful to my editor, Lauren Bourque, who was very patient and provided stalwart guidance while working with someone writing their first book.

Finally, I need to mention my family. I am so appreciative of my parents who taught my sisters and me to see each person as the individual that they are, regardless of their multiple identities. While my immediate family are no longer with me, I feel their presence and support every single day in every thing I do, cheering me on. My incred-